GOPAL KRISHNA GOKHALE

GOPAL KRISHNA GOKHALE

Edited by

M.K. SINGH

ANMOL PUBLICATIONS PVT. LTD.

NEW DELHI - 110 002 (INDIA)

ANMOL PUBLICATIONS PVT. LTD.
H.O.: 4374/4B, Ansari Road, Darya Ganj,
New Delhi-110 002 (India)
Ph.: 23278000, 23261597
B.O.: No. 1015, Ist Main Road, BSK IIIrd Stage
IIIrd Phase, IIIrd Block,
Bangalore - 560 085 (India)
Visit us at: www.anmolpublications.com

Gopal Krishna Gokhale

First Published, 2008
ISBN 978-81-261-3511-0

PRINTED IN INDIA

Printed at Mehra Offset Press, Delhi.

CONTENTS

PREFACE

Gopal Krishna Gokhale was a great son of Mother India, about whom nation can feel proud. He had the privilege of guiding nation during his times and taking forward the millions of Indian on the path of self-government. Being a Liberal he had full faith in British sense of justice and wished that the Indians should give maximum co-operation to the British in its efforts to take India on the path of constitutional development. He believed that most of the Britishers who were incharge of administration were ignorant of India's problems and efforts were needed to make them appreciate and realise our difficulties. He had also faith in the capacity of Indians to improve their conditions and come out of grinding and growing poverty. He was both a politician, social reformer and an economist. He was also one of the most brilliant parliamentarians which India produced at that time. He was an educationist and political guru of even Mahatma Gandhi. He founded the servants of Indian Society to train the young people of India for noble cause of devoting themselves to the service of their Motherland. Gokhale was not only a politician or political thinker but he also studied economic problems of India with keen interest. He started with the basic presumption that in India agricultural land was not producing to the desired extent, with the result that India though predominantly an agricultural country, was agriculturally backward.

The book comprises a detail on Gokhale includes his Life Sketch, On Path of Politcs, His Plans and Programmes for Congress, the Guru of Gandhi, Self-Government and Swadeshi, Gokhale on Religious Issues, Constitutional Reforms and an Overview etc.

The book is of great magnitude for the students, scholars, teachers as well as researchers.

1

Gopal Krishna Gokhale : Life Sketch

Gopal Krishna Gokhale was born on May 1, 1866 in Chitpavan community in Ratnagiri District. He was hardly 13, when his father died and by the force of circumstances his mother was obliged to leave the village and shift to Kolhapur where her elder son was employed on a meagre monthly salary of fifteen rupees. It was a very critical time for this small family which even could not afford the education of the young boy who subsequently became the world famous parliamentarian, social reformer and politician. The extent of poverty can be well imagined from the fact that Gokhale had to sit beneath the street lights to study at night. After completing his early education, he joined Deccan College, Poona and Elphinstone college Bombay from where he graduated at the age of 18. After his graduation he decided to join Deccan Education society where he, on his own, accepted a meagre salary of seventy five rupees per month for a period of 20 years.

His this decision was opposed in the initial stages by his brother to which subsequently he reconciled. During his stay in the society he worked as its secretary and became so much close to it that he became its soul and life. He had the opportunity of visiting England 7 times and each time he left an impression of his ability on the people there. In 1897 he went there to give his evidence before Welby Commission which had been set up by the government to enquire into the Indian finances. In 1905 he was one of the members of the delegation sent by the Congress to persuade the British government not to go ahead with the proposal of the partition of Bengal. In 1908 he gave evidence before Hobhouse Decentralisation Commission and in 1912 he became the member of Islington Commission which was set up to enquire into the working of civil services in India. In 1912 he had to go to England in connection with the working of P. S. Commission. During one of his visits to England, Gokhale seized the opportunity of meeting Lord Morley and convinced him about the need and necessity of giving constitutional reforms to India. Perhaps no one will deny that it was due to his efforts and influence that India got her first dose of constitutional reform in 1909.

During his college career, Gokhale was much impressed by Edmund Burke's scholarly work on Reflections on the French Revolution. He very often quoted line after line from this work during the college debates and greatly impressed upon his audience. Students and teachers always showered their love and respect for him. After graduation, some of his friends suggested to him to compete for the Indian Civil Service examination, but he knew very well about his financial resources which did not permit him to travel abroad. He ultimately joined as a teacher in the New English School on a salary of Rs. thirty five per month and also decided to study law. Now with these financial resources, he could not only relieve the economic burden of his elder brother but also helped his mother and her family members.

Among these institutions typical of Maharashtra, the Deccan Education Society of Poona, the centre of Mahratta patriotic activities, takes a very high rank. It was in 1879 that a few enthusiastic young men like the late Mr. V.K. Chiplunkar, the late Mr. M.B. Namjoshi, the late Mr. G.G. Agarkar, and Mr. B.G. Tilak, with the advice and approval of leading people like Mr. Mandlik and Mr. Ranade, started the New English School at Poona with the object of cheapening and facilitating education and making it available for all classes by opening schools and colleges under private management. That small seed steadily grew into a large tree under whose genial shade thousands of young men were comfortably drinking at the inspiring fountain of education. The Deccan Education Society, established in 1884 to give a regular shape to this educational activity, was a unique institution in India. The life Members, those who conduct the Fergusson College, the schools and other institutions of the Society, bound themselves to serve for a period of 20 years on a small salary which was but a subsistence allowance. Their sacrifice had enabled them to develop the educational institutions under their charge to such an extent that no less than 3,600 pupils were then receiving their education in the college and schools of the D.E. Society. In the New English School, Gokhale was to coach 4th and 5th standards. He was a teacher of English and Mathematics. His fluency in English was marked with proper accent. He knew the text books by heart and with his immense knowledge which he gathered by reading works of Milton, Burke and several other writers, he injected a new academic phraseology in the minds of young students. At this point of time, Tilak, Apte and Agarkar had come into lime light on account of their social and educational activities in the region. The foundation of the Fergusson College made them realise the fact that Gokhale should join this institution. He agreed to accept this appointment, and he taught English with a sense of highest degree of brilliance. His students like R.P. Paranjpye, T.K. Shahani and several others paid rich tributes to his academic qualities? Besides he showed much interest in economics. He soon became well-conversant with the economic condition of a common Indian. In this connection, he learnt much about the subject with his deep connection with Ranade. In fact both discussed several economic issues for hours together and thus Gokhale enhanced his knowledge which paid him rich dividends when he was a Member in the Bengal Council as well as in the Central Assembly. He would argue well on budget and several other issues of economic aspects. The main aim of the Deccan Education Society was to promote education at various levels.

Undoubtedly the members were inspired with a sense of sacrifice and each and every action was a model to the students in the institutions managed by this society. The other aim of the Society was, prepare students to liberate their country from foreign domination. Gokhale remained in the society for fifteen years. Gokhale was a fine writer and contributed several articles in the Kesari and the Mahratta. He also contributed a lot in Sudharak founded by Agarkar. On account of his comprehensive journalistic contribution, M.G. Ranade requested him to take charge of the Quarterly Journal of the Sarvajanik Sabha. Whereas Gokhale was a rising star in social and political life of our country, his domestic life was not happy one. He was only 14 when he was married. His wife suffered from leucoderma. His elder brother and sister-in-law prevailed upon him to marry again. He did not agree at first but having got his wife's consent he agreed to marry again.

The second marriage was happy though it could not last for a long time. The second wife died in 1900, leaving behind a son and two, daughters. The son also died at on early age.' A fine sportsman as he was he played cricket, tennis and billiards. He also loved cards and chess and these he adopted as pastime. Although a good speaker, he never claimed to be a mass orator. His speeches were fairly comprehensive in contents, and touched upon the problems of a common man. He was a member of the University Senate, Bombay for several years and regularly participated in all the deliberations which had linkage with the promotion of education in the presidency. He always advocated the idea that the issues raised in the University Senate should not be weighed in the balance of politics. He argued that this kind of style would retard the progress of education and ultimately it would be a serious setback for out society. He was indeed a tireless worker and always worked at the cost of his health. For any meeting, public or official, be got himself fully prepared and the minutest detail about any issue, big or small, did not escape his searching eyes. He knew how to answer any ticklish issue and very often he answered well. In the Bombay Council as well as in the Central Assembly, his contribution on several problems facing the Indian subcontinent was quite unique. He was heard by the Raj officials, with full attention and very often his queries put the government officials into difficulty. As a Congress leader, he was in the group of moderate leaders. He did not wish to adopt a posture as was adopted by Bal Gangadhar Tilak, Aurobindo Ghose, B.C. Pal and Lala Lajpat Rai. He was well-aware of the fact that a constitutional posture was best suited to attain substantial constitutional concessions for his people. He, therefore, did not believe in direct confrontation with the bureaucracy. He was, however, critical of the ways the bureaucracy behaved at a particular moment in order to resolve any issue and it was his temperament to call spade a spade and not to shirk his moral or social responsibility. While he was in the Fergusson College, there were other activities which shared his attention with educational work. About the time that he entered the Fergusson College, Mr. Gokhale came under the influence of the late Mr. Justice Ranade by whom, more than by any other, we may say that the life and character of Mr. Gokhale have been moulded.

Under the masterful guidance of Mr. Ranade, Mr. Gokhale devoted himself to the study of political economy for over twelve years, with the result that today, Mr. Gokhale was one of the few men in India who could speak with authority on economical problems. No wonder Mr. Gokhale entertained the highest reverence for the late Mr. Ranade and regarded him as his guru. In 1887, in compliance with Mr. Ranade's wish, Mr. Gokhale became the editor of the Quarterly Journal of the Poona Sarvajanik Sabha. Subsequently he became Honorary Secretary of the Deccan Sabha. He was also one of the editors of the Sudharak, an Anglo-Marathi weekly, of Poona. He was Secretary of the Bombay Provincial Conference for four years and of the Indian National Congress held at Poona in 1895. His earnestness and knowledge of public affairs became so well known and appreciated that he was called the Rising Star of the Deccan. It was natural, therefore, that in 1897 he was selected along with Mr. Wacha by the Bombay public to go to England and give evidence before the Welby

Commission on Indian expenditure. The very valuable evidence which he gave showed what a mastery he had acquired of the problems which British rule in India presents. The most note worthy point in the evidence was, perhaps, his insistence or the emasculation which British rule entails upon the Indian people—a point which our revered countryman Dadhabai Naorojee was never weary of emphasising.

Mr. Gokhale pointed out how, to use his own favourite expression, under British rule in India the tallest had to bend in order that the exigencies of the situation might be satisfied. While, in England, he delivered several speeches on Indian affairs. He also published a scathing condemnation of the plague policy, of the Bombay Government and the atrocities of soldiers on plague duty. The criticism provoked a howl of indignation and he was assailed by abuse and obloquy from all sides. When he returned to India he was called upon to substantiate his charges and on friends who had furnished him with information refusing to come forward to support him, he could do nothing but tender an apology to the Bombay Government. Sometime after he was elected a member of the Bombay Legislative Council. In 1902, he retired from the Principalship of the Fergusson College on a pension of Rs. 25 a month, and about the same time he was elected to represent Bombay on the Supreme Legislative Council in place of Sir Pherozeshah Mehta, whose ill health prevented his continuing in the office; and so well has Mr. Gokhale acquitted himself that he was, re-elected successively. Mr. Gokhale joined the Congress movement at an early stage of its career.. He was present at most sessions of the Congress and delivered several speeches on the Congress platform. One of the most notable of these was the speech that he delivered at the Bombay Congress in 1904 on 'Surpluses,' a speech which, according to Sir Henry Cotton, would compare favourably with the best speeches heard in the House of Commons.

In 1905 he was sent as a delegate to England by the Bombay public, to explain the political situation in India to the British electorate. He discharged his mission most satisfactorily delivering no less than 45 speeches in the course of 50 days. Many competent men who heard him in England expressed themselves as charmed by his presentation of the Indian view of the British Government in India. Before he left for England he has been chosen President of the National Congress, which was to meet in the following December in the sacred city of Benares. His work in England put such a strain upon his powers that his health was affected, and he had to undergo a throat operation before returning to India to preside over the deliberations of the Benares Congress. His Presidential Address at the Benares session was a most lucid and masterly performance.

The most remarkable passage in the address was perhaps where he indicated the immediate reforms on which the Congress should concentrate its attention, the irreducible minimum, as it were, which alone would satisfy the political aspirations of educated Indians. Shortly after the Benares Congress was over, he proceeded again to England and this time he had several interviews with Mr. John (now Lord) Morley which inspired him with great faith in the Liberal Ministry, a faith which must have been severely tried by subsequent events. He once again went to England in 1908 in view of the Reform Proposals of Lord Minto. Gokhale's Speech delivered at a public meeting of 1894 in Poona during farewell to Mr. A.O. Hume. Mr. Gokhale began by saying that it was a high privilege to be asked to offer welcome to so eminent a benefactor of India as Mr. Hume, and the welcome that he offered was offered not only on behalf of the people of Poona, but in the name of the entire Deccan, representatives from the various districts of which had thought it their duty to be present on that occasion. It was impossible for him to adequately express how deeply grateful they all felt to Mr. Hume for the immense sacrifice of personal comfort and convenience at which he bad snatched, in his indifferent state of health and after a very fatiguing journey, a few hours to gratify their dearly cherished wishes and honour their city with that visit.

The speaker, however, wanted to say that no one was surprised at the trouble Mr. Hume had taken; because his conduct in that matter was only in keeping with that absolute disregard of self which had all along been the guiding principle of his life. Mr. Gokhale was aware that nothing was more repugnant to Mr. Hume than any demonstration or even an expression of the feelings by which he was regarded by the people of the country; but he would ask him to remember that, when the gratitude of the heart was deep and strong, it gave an irresistible impulse to the tongue to speak. And if, therefore, in what little he intended to say, he appeared not to act quite in accordance with Mr. Hume's wishes, he trusted Mr. Hume would excuse him on the ground, that what he wanted to say came straight from the heart and there was no art about it. Any one who compared the India of today with what she was seven or eight years ago, would at once realize the enormous nature of the services rendered by Mr. Hume to the country. All that the Indian National Congress had done during the seven years of its existence was principally Mr. Hume's work. What it was exactly that the Congress had achieved it was unnecessary for the speaker to state at length, first, because that question had been repeatedly dealt with in an infinitely abler and more eloquent manner than any he could ever hope to attempt, by successive Presidents of past Congresses, and secondly, to speak of that in the presence of the Father of the National Congress was something like holding up a candlelight to the face of the eternal and glorious source of all light. Mr. Gokhale, however, wanted briefly to refer to four results which were principally due to the Congress. First, the Congress had welded together all the influences in the country which were struggling, scattered, to create throughout India a sense of common nationality. The influences had not been created by the Congress. They had come into existence along with British rule in this country, and they had been tenderly nursed by the wise and large hearted policy of successive generations of statesmen, and notably that of the Marquis of Ripon. But although the influences were already in existence, it was reserved for the Congress to unite them together and produce a result owing to which the heart of Bombay throbbed today in unison with that of Bengal or Madras in matters of national welfare.

The Congress had also made public opinion in India more enlightened and more influential. The movement had spread far and wide in the land a considerable knowledge of the main political questions, and the result was that public opinion was better informed now than before. It also carried more weight with Government and no more eloquent testimony on the point was required than the fact that Lord Lansdowne himself had recognised in the Congress the Liberal party of India. Then owing to the Congress movement, the main political questions of the country were advancing, some slowly, some rapidly, but all of them advancing towards a state of satisfactory solution. And lastly, the Congress supplied a ready machinery to those English politicians who realized their vast responsibilities in connection with India and who were anxious to do their duty by the people of this country. One peculiarly glorious circumstance connected with British rule, according to Mr. Gokhale, was that this country had never lacked distinguished, disinterested advocates of her cause in England. The speaker mentioned the services rendered by Edmund Burke to this country a century ago, and said that it was for such services that the names of Bright and Fawcett-and, last but not least, Bradlaugh—had become household words with the people. The four results mentioned by the speaker were the work of the Congress and as such they were principally the work of Mr. Hume's hands; and surely it was not given to a single individual to achieve more.

Mr. Hume's path, again, had not been smooth. He had to work amidst the repeated misunderstandings of well-meaning friends and the unscrupulous attacks of determined enemies. But as though those difficulties had not been sufficient, it had pleased Providence to send him more trying ordeals. In the space of the past two, years a domestic affliction, sad and heavy at all times, but peculiarly sad and heavy in old age when the mind of man is rather conservative in its attachments, had rendered his home desolate and his hearth cheerless; while his public life was embittered by the sad and untimely loss of his best and most eminent co-worker in England and his most beloved and trusted collaborator in India. The difficulties and misfortunes mentioned by the speaker were more than sufficient to break the spirit of most men; but Mr. Hume continued, in spite of them all, to walk firmly and unshaken in the path of duty chosen by himself. When the people of India contemplated all that, naturally their hearts overflowed with feelings of gratitude and admiration and veneration and love. For Mr. Hume had enabled India, for the first time in her history, to breathe and feel like one nation by bringing together men of enlightenment and patriotism for the various parts of the country to work in a common cause. He had tried to steady their faltering footsteps and turn their weak accents into firm speech. He had toiled for them in the midst of calumny and contumely of every kind, amidst the wicked attacks of avowed enemies and the more wicked stabs of false friends. For their sake he had denied himself the comforts which old age demanded and to their service he had devoted his time, his energy, his talents, his purse, his all. Above all, he had set them a high and glorious example as to how they should labour for the regeneration of their motherland.

Such had been Mr. Hume's services and they were above any memorial or reward. Rather their own reward they were, and in themselves they constituted a memorial more lasting than brass and more enduring than marble. In conclusion, Mr. Gokhale expressed the great regret of all assembled there that Mr. Hume was not coming out for the next Congress. The melancholy circumstances of Pandit Ajudhyanath's death rendered it, in the speaker's opinion, necessary that the next Congress should have the guidance of Mr. Hume's hand. However, as Mr. Hume's decision had been already finally made in the matter, they had to bow to it as meant for the best. Mr. Gokhale was also very sorry that Mr. Hume's stay in Poona should have been so extremely short that they had to blend their welcome and their farewell together. But as even in that matter Mr. Hume had already made final arrangements, nothing remained for him but to wish Mr. Hume and his daughter a happy voyage and a very happy time in England. Gokhale moved the following Resolution at the Dharwar on the elevation of the depressed classes.' Mr. President and Gentlemen—The proposition which has been entrusted to me runs thus : That this Conference holds that the present degraded condition of the low castes is in itself and from the national point of view unsatisfactory, and is of opinion that every well-wisher of the country should consider it his duty to do all be can to raise their moral and social condition by trying to rouse self-respect in these classes and placing facilities for education and employment within their reach. Gentlemen, I hope I am not given to the use of unnecessarily strong language and yet I must say that this resolution is not as strongly worded as it should have been.

The condition of the low castes-it is painful to call them low castes—is not only unsatisfactory as this resolution says—it is so deeply deplorable that it constitutes a grave blot on our social arrangements; and, further, the attitude of our educated men towards this class is profoundly painful and humiliating. I do not propose to deal with this subject as an antiquarian; I only want to make a few general observations from the standpoint of justice, humanity, and national self-interest. I think all fair minded persons will have to admit that it is absolutely monstrous that a class of human beings, with bodies similar to our own, with brains that can think and with hearts that can feel, should be perpetually condemned to a low life of utter wretchedness, servitude and mental and moral degradation, and that permanent barriers should be placed in their way so that it should be impossible for them ever to overcome them and improve their lot.

This is deeply revolting to our sense of justice. I believe one has only to put oneself mentally into their place to realise how grievous this injustice is. We may touch a cat, we may touch a dog, we may touch any other animal, but the touch of these human beings is pollution ! And so complete is now the mental degradation of these people that they themselves see nothing in such treatment to resent, that they acquiesce in it as though nothing better than that was their due. I remember a speech delivered seven or eighty ears ago by the late Mr. Ranade in Bombay, under the auspices of the Hindu Union Club. That was a time when public feeling ran high in India on the subject of the treatment which our people were receiving in South Africa. Our friend, Mr. Gandhi, had come here on a brief visit from South Africa and he was telling us how our people were treated in Natal and Cape Colony and the Transvaal-how they were not allowed to walk on footpaths or travel in first-class carriages on the railway, how they were not admitted into hotels and so forth.

Public feeling, in consequence, was deeply stirred, and we all felt that it was a mockery that we should be called British subjects, when we were treated like this in Great Britain's colonies. Mr. Ranade felt this just as keenly as any one else. He had been a never failing adviser of Mr. Gandhi, and had carried on a regular correspondence with him. But it was Mr. Ranade's peculiar greatness that he always utilized occasions of excitement to give a proper turn to the national mind and cultivate its sense of proportion. And so, when every one was expressing himself in indignant terms about the treatment which our countrymen were receiving in South Africa, Mr. Ranade came forward to ask if we had no sins of our own to answer for in that direction. I do not exactly remember the title of his address. I think it was "Turn the search-light inwards," or some such thing. But I remember that it was a great speech one of the greatest that I have ever been privileged to hear. He began in characteristic fashion, expressing deep sympathy with the Indians in South Africa in the struggle they were manfully carrying on. He rejoiced that the people of India had awakened to a sense of the position of their countrymen abroad, and he felt convinced that this awakening was a sign of the fact that the dead bones in the valley were once again becoming instinct with life. But he proceeded to ask : Was this sympathy with the oppressed and down trodden Indians to be confined to those of our countrymen only who had gone out of India ? Or was it to be general and to be extended to all cases where there was oppression and injustice ? It was easy, he said, to denounce foreigners, but those who did so were bound in common fairness to look into themselves and see if they were absolutely blameless in the matter. He then described the manner in which members of low caste were treated by our own community in different parts of India. It was a description, which filled the audience with feelings of deep shame and pain and indignation. And Mr. Ranade very justly asked whether it was for those who tolerated such disgraceful oppression and injustice in their own country to indulge in all that denunciation of the people of South Africa. This question, therefore, is in the first place a question of sheer justice: Next, as I have already said, it is a question of humanity. It is sometimes urged that if we have our castes, the people in the West have their classes, and after all, there is not much difference between the two.

A little reflection will, however, show that the analogy is quite fallacious. The classes of the West are a perfectly elastic institution, and not rigid or castiron like our castes. Mr. Chamberlain, who is the most masterful personage in the British Empire today, was at one time a shoemaker and then A screw-maker. Of course, he did not make shoes himself, but that was the trade by which he made money. Mr. Chamberlain today dines with Royalty, and mixes with the highest in the land on terms of absolute equality. Will a shoemaker ever be able to rise in India in the social scale in a similar fashion, no matter how gifted by nature he might be ? A great writer has said that castes are eminently useful for the preservation of society, but that they are utterly unsuited for purposes of progress. And this I think is perfectly true. If you want to stand where you were a thousand years ago, the system of castes need not be modified in any material degree. If, however, you want to emerge out of the slough in which you have long remained sunk, it will not do for you to insist on a rigid adherence to caste. Modern civilisation has accepted greater equality for all as its watchword, as against privilege and exclusiveness, which were the root ideas of the old world. And the larger humanity of these days requires that we should acknowledge its claims by seeking the amelioration of the helpless condition of our down-trodden countrymen. Finally, gentlemen, this is a question of National Self interest. How can we possibly realise our national aspirations, how can our country ever hope to take her place among the nations of the world, if we allow large number of our country men to remain sunk in ignorance, barbarism, and degradation ? Unless these men are gradually raised to a higher level, morally and intellectually, how can they possibly understand our thoughts or share our hopes or co-operate with us in our efforts ? Can you not realize that so far as the work of national elevation is concerned, the energy, which these classes might be expected to represent, is simply unavailable to us ? I understand that great thinker and observer-Swami Vivekananda—held this view very strongly. I think that there is not much hope for us as a nation unless the help of all classes, including those that are known as low castes, is forth-coming for the work that lies before us. Moreover, is it, I may ask, consistent with our own self-respect that these men should be kept out of our houses and shut out from all social intercourse as long as they remain within the pale of Hinduism, whereas the moment they put on a coat and a hat and a pair of trousers and call themselves Christians, we are prepared to shake hands with them and look upon them as quite respectable ? No sensible man will say that this is a satisfactory state of things.

Of course, no one expects that these classes will be lifted up at once morally and intellectually to a position of equality with their more favoured countrymen. This work is bound to be slow and can only be achieved by strenuous exertions for giving them education and finding for them honourable employment in life. And, gentlemen, it seems to me that, in the present state of India, no work can be higher or holier than this. I think if there is one question of social reform more than another that should stir the enthusiasm of our educated young men and inspire them with an unselfish purpose, it is this question of the degraded condition of our low castes. Cannot a few men-five per cent, four per cent, three, two, even one per cent—of the hundreds and hundreds of graduates that the University turns out every year, take it upon themselves to dedicate their lives to this sacred work of the elevation of low castes ? My appeal is not to the old or the middle aged—the grooves of their lives are fixed but I think I may well address such an appeal to the young members of our community-to those who have not yet decided upon their future course and who entertain the noble aspiration of devoting to a worthy cause the education which they have received. What the country needs most at the present moment is a spirit of self-sacrifice on the part of our educated young men, and they may take it from me that they cannot spend their lives in a better cause than raising the moral and intellectual level of these unhappy low castes and promoting their general well-being.'

Constitution of the Servants of India Society founded by. G.K. Gokhale, at Poona is as follows : For some time past, the conviction has been forcing itself on many earnest and thoughtful minds that a stage has been reached in the work of nation-building in India, when, for further progress, 'he devoted labour of a specially trained agency, applying itself to the task in a true missionary spirit, are required. The work that has been accomplished so far has indeed been of the highest value. The growth during the last fifty years of a feeling of common nationality, based upon common traditions and ties, common hopes and aspirations, and even common disabilities, has been most striking.

The fact that we are Indians first and Hindus, Mahomedans, Parsees or Christians afterwards, is being realised in a steadily increasing measure, and the idea of a united and renovated India matching onwards to a place among the nations of the world, worthy of her great past, is no longer a mere idle dream of a few imaginative minds, but is the definitely accepted creed of those who form the brain of the community—the educated classes of the country. A creditable beginning has already been made in matters of education and of local self-government; and all classes of the people are slowly but steadily coming under the influence of liberal ideas.

The claims of public life are every day receiving wider recognition, and attachment to the land of our birth is growing into a strong and deeply cherished passion of the heart. The annual meetings of Congresses and Conferences, the work of public bodies and associations, the writings in the columns of the Indian Press—all bear witness to the new life that is coursing in the veins of the people. The results achieved so far are undoubtedly most gratifying, but they only mean that the jungle has been cleared and the foundations laid. The great work of rearing the superstructure has yet to be taken in hand and the situation demands on the part of workers devotion and sacrifices proportionate to the magnitude of the task. The Servants of India Society has been established to meet in some measure these requirements of the situation. Its members frankly accept the British connection as ordained, in the inscrutable dispensation of Providence, for India's good. Self-Government within the Empire for their country and a higher life generally for their countrymen is their goal. This, goal, they recognise, cannot be attained without years of earnest and patient effort and sacrifices worthy of the cause. Much of the work must be directed toward building up in the, country a higher type of character and capacity than is generally available at present and the advance can only be slow. Moreover, the path is beset with great difficulties; there will be constant temptations to turn back; bitter disappointments will repeatedly try the faith of those who have put their hand to, the work. But the weary toil can have but one end, if only the workers grow not faint-hearted on the way.

One essential condition of success in this work is that a sufficient number of our countrymen must now come forward to devote themselves to the cause in the spirit in which religious work is undertaken. Public life must be spiritualized. Love of country must so fill the heart that all else shall appear as of little moment by its side. A fervent patriotism which rejoices at every opportunity of sacrifice for the motherland, a dauntless heart which refuseand to be turned back from its object by difficulty or danger, a deep faith in the purpose of Providence which nothing can shake equipped with these, the worker must start on his mission and reverently seek the joy which comes of spending oneself in the service of one's country. The Servants of India Society will train men prepared to devote their lives to the cause of the country in a religious spirit, and will seek to promote, by all constitutional means, the national interests of the Indian people. Its members will direct their efforts principally towards (1) creating among the people, by example and by precept, a deep and passionate love of the motherland, seeking its highest fulfilment in service and sacrifice; (2) organising the work of political education and agitation, basing it on a careful study of public questions, and strengthening generally the public life of the country; (3) promoting relations of cordial goodwill and cooperation among the different communities; (4) assisting educational movements, especially those for the education of women, the education of backward classes and industrial and scientific education; (5) helping forward the industrial development of the country; and (6) the elevation of the depressed classes. The headquarters of the Society will be at Poona, where it will maintain a Home for its members, and, attached to it, a Library for the study of subjects bearing on its work. The following constitution has been adopted for the Society :

1. The Society shall be called "The Servants of India Society."
2. The objects of the Society are to train national missionaries for the service of India and to promote by all constitutional means, the true interests of the Indian people.
3. The Society will consist of, (a) a First Member or President, (b) Ordinary Members, and (c) Members under training.
4. The First Member or President will be the Head of the Society.
5. Every member, on admission, shall undergo a special training for a period of five Years. During this period, he will be known as a 'Member under training.' When a member has completed his five years' discipline, he will be styled an 'Ordinary Member' of the Society.
6. Subject to rules 12 and 13, every ember of the Society shall be a member for life.
7. The affairs of the Society will be managed, in accordance with byelaws framed for the purpose, by the First Member or President assisted by a council of three

Ordinary Members, who shall be elected by the Ordinary Members of the Society. Every year one member of the Council, whose name shall be drawn by lot, shall retire; but he will be eligible for re-election.

8. No person will be admitted as a member of the Society, unless his admission is recommended by the Council and the recommendation accepted by the First Member or President.

9. Every member at the time of admission shall take the following seven vows :

   (i) That the country will always be the first in his thoughts and he will give to her service the best that is in him.

   (ii) That in serving the country he will seek no personal advantage for himself.

   (iii) That he will regard all Indians as brothers and will 'work for the advancement of all, without distinction of caste or creed.

   (iv) That he will be content with such provision for himself and his family, if he has any, as the Society may be able to make. He will devote no part of his energies to earning money for himself.

   (v) That he will lead a pure personal life.

   (vi) That he will engage in no personal quarrel with anyone.

   (vii) That he will always keep in view the aims of the Society and watch over its interests with the utmost zeal, doing all he can to advance its work. He will never do anything which is inconsistent with the objects of the Society.

10. Every member under training ,hall, during the time that he is under training, place himself under the entire guidance and control of the First Member of President

and shall do such work and devote himself to such studies as the First Member or President may direct.

11. An Ordinary Member may be sent by the First Member or President and Council to any part of India on special duty or for general work in connection with the Society. He will be bound to do the work assigned to him under the general direction of the First Member or President and Council, and will obey all orders and instructions that may be received from them.

12. The Society may release a member from his vows and permit him to resign his membership on the ground of continued ill-health or for other sufficient cause on a recommendation to that effect being made by the Council, with the concurrence of not less than three-fourths of the members of the Society, and the recommendation being accepted by the First Member or President.

13. The Society may remove the name of any member from its roll of members on a recommendation to that effect being made by the Council, with the concurrence of not less than three-fourths of the members of the Society, and the recommendation being accepted by the First Member of President.

14. The First Member will hold office for life.

It will be the duty of the First Member to recommend in writing to the Council the names of three Ordinary Members, out of whom the members of the Society shall elect a successor to him as First Member on a vacancy occurring. If no such recommendation has been received by the Council when the vacancy occurs, the members of the Society may elect any Ordinary Member, or, in the absence of a suitable Ordinary Member, any member to succeed as First Member.

In case, however, it appears undesirable to elect any member as First Member, the members may elect one of their number to be President of the Society for a period of three years.

15. When a vacancy occurs in the First Membership or Presidentship of the Society, the Council for the time being shall exercise all the powers vested by the rules in the First Member or President singly or the First Member or President and Council until such time as a new First Member or President is duly elected, and any act done by the Council, during such time shall be deemed valid, provided that the Council takes steps with all reasonable despatch to arrange for the election of a new First Member or President under rule 14.

16. In special circumstances, the First Member or President and Council may exempt, for reasons to be recorded in writing, any member of the Society from the operation of any rule, save rule No. 9.

17. An applicant for membership may be required to pass through a period of probation before admission as a member and may, in that case, be enrolled as a Probationer on such terms and for such period as the First Member or President and Council may determine.

18. The First Member or President and Council may remove the name of any Probationer from the list of Probationers before the expiry of the period of probation. The Society will not be bound to disclose the reasons for such removal.

19. The First Member or President and Council may admit any person, who in their opinion is capable of being trained to assist efficiently members of the Society in their work and who is prepared to devote his life to such work, as a Permanent Assistant of the Society, on such terms as the First Member or President and Council may determine. Permanent Assistants will be divided into two classes-Senior and Junior according to their educational and other qualifications.

20. A Permanent Assistant may, on grounds of special fitness and after a period of approved service of not less than three years, be admitted as a member of the Society.

21. The First Member of President and Council may remove the name of any Permanent Assistant from the list of Permanent Assistants of the Society. The Society will not be bound to disclose the reasons for such removal.

22. The First Member or President and Council may admit any person, who is in full sympathy with the objects of the Society and is prepared to devote his life to such work as may be assigned to him for the benefit of the Society, as an Attache of the Society on such terms and under such control as the First Member or President and Council may determine.

23. The First Member or President and Council may remove the name of any Attache from the list of Attaches of the Society. The Society will not be bound to disclose the reasons for such removal.

24. The First Member or President and Council may enrol any person, who is in full sympathy with its objects and who is prepared to devote a portion of his time and resources to the furtherance of its work, as an Associate of the Society.

25. Probationers, Permanent Assistants, Attaches and Associates will have no voice in the management of the affairs of the Society and no interest in the Society's property or funds.

26. All property of the Society shall belong to the Society in its corporate character, and no member, in his individual capacity, nor the heirs, executors or assignees of any member shall have any right to any portion of it.

27. The property of the Society shall be held by three trustees, one of whom shall be the First Member or President for the time being and the other two, such Members as may be elected by the Members of the Society for the purpose.

28. All contracts, entered into for and on behalf of the Society, shall be in the name of the First Member or President.

In all suits brought by or against the Society, the Society shall be represented by the First Member or President.

29. The Society shall not be dissolved by the death, secession or removal of any member.

30. The First Member or President may, with the concurrence of a majority of the Ordinary Members of the Society, make after or rescind, any bye-laws for (1) the management of the affairs of the Society and the conduct of its business; (2) the custody, disposal and control of the funds of the Society; (3) the provision to be made for members of the Society and their families and the grant of special allowances to them, in special circumstances; (4) the grant of leave to members of the Society; (5) the grant of allowances to Permanent Assistants and Attaches of the Society; and (6) the carrying out in other ways of the objects of the Society.

31. The first Member or President and Council shall have the power to take whatever steps may be deemed necessary in the interest of the Society, provided that they are not inconsistent with the objects of the Society or with the provisions or spirit of any of the rules or byelaws at the time in force.

32. No alteration shall be made in this constitution, unless, it is recommended by the Council with the concurrence of not less than three-fourths of the members of the Society and the recommendation accepted by the First Member or President.

The following Bye-Laws have been made under rule 30 :

(1) The Society shall, as circumstances permit, establish Branches for work in different parts of the country. At the head of each Branch there shall be a Senior Member whose appointment and removal shall vest in the First Member or President and Council. The affairs of each Branch shall be managed by a Board consisting of the Senior Member and the. Ordinary Members belonging to it.

(2) (a) Every Member under training will be granted an allowance of Rs. 30 a month for the first two years of his training and Rs. 35 for the next three.

(b) Every Ordinary Member will be granted an allowance of Rs. 55 a month for the first five years, Rs. 60 for the next five years and Rs. 65 afterwards.

(c) All Members, whether under training or Ordinary will be granted a personal allowance of Rs. 10 per month in addition to the allowances mentioned above.

(d) The Senior Member of a Branch will be granted a special allowance of Rs. 10 a month.

(e) A rent allowance, not exceeding Rs. 15 a month in Bombay and Rs. 10 elsewhere, or the actual rent paid if less, will be granted 'to Ordinary Members, in case three are no quarters available on the premises of the Society.

(f) The allowance of Junior Permanent Assistants will be Rs. 15 to Rs. 20 and that of Senior Permanent Assistants Rs. 20 to Rs. 30 per month.

(3) (a) A Member under training is entitled to two months' leave every year, which can be granted by the First Member or President, and, if the applicant is attached to a Branch the Senior Member of that Branch.

(b) Ordinary Members are entitled to a month's leave every year, which can be granted by the First Member or President, and, if the applicant is attached to a Branch, the Senior Member of that Branch.

(c) Ordinary Members of the Central Provinces and Berar are entitled to one month and ten days' privilege leave if they go on leave on the Ist of May.

(d) All members are entitled to twenty days' casual leave in a year.

(e) Both casual and privilege leave mentioned above will only be sanctioned if the work of the Society permits.

(4) (a) The life of every member will, on admission, be assured by the Society, in favour of the First Member or the President for the time being, for a sum of Rs. 3' 000 payable at death. If no Insurance Company accepts the life of any member for assurance, the First Member or President and Council may make such other arrangement as they deem fit to secure, in the case of such member, The object of this Bye-Law.

(b) On the death of a member, whose life has been assured, the First Member or the President shall pay the amount recovered on the life policy of the deceased to such member or members of his family as the deceased member may, by will or otherwise in writing, have directed. In the absence of such direction, the First Member or the President and Council shall have the power to determine whether the amount recovered maybe paid to any member or members of the deceased's family, and if so, to whom.

(5) The First Member or President and Council may grant, in special circumstances, a special allowance to a member, suited to the requirements of his case.

(6) If a member secedes from the Society he and his family shall forfeit all claim to the benefit secured to him or them under these Bye-Laws."

[The following is the full text of the speech delivered by the Gokhale at the National Liberal Club, London.]

Sir Henry Cotton, Ladies and Gentlemen—I feel very grateful to the Political Committee of the National Liberal Club for their kind invitation to me to address them this evening on the subject of India. Political reformers in India are, in one sense, the natural allies of the Liberal Party in England; for we, in India, are struggling to assert in our own country those very principles which are now the accepted creed of the Liberal Party in England. Peace, retrenchment and reform are our watch-words, as they are yours. We are like you seeking to throw open to the unprivileged many the advantages which at present are a monopoly of the privileged few; and we are fighting against the predominance of the interests of a class over those of the mass of the people. It is true that I use the word 'allies' only in a limited sense—in the sense of parties that have a common aim, even though they do not take joint or common action in pursuing that aim. And I recognize that, a, things are, we can't claim to be allies of the Liberal Party in any fuller sense of the term, for the simple reason that we have nothing to offer the Liberal Party in return for what it can do for us, except the gratitude and attachment of a helpless people, and this may not count for much in the eyes of many.

However, of one thing I am certain-that we are entitled to look for sympathy and support from the Liberal Party when we address our appeal to that party for a large and steadily increasing measure of self-government being conceded to the people of India. Ladies and gentlemen, it is now, roughly speaking, a hundred years since the destinies of India and England came to be linked together. How we came under your rule is a question into which no useful purpose will be served by enquiring on an occasion like this. But two things I wish to say for my countrymen. First, that because we came under the rule of foreigners, it does not mean that we are like some savage or semi-civilized People whom you have subjugated. The People of India are an ancient race who had attained a high degree of civilization long before the ancestors of European nations understood what civilization was. India has been the birth-place of great religions. She was also the cradle and long the home of literature and philosophy, of science and arts. But God does not give everything to every people, and India in the past was nor known for that love of liberty and that appreciation of free 1. institutions which one finds to be so striking a characteristic of the West. Secondly, because the Indians are under the rule of foreigners, it does not follow that they are lacking in what is called the martial spirit; for some of the best troops that fight the battles of the Empire today are drawn from the Indians themselves. I mention these two things because I want you to recognize that though we have lost our independence, we have not, on that account, quite forfeited our title to the respect and consideration of civilized people. Your earlier race of statesmen, indeed, never failed to recognize this freely. They perceived the finger of Providence in the succession of events which ultimately set a small island at one end of the world to rule over a great country at another end of the world; and they were quite sincere when they stated that they regarded India as a solemn trust and that they would administer the country in the spirit in which all trust ought to be administered, i.e., with the sole object of promoting the best interests of the Indians themselves.

Well, a hundred years have now elapsed since then and no one can charge us with being in a hurry to pronounce an opinion, if we now pass under review the results of your hundred years' rule in India. The first task that confronted your statesmen in India was naturally the consolidation of your rule, and this they proceeded to effect by introducing into that country the appliances of your material civilization and by elaborating there an administrative machinery conforming to the type that prevails in the west. And, on the whole, this work has been extremely well done. The country is now covered with, Railways and Post offices and Telegraphs. Peace and order reign throughout the land. Justice, though costly, is fairly administered as between Indian and Indian, though, when it comes to be a matter between Indian and Englishman, it is another story. Of course, the machinery of administration that has been evolved is by no means perfect-there are obvious defects of a serious character which need not be there-but, on the whole, I repeat, this part of your work has been extremely well done and you are entitled to regard it with a just sense of satisfaction. Side by side with consolidation, your statesmen had to undertake another work-that of conciliation. And this work of reconciling the people of India to the rule of foreigners—a difficult and delicate task-has also been satisfactorily accomplished. This result has been achieved by the Parliament and the Sovereign of England enunciating a noble policy towards India and by the introduction into that country of what is known as Western education—the same kind of education that is given to your youths in your schools and colleges-an education that, among other things, inspires one with a love of free institutions. Three-quarters of a century ago, your Parliament passed an Act, known as the Charter Act of 1833, laying down the principles on which the government of India was to be based. And twenty-five years later, the late Queen addressed a Proclamation to the people of India reiterating the same policy.

The Charter Act of 1833 and the Proclamation of 1858 pledge the word of your Parliament and your Sovereign to the people of India—and these are the only two authorities that can speak in your name—that the sole aim of British rule in India is the promotion of the interests of the Indian people and that, in the government of the country, there would be equality for the two races, no disability of any kind being imposed on any one by reason merely of race or colour or creed.

A policy so enunciated was bound to win all hearts and it went a long way to reconcile the people of India to your rule. Along with this enunciation of the principles of your government, came the opening of schools and colleges such as you have in your own country, and it is a remarkable fact that the three older Universities of India were established almost during the dark days of the Mutiny. Be it remembered, also, that the gates of Western knowledge were thrown open to us with a clear anticipation of the results that were likely to follow; and in a well-known speech Lord Macaulay used memorable language in this connection. He observed that it was, perhaps, inevitable that the people of India, having been brought up in Western knowledge, would in course of time demand European institutions in the government of their country, and he said : Whether such a day will ever come I know not; but never will I attempt to avert or retard it. Whenever it comes, it will be the proudest day in English history. Thus, you declared Policy towards India and the introduction of Western education, joined to your higher Western standards of government, effected the work of conciliation in a satisfactory manner, and twenty years ago, an Englishman going out to India would have found on every side a frank acceptance by the people of British rule as their national rule, as they then fully believed that, under that rule, they would be allowed to work out their own salvation and eventually attain the colonial type of government—so that they could remain within your Empire and yet have a position worthy of their self-respect. And if today this faith has been seriously weakened, it is because your statesmen have now been hesitating at the third stage that has become inevitable after consolidation and conciliation-the stage of reconstruction. When you first started your work in India, when Western standards of administration had to be introduced into the country and there was no Western education to enable us to understand those standards' it was, perhaps, indispensable that all power should be lodged in the hands of a few English officials. But now that the schools and colleges and universities have been doing their work for half a century and more, and when a large and steadily increasing class of men educated after the Western model—a class qualified and anxious to take part in the administration of the country-has come into existence, you must reconstruct the foundations of your rule so as to find room for these men inside the administration, if the pledges given in your name are intended to be redeemed. Unfortunately it is here that the statesmen responsible for the government of India are hesitating with results which already threaten to be disastrous. Twenty-five years ago, indeed, a noble attempt was made by a great Englishman, who went out to rule there as Viceroy, at such reconstruction and his name is cherished to the present day with feelings of the deepest affection and gratitude throughout India.

Lord Ripon-that is that Viceroy's name—strove hard and manfully for five years to liberalise the foundations of British rule in India and introduce, to some extent, those changes in the administration of the country which the people had been led to expect and which the spread of Western education among them had rendered inevitable. He gave the country a little local self-government; he gave an important stimulus to education; and he tried to remove some of those glaring inequalities between the Indian and Englishman which at present prevail in that country.

What was the result ? He exposed himself to such fierce persecution at the hands of his own countrymen in India, that no successor of his has ventured to repeat his experiment. Not only that; during the last few years, a reactionary policy has been pursued towards the educated class of the country and this reaction has taken the form of active repression during the last three years of Lord Curzon's administration.

Now, I want you to see that such repression can never succeed. According to the last census, there are a million men in India today who have come under the influence of some sort of English education. You cannot hope to keep this large and growing class shut out completely from power, as at present. Even if it were possible to perpetuate the present monopoly of power by the bureaucracy, your national honour demands that such an attempt should not be made. But it is not possible, and any attempt to achieve the impossible can only end in disaster. Already great harm has been done. The faith of my countrymen in British rule, so strong at one time, has been seriously weakened and large numbers of young men are coming forward who do not believe in it at all. The situation is one that must fill all thoughtful minds with serious apprehensions about the future, and unless you here realize it properly, it is difficult to see how it is to mend." Ladies and gentlemen, I have admitted that your countrymen are entitled to great credit for having introduced into an Oriental country the Western type of the machinery of administration. But, after all, such machinery is a means to an end-it is not the end in itself. It is, therefore, necessary to consider how far the best interests-material and moral—of the people of India have been promoted by your administration during the last hundred years. This, in reality, is the main test-I had almost said the supreme test. If the results, judged by this test, were satisfactory, however much one might object on principle to the present form of government maintained in India, there would be something to be said in its favour. If, on the other hand, these results are found to be on the whole unsatisfactory, for the sake of your national honour as also in the interests of the Indian people themselves, a reconsideration of the existing arrangements becomes necessary. Let us first consider the moral results. These, it will be found, are of a mixed character. There is a great deal in them which you may regard with satisfaction and even pride. The blessings of peace, the establishment of law and order, the introduction of Western education, and the freedom of speech and the appreciation of liberal institutions that have followed in its wake all these are things that stand to the credit of your rule. On the other hand, there are great evils too, and of these none, to my mind, is so great as the continuous dwarfing or stunting of our race that is taking place under your rule. Our rigorous exclusion from all power and all positions of trust and responsibility, on a scale never before attempted in the history of humanity, involving, as it does, an enforced disuse of our national abilities-is leading to a steady deterioration of our race, and this, I venture to think, is a cruel, an iniquitous wrong you are inflicting upon us.

According to a Parliamentary return published in 1892, there are in India altogether about 2,400 officers carrying a salary of £ 700 and upwards, and of these only about 60 are held by Indians, and even most of these are of a comparatively low level. Another great evil is indicated by the present political status of the India people. All the three hundred millions of them put together have not got, under the constitution, as much power as a single elector in England to affect the position of the Government. Then the entire population is kept disarmed and as though it was not enough humiliation to the Indians to be deprived thus of their natural right to bear arms in defence of their hearths and homes, England has recently entered into an alliance with another Oriental nation—a nation that has borrowed much in the past from India-to repel foreign aggression on the borders of India and, incidentally, to perpetuate the present state of bondage for the Indians themselves. This is our position in our own country. If we go to your self-governing Colonies like Natal, we are treated as outside the pale of civilisation, and they object to our walking on the footpaths, or travelling in first-class carriages, or in seeking accommodation at hotels ! In Crown Colonies like the Transvaal, our humiliation is even more complete.

Among the reasons for which you went to war with those two Boer Republics, wiping them, in the end, out of existence, you made rather prominent mention of certain ordinances which the Boer Governments had promulgated against the Indians residing within their territories. But though these ordinances existed on paper in the time of the Boer Republics, they never were actually enforced, because those Governments were afraid of the mighty arm of England that they thought was behind the Indians. But now that the territories have become Crown Colonies, and are under the control of the English Colonial office, these same ordinances, incredible as it may seem, are being rigorously enforced against us. If this is our position in your Empire after our having been a hundred years under your rule, I am sure no one will pretend that the moral results of your rule may be regarded with satisfaction. Let us now turn to the material results, and here, I am sorry to say, the verdict is even more emphatic against your rule. I firmly believe, and I say this after a careful study of about twenty years of the question, that the economic results of British rule in India have been absolutely disastrous. That the mass of the people India are at present sunk in frightful poverty is now admitted by all, including the most inveterate official optimist.

A few facts, however, may be mentioned to bring this home clearly to your minds. Your average annual income has been estimated at about f 42 per head. Ours, according to official estimates, is about f 2 per head and according to non-official estimates, only a little more than f I per head. Your imports per head are about f 13; ours about 5s. per head. The total deposits in your Postal Savings Bank amount to 148 million sterling and you have in addition in the Trustees Savings Banks about 52 million sterling. Our Postal Savings Bank deposits, with a population seven times as large as yours, are only about 7 million sterling and even of this a little over one-tenth is held by Europeans. Your total paid-up capital of joint-stock companies is about 1,900 million sterling. Ours is not quite 26 million sterling and the greater part of this again is European. Four-fifths of our people are dependent upto agriculture and agriculture has been for some time steadily deteriorating. Indian agriculturists are too poor and are, moreover, too heavily indebted to be able to apply any capital to land, and the result is that over the greater part of India agriculture is, as Sir James Card pointed out more than twenty-five years ago, only a process of exhaustion of the soil. The yield per acre is steadily diminishing, being now only about 8 to 9 bushels an acre against about 30 bushels here in England; the losses of the agricultural community during the famines of the last eight years in crops and cattle have, according to a competent Commission, amounted to 200 million sterling. Forty millions of people, according to one great Anglo-Indian authority-Sir William Hunter-pass through life with only one meal a day. According to another authority-Sir Charles Elliot seventy millions of people in India do not know what it is to have their hunger fully satisfied even once in the whole course of the year. The poverty of the people of India thus considered by itself, is truly appalling. And if this is the state of things after a hundred years of your rule, you cannot claim that your principal aim in India has been the promotion of the interests of the Indian people. But this is not all. I think there is ample evidence to show that even this deplorable condition of the mass of people in India has been further deteriorating steadily.

Thus, famines are growing more frequent, their extent is larger and the suffering they occasion more acute and widespread. Then during the last seven years, the plague has been ravaging the country in addition to famines. Now to those who consider the matter superficially, the plague may appear to be only a Providential scourge. But it really carries away hundreds or thousands 'of people, because, owing to constant under-feeding, the people have not got the stamina to resist the attacks of plague. Then it will be found that in the last decade of the 19th century, the population in the older provinces of India has been stationary and in some of them it has even declined ! But the most conclusive testimony on this point—a testimony that there is no getting over-is supplied by the death-rate of the country. Let us take the last twenty years—I take this long period of twenty years, because we shall not then be open to the charge that we have only taken a few years rendered abnormal by famine or plague—and to emphasize the situation, let us compare the movement of the death-rate in India with that of the death-rate in England during the same time. Let us divide these twenty years into four periods of five years each that is the only way to present a fairly reliable generalization and what do we find ? In the first period of five years, an average annual death rate was between 24 and 25 per thousand; yours at that time was about 20 per thousand. In the next five years, ours rose form under 25 to about 28 per thousand. Yours, on the other hand, owing to the greater attention paid to the condition of life of the working classes, fell from 20 to between 18 and 19. In the third period of five years, our death-rate further mounted from 28 to 30 per thousand. Yours again came down from over 18 to about 17.

Finally, in the last period, ours went up still higher-from 30 to about 32, while yours has fallen still further from 17 to less than 16. For the last year it stands according to the Statistical Abstract for British India recently published, at about 35 per thousand. Thus, during the last twenty years, while your death-rate has been steadily declining, ours has risen by no less than 10 per thousand, which on a population of three hundred millions means three million deaths annually more than was the case twenty years ago. Surely this is a frightful sum of human misery and you must find out where the responsibility for it is, for there must be responsibility somewhere. I think I need not say anything more on the subject of the material condition of India. To any one who looks beneath the surface, this fearful impoverishment was bound to result from the peculiar character of British rule. The administration by a foreign agency is so costly and the dominant position of the Englishman's position in every field gives him such an advantage in acquiring wealth in India, that a large drain of wealth has continuously gone on for years and years from India to England. During the last forty years, the net excess of our exports over imports has amounted to about a thousand million pounds. No country-and least of all a poor country like India-can stand so large a drain; and steady impoverishment has been the natural consequence. Well, things cannot go on at this rate for long, and the only remedy for the state of things must be sought in the steady association of the people of India with the administration of their own affairs till at last the colonial type of government is reached.

As things are managed at present, the real interests of the people do not occupy the first place not the second place nor even the third place on the slate of Government. Nearly half the net revenue is eaten up by army charges. Large salaries are paid to English officials and the charge on their account is steadily rising. Nearly one-third of the net revenue is withdrawn from India to be spent in this country for purposes of the Government... Railway extension has taken precedence of irrigation in the past, because English capitalists are interested in the former. The progress of the people is obviously bound up with the spread of primary education-but how little so far has been done may be seen from the fact that, at the present moment; four villages out of every five are without a school-house and seven children out of eight are growing up in darkness and all the moral helplessness which comes of such darkness. The greatest need of the hour at present in India is industrial education, and yet there is not a single decent technical institute in the whole country. The truth is, there is nobody at present in the Government of India whose interests are permanently identified with those of the people. As long as this state of things continues, it is hopeless to expect that large questions which are urgently pressing for solution and which must be dealt with in a statesmanlike manner with the sole aim of promoting the interests of the people-such as the spread of primary education and of industrial education, the fearful indebtedness of the peasantry and such others will receive the attention they require.

2

GOKHALE AT FERGUSSON COLLEGE

Fergusson College was located in the old Gadre Wada in Shaniwarpeth with its old-world ornamental arches and overcrowded benches. It offered a complete contrast to the government-owned Deccan College. It could not boast of a hostel, a library or even a playing field; its teachers were young, inexperienced and without the high qualification and prestige of the English Principal and professors of the Deccan College. 'A tinpot college' was how the students of the Deccan College described the Fergusson College. However, the Fergusson College more than made up for what it lacked in amenities in the enthusiasm of its teachers and students; they were proud that theirs was a wholly 'indigenous institution', run entirely by Indians fired with a missionary zeal. Sir James Fergusson, the Governor of Bombay, after whom the college was named, had encouraged its promoters; he visited the New English School and presided over its prize-distribution ceremony in 1884. There was even a proposal to turn over the management of the government-owned Deccan College to the Deccan Education Society, formed to run the New English School, the Fergusson College and other such institutions. Anglo-Indian critics, however, did not take long to scent the dangers inherent in colleges run entirely by Indians.

'The minds of the present generation of educated natives', wrote the Times of India, on 10 March 1895, 'have been moulded by European scholars with whom they have been associated. The minds of future generations will be moulded by men who have founded a college on the historic site of the Peshwa's palace and have strong views about patriotism.' The official attitude towards the Fergusson College gradually changed from one of sympathy to suspicion, and in August 1890 we find Governor Harris confiding to the Secretary of State that the Fergusson College was a 'nest of disaffection'.' Seven years later, the Bombay Government openly frowned on the Fergusson College and sought to clip the wings of its teachers. Gokhale started his career at the Fergusson College as a lecturer in English literature. When Tilak resigned in 1890, Gokhale was asked to take the mathematics classes. The following year, D. K. Karve, who was Gokhale's classmate in Elphinstone College, joined Fergusson College and relieved him of the mathematics classes. Gokhale seems to have found little difficulty in switching from literature to mathematics and from mathematics to history and political economy.

A little book he wrote on arithmetic for schools proved extremely popular, and did for him what the Autobiography did for Jawaharlal Nehru :2 it made him financially secure. The study of mathematics was a useful discipline for Gokhale; it gave a statistical bias to his study of economic and financial problems and lent clarity and trenchancy to his criticisms of official policies. The close reasoning and the great precision which were to characterize his writings and speeches on economic matters may have owed something to his training in mathematics in his youth. But he also had unique opportunities for intimate discussion with two of the most knowledgeable critics of the Indian economic scene: G. V. Joshi and M. G. Ranade. From them Gokhale learnt the value of the Blue Books and official reports for analysing and assailing the policies of the government. For an admirer of Edmund Burke and Robert Browning, wading through statistical tables and official verbiage may not have been a wholly pleasant pastime, but, as we shall see later, it paid rich dividends. Gokhale was an exceedingly conscientious teacher. If we ire to believe the recorded recollections of some of his students, he hardly ever laughed in the classroom. Lack of humour does not, however, seem to have been a serious handicap to him. He was well liked by his students, who found him accessible and helpful. They were spellbound by his clear and eloquent exposition in the classroom. 'The bell that tolled the close of the period', recalled one of them many years later, 'often came as a deep disappointment'.3 Gokhale did not treat the study of history and economics merely as an intellectual exercise; he made it a key to the understanding of contemporary problems. In his lectures on economics, he stressed the necessity of a protective tariff for India's nascent industries. In his lectures on history, he drew telling parallels between Ireland and India; he felt sure that the tide of liberalism and democracy which had swept across nineteenth century Europe was bound to reach Asia.

Dhavle, who graduated from the Rajaram College at Kolhapur and attended some of Gokhale's lectures on Indian history at the Fergusson College, recalls: 'He spoke on the Peshwas. He marshalled his facts with great skill, gave opinions of Marshman, Hunter and Grant Duff, but said that the opinions of these English historians should not be considered the last word on the subject.14 Gokhale wanted his students to prepare themselves for the great responsibilities which awaited them. Such was his preoccupation with the political and economic problems of India that he went out of his way to discourage promising students from taking up the study of science. Conditions in India, he told them, were not propitious for specialization in industrial and scientific studies. 'The study of history, economics and politics', he argued, 'would balance our judgements, widen our sympathies and broaden our vision... and if we have a large class of men well-read in these subjects, the level of public life will, of necessity, be raised.' As a teacher, Gokhale never seemed to be in a hurry. He explained every passage and argued every problem from different angles. Though he spoke and wrote chaste Marathi, his real medium was English, which he wielded with an uncommon facility and elegance. He had closely studied the works of Edmund Burke, John Stuart Mill and John Morley.

Such was his sensitivity to a good English style that he tended to form a favourable first impression of any unknown correspondent who sent him a wellcomposed letter. For this weakness he had sometimes to pay dearly, by being saddled with 'the company of undesirable persons who first approached him by means of a fluent letter in imitation of Macaulay or Burke'. Gokhale was never slipshod in his thinking or expression. Sometimes he would walk up and down the room ('like a tiger in a cage' as his friend and pupil R. P. Paranjpye once put it) to think out the precise word or phrase he wanted to use. His speeches and articles were well-argued and compact. As a student, Gokhale was nervous and halting in his speech, but he resolved to overcome this handicap after he became a teacher. He memorized many famous speeches. While at the Deccan College, he is reputed to have committed to memory portions of Burke's Reflections on the French Revolution. The result was that in his early twenties he was able to make a mark as a speaker, and was much in demand at meetings organized in Poona by the Fergusson College, the Deccan Education Society, and the Sarvajanik Sabha-and later at the annual sessions of the Indian National Congress. In 1896, he was invited to deliver the annual address of the Bombay Graduates Association. This was a signal honour, as among the speakers in previous years had been such eminent figures as Pherozeshah Mehta and Ranade.

Like Ranade, Gokhale usually wrote his speeches; with his excellent memory he could, however, effortlessly deliver them without any notes. His close reasoning, polished diction, poetical allusions and apt quotations delighted a generation of educated Indians who studied English classics with greater care and enjoyment than we can imagine today. It did not take Gokhale long to discover that it was not easy to be at once a conscientious teacher, journalist and politician. What it meant in terms of hard work may be gathered from a letter which he wrote to G. V. Joshi in 1891. He was lecturing twenty hours a week and also correcting students' notebooks. His week-ends were almost entirely taken up by the editing of the Sudharak and the Quarterly Journal and by the secretarial work of the Sarvajanik Sabha. In addition to this back-breaking schedule, he had to keep himself posted with current affairs in India and abroad, and to read the Kesari, Mahratta, Dnyanaprakash, the Times of India and other newspapers and magazines. He subscribed to the Dublin Freeman, and The Times [London]. He read the proceedings of legislative councils, and official reports, without which it would have been impossible for him to function effectively as an editor and politician. In 1895, Gokhale was elected to the senate of the Bombay University of which he remained a member for nearly twenty years.

He was appointed the examiner in history and political economy by the Bombay University, an honour then rare for an Indian professor. It brought him an additional burden, but gave much satisfaction to the Indian academic community which resented the virtual monopoly of examinerships by European professors. 'I have heard of grumblings in some Anglo-Indian newspapers', wrote Paranjpye to Gokhale, 'about some of these appointments [of Indians] owing to their being natives, but they are incomparably better than insulting us by appointing the average two-penny, half-penny Englishmen whose only qualification is their white skin as examiners in all conceivable subjects.' All this added up to a heavy load, but in 1892 Gokhale also became the secretary of the governing body of the Council of the Deccan Education Society. It was a great honour, but it brought additional worries. A new building for the Fergusson College was planned; the foundation stone had been laid in 1892. Funds had to be raised, and Gokhale had to spend some week-ends and summer vacations contacting potential donors in Bombay and Gujarat.

Thanks largely to Gokhale's efforts, Fergusson College moved into the new building in 1895. His health was nearly shattered in the process, but the experience was useful. Many years later when he was called upon to collect funds for the Indian National Congress or the Servants of India Society, the contacts he had made in the mofussil stood him in good stead. When Gokhale was the secretary of the Council of the Deccan Education Society, its president was F. G. Selby, Principal of the Deccan College. Selby was a remarkable Englishman who had come to India in 1877 after taking his degree from the University of Oxford. He had edited Bacon's Essays and Aristotle's Ethics, but his popularity with the Indian elite in Poona was due less to his scholarship than to his great amiability and complete freedom from racial prejudice. To many Indians he seemed the epitome of the best qualities of an

Englishman. Even though he was the Principal of the rival Deccan College, he was elected to preside over the governing body of the Fergusson College. Gokhale's wrote a letter to Selby who was his friend :

Throughout these years, I have felt for you the reverence and affection that one feels for a teacher, and if my attitude of mind towards Englishmen generally is today more friendly and more appreciative than that of many of my colleagues, it is largely due to what I have seen of Englishmen in you. The thought that what I said or wrote would perhaps meet your eye has always increased my sense of responsibility and exercised a sobering and restraining influence on my thoughts and words. Gokhale had inherited a good constitution. As a student he was no bookworm. He took long walks and played cricket and tennis. He enjoyed a good game of cards, billiards or chess. If he had continued to balance mental toil with physical exercise and recreation, all would have been well. The seduction of politics and his youthful ardour, however, made him careless of his health. He tended to take too much upon himself and to take everything too seriously. If there was an important speech or article to prepare, he postponed it till the last day, and then sat up the whole night to complete it. He did not realize the risks he was running by curtailing his sleep. His food habits were also not very admirable. He disliked ghee, but could hardly resist food seasoned with chillies. His hair-trigger sensitivity to criticism added an emotional strain to the burden of his work and responsibility.

An uncharitable comment in the Kesari or the Times of India, a careless remark by a friend, or a malicious innuendo by a political opponent could throw him into a fit of despair. Politics is a rough game and requires, even from its luckiest practitioners, not only intellectual toughness but a thick skin. It is a strange paradox that Gokhale, who was initiated into journalism and politics almost in his teens, should have remained all his life so sensitive and vulnerable to criticism. So much of a prominent politician's life is sometimes lived in public that one may be tempted to imagine that he has no life of his own apart from politics. In India there is the further difficulty that we know very little about the private lives of our public figures; it is not part of decorum to talk or write about one's intimate life even to one's closest friends. The barest facts of Gokhale's domestic life have therefore to be pieced together from stray references in his correspondence, and the recorded recollections of his friends and relatives. He was married early (at the age of fifteen) as was customary at that time among the Brahmans of Maharashtra.

About his first wife, Savitribai, we know little except that she suffered from leprosy and never lived with her husband. In 1887, at twenty-one, Gokhale was persuaded by his mother and elder brother to marry again. Savitribai, whose malady was incurable, is said to have given her consent. Her gesture was reciprocated by Gokhale and his second wife, Radhabai, both of whom treated Savitribai with much kindness and arranged for her treatment and care until she died a few years later."

The second marriage of Gokhale was a happy one. Radhabai gave birth to a daughter, Kashibai, in 1893. Three years later, in 1896, another girl, Godavari, was born. It is doubtful if Radhabai knew more than the rudiments of Marathi, or understood the great world of literature and politics which absorbed her husband. To live with a man who was wedded to intellectual pursuits, voluntary poverty and political ambition could not have been easy.

The relentless schedule which Gokhale imposed upon himself left him little time to spend with his family. This may not have weighed heavily on Radhabai; a Hindu wife of her age and class could fulfil herself by serving her husband and children, dividing her time between the home and the temple, and remain remarkably undemanding and uncomplaining. One wonders if Radhabai sensed the special position that her young husband occupied not only in the Fergusson College but in Poona. There is some evidence that she tried to share her husband's responsibilities. Dr Krishnabai Kevalkar, the first girl to join the Fergusson College in 1894, recalled many years later that Gokhale had helped her in securing admission and that 'Mrs Gokhale was very sympathetic towards me throughout my career'. Politics brought to Gokhale moments of great excitement and exaltation as well as of disillusionment and despair. Of his attachment to his wife and children, we get brief but revealing glimpses in the recollections of Wacha, who accompanied him to London in 1897, and of Mrs Congreve, who nursed him back to health after a serious illness in England. For a man who was so earnest, so ambitious, and so sensitive, that little house in Bhatwadekar Wada in Poona, where Radhabai was bringing up their two little daughters, must have been a little haven. The haven was not to last long. On 18 October 1900, Radhabai gave birth to a child. Neither the mother nor the child lived.

Association with Congress

The visits of Hume and Naoroji were reminders of the ties between Poona and the Indian National Congress. It was at the annual sessions of the Congress that Gokhale experienced a sense of participation in national politics. In November 1888, even before he was elected secretary of the. Sarvajanik Sabha, Gokhale attended the first Provincial Conference at Poona, which elected delegates to the Allahabad Congress. He moved one of the important resolutions at the Provincial Conference and was elected its joint secretary.' Gokhale could not, however, attend the Allahabad Congress.

The following year, in the Christmas week of 1889, when the Congress met at Bombay with Sir William Wedderburn in the chair, the large contingent of fifty-nine delegates from Poona included (to quote from the official report of the proceedings) 'Mr Gopal Krishna Gokhale, B.A., Brahmin, Teacher and Professor, Fergusson College, Joint Secretary, Provincial Congress, Joint Editor, Sudharak, Editor, Quarterly Journal, Sarvajanik Sabha'. Among his fellow delegates were three of his colleagues in the Fergusson College, B. G. Tilak, V. S. Apte and G. G. Agarkar. Gokhale's maiden speech on the Congress platform was delivered on 27 December 1889. He spoke in support of an amendment moved by Tilak to a resolution on the reform of the Governor-General's Legislative Council. It was an uninspiring performance, but on the following day when Gokhale criticized the Government of India's action on the report of the Public Service Commission, he gave ample proof of his gifts as a speaker.

Recalling the 'noble promises' of the Charter of 1833 and the Queen's Proclamation of 1858, he argued that those who shrank from fulfilling them 'must be prepared to face the painful dilemma of hypocrisy or treachery, must be prepared to admit that England was insincere when she made those promises or that she is prepared to break faith now'. He compared 'the present struggle' between Anglo-Indians and Indians to the struggle between the 'patricians and plebians' in ancient Rome and between 'the classes and the masses' in modern Britain. He reiterated the demand that the I.C.S. examination should be held simultaneously in India and England: 'For posts in our own country, if we are not to be examined in our own country, I do not know what justice and equity are.' The young professor-politician was developing his style as a speaker: mastery of facts, marshalling of arguments, a repertoire of literary and historical allusions and a felicitous English style which was calculated to fascinate a generation of educated Indians. His diction was elegant, but he did not hesitate to call a political spade a spade. The January 1890 issue of the Quarterly Journal of the Poona Sarvajanik Sabha carried an article on the Bombay Congress which was evidently from Gokhale's own pen: 'The Fifth National Congress was in many ways the most remarkable of all the Congresses hitherto held. In point of number-nearly 1900 delegates- and in point of the variety of subjects on which resolutions were passed, no other Congress has approached it; while in regard to the eloquence displayed on the platform and enthusiasm pervading the general ranks of the delegates, it has, to say the least, fully maintained its traditions of previous years.' With Sir William Wedderburn in the chair and with Charles Bradlaugh on the platform, the atmosphere of the Bombay Congress was charged with great enthusiasm. In half an hour, a sum of Rs. 63,000 was raised for the work of the Congress. Gokhale's article stoutly defended the representative character of the Congress. He analysed the motives of its detractors. Foremost among them were the Anglo-Indian gentlemen, 'whose illiberality of mind and narrowness of vision are equalled only by the selfishness of their aims and the elasticity of their conscience, and who are therefore bitter and uncompromising foes of all political and educational progress of the Natives of this country'. Then there were those 'wellmeaning but timid souls, who can never contemplate the prospect of any change in the constitution without trembling'. Finally, there were the 'aspiring officials, and self-seeking sycophants, and spiteful cavillers and misguided simpletons... fit only to be tools in the hands of the designing persons'. Gokhale refuted the charge that Muslims and Parsis were keeping away from the Congress.

A few Parsis had been critical, but the Parsi community-on the basis of its population was well-represented in the rank and file of the Congress as well as in its leadership. As for the Muslims, they had so lagged behind in education that the wonder was 'not that more Mahomedan delegates are not seen in the Congress, but so many are'. Gokhale also answered the charge that the Congress did not represent the interests of the mass of the people. He could not see how the Congress demands were opposed to the real interests of the Indian masses. How could the masses be hurt by election, rather than nomination of some of the members of the Legislative Councils?

In whose interest, if not that of the masses, was the reduction of the salt duty, the establishment of technical schools, the separation of the judiciary and the executive, and the reform of the police and revenue administration ? Gokhale affirmed that the interests of the educated and uneducated classes were not basically antagonistic. Education had 'merely put a tongue into the mouths that were dumb before'; the educated classes were merely the spokesmen of their countrymen. In any case it was presumptuous on the part of 'Anglo-Indian administrators, whose life passes in the seclusion of their bungalows or in the exclusive atmosphere of their offices, or in the shikar of wild beasts', to claim that they knew more of the wants and wishes of the masses of India than educated Indians who were in daily contact with their countrymen. A year later, when the Indian National Congress met at Calcutta, Gokhale spoke eloquently in favour of reducing the salt tax. The tax which had been increased pressed heavily on the Indian peasantry, living on the 'borderland of famine', to whom Gokhale applied (with a slight alteration) the lines of the Corn Law poet: Landless, joyless, helpless, hopeless, Gasping still for bread and breath; To their graves, by troubles haunted, India's helots toil till death. He reminded the delegates of the Calcutta Congress that the poor people in the villages had 'as much right to the comforts of this God's earth as you or I or anyone else'. 'I dare say', he said, 'there is not a single person present, not a single member of those who are called the middle and upper classes who have consumed during the last three years, one grain of salt less than he would have done if there had been no enhancement [of the salt tax].' He recalled that when the income-tax was imposed, official spokesmen had argued that the poorer classes were already bearing more than their share of the tax burdens. Why was the salt tax raised? asked Gokhale. Was it because 'the masses were almost certain to suffer silently without protest... whereas their wealthier brethren were... certain to denounce any taxation on them in the public press and at St. Andrew's dinner speeches?' 'We are appealing', declaimed Gokhale, 'to the sense of justice of the Government of India. We are appealing to their statesmanship, to their righteousness, and I even go further and say, to their mercy....' As Gokhale spoke at Congress sessions year after year, he gained in selfconfidence.

Whatever the subject under discussion he gave a good account of himself. He appealed to the better side of the ruling race, but was unsparing in his criticism of the authorities. Speaking at the Allahabad Congress (December 1892) on the Indian share in the higher ranks of the administration, he burst out: 'If ever a mountain was in labour and brought forth a mouse, it was in the present instance of the Public Service Commission.... I say it would be well for them [the British] to openly and publicly fling into flames all these promises, and pledges as so much wastepaper and tell us once for all that after all we are a conquered people and can have no rights or privileges.' At the Lahore Congress (December 1893), Gokhale charged the Government of India with pursuing 'a policy of retrogression', and treating the educated classes 'with increasing jealousy'. He criticized the rules for the Legislative Councils framed under the Act of 1892 and dwelt on the inequitable distribution of financial burdens between India and England. A recent debate in the House of Commons had revealed the raw deal India had received at the hands of the British War office and the Treasury. 'If ever the Government of the country were put on its trial', said Gokhale, 'I should be content to frame the indictment on those admissions [of responsible British statesmen].' The financial and economic partnership between India and England reminded him of the dwarf and the giant in Goldsmith's The Vicar of Wakefield. From 1889 onwards Gokhale attended the Congress sessions regularly. At the Nagpur Congress (189 1), he was elected a member of the 'Subjects Committee', the inner forum for the selection of subjects and speakers for the plenary session of the Congress. It was in the Subjects Committee that he had opportunities of meeting the senior leaders who decided the strategy and commanded the patronage of the Indian National Congress.

As the secretary of the Poona Sarvajanik Sabha and the editor of its journal, he was already acquainted with the leaders of western India; but it was at the annual Congress gatherings that he came to know the leaders from other provinces and acquired the reputation of a young, able and eloquent politician who was deferential towards his seniors but in dead earnest about politics. When the Indian National Congress met at Poona, Gokhale was one of the secretaries of the Reception Committee. The Poona Congress brought into the open a bitter rift in the body politic of Maharashtra, the roots of which lay in personal and social rather than in political issues.

Controversy on Social Reforms

In the long-drawn-out controversy between Agarkar and Tilak differences on social reform had not figured prominently, though they undoubtedly contributed to mutual misunderstanding and bitterness. After Tilak was forced out of the Deccan Education Society in 1890, social reform increasingly became a wedge in the public life of Poona. It is not easy for us to imagine the feelings of those who attacked and those who defended orthodox customs and ritual eighty years ago. Under Muslim rule, Hindu society had developed a defensive dogmatism and rigidity. As a system of thought Hinduism continued to be liberal, but as a social system it became increasingly exclusive and intolerant. Caste distinctions hardened; the professional priestly caste gained in authority; religion tended to be reduced to mechanical formulae; superstition and fatalism were at a premium.

A contemporary of Gokhale, G. S. Sardesai, the historian, has recorded how as a child he was required to take a bath if he happened to touch a person of the lowest caste, to wear at mealtimes clothes made only of 'pure textiles' (silk or wool) and to have a hair-cut only on an 'auspicious' day.' Little boys had to get their ear-lobes pierced; such was the importance attached to this custom that in Marathi nonHindus were often referred to by a term (avindh) meaning 'without the pierced earlobe'. Instructions on what, how and where to eat were carried to ludicrous lengths, not only by unsophisticated people in the villages but by the educated e lite. Some of the delegates to the meetings of the Indian National Congress carried or cooked their own food and ate behind closed doors to avoid the unholy gaze of their colleagues.

The more prosperous of them asked not only for Brahman cooks, but for Brahman cooks of particular sub-castes. In Bengal the eating of biscuits was at one time a serious enough transgression to merit excommunication from the caste.4 Excommunication was a deadly weapon, a sword of Damocles hanging over the head of anyone who dared to defy the canons of Hindu orthodoxy. In 1883 no Hindu youth in the whole of Bombay Presidency came forward to avail of a Parsi magnate's generous offer of a scholarship for qualifying as a barrister in England. The taboo on foreign travel was so strong that even Tilak, a devout and scholarly Hindu, had to undergo a penance when he returned from a visit to Burma in 1899. It was quite natural that contact with the West should have produced impatience with the strait-jacket of caste, custom and superstition. 'Our system is to a great extent become petrified...', complained Telang; 'the moral conceptions which once informed it have long since vanished and... we are now hugging the mere outer shell as if that were all in all.' 'A kind of death-in-life' was how N. G. Chandavarkar, another prominent figure in the social reform movement, described the state of Hindu society. 'We are neither Vedantists... nor Pauranics nor Tantrics', declared Swami Vivekananda. 'We are just "Don't-touchists". Our religion is in the kitchen. Our God is the cooking-pot, and our religion is "Don't touch me, I am holy." If this goes on for another century, every one of us will be in a lunatic asylum. Of the evils which were corroding Hindu society, none seemed graver than those which stunted the growth of Indian womanhood, Ranade's wife has recorded" how as a child she was forbidden to enter the front apartments of her own home and be seen in the preence of even her father. Singing and playing were unthinkable for girls, and so were reading and writing. One of her sisters was married at the age of five, another at seven; she was lucky to be married relatively late, at eleven. Pandita Ramabai, the Christian missionary who founded the Sharda Sadan in Poona, told the Education ComMission that no more than one in five hundred Indian women was literate. Early marriage was the root cause of illiteracy; it also resulted in another terrible institution; that of the child widow. Little girls, who hardly knew the meaning of marriage, were condemned to lifelong mourning when their boy-husbands, on whom they had hardly set their eyes, died. The condition of the infant widows, Ranade wrote in 1886, was 'a scandal and a wrong which is a disgrace to any well-regulated society'. The efforts of the great Bengali reformer, Iswarchandra Vidyasagar, culminated in the passage of the Hindu Widows Remarriage Act of 1856, but it afforded little real relief to the widows.

Thirty years after the passage of the Act, a child-widow, Godubai (who later married D. K. Karve the centenarian reformer of Poona), discovered that she was virtually a slave in the home of her deceased husband. To expiate the alleged sins of a past life which had robbed her of her husband, her head was shaved; she was made to wear a red sari, the widow's garb; she had to do all the menial tasks in the house, and on the farm. That the unfortunate victims of this tyranny were not few was shown by a statistical analysis in the Quarterly Journal of the Poona Sarvajanik Sabha. The article showed that among the Deccan and Konkani Brahmans, one Woman out of five was a widow, and one out of every thirty widows was under nine years of age. The biggest hurdle in the way of reforms was the intimate connection between marriage customs and religious beliefs: suggestions for reform instantly evoked the cry of 'Hinduism in danger'. The social reformers of western India were usually good and even devout Hindus. Unlike most of their counterparts in Bengal, they did not take to European ways. Nor did they cut themselves off from the common people. K. T. Telang, a distinguished Sanskrit scholar, affirmed with all sincerity that he was first and last a Hindu. Ranade was deeply religious, and anxious to conserve the best elements in Hindu thought and practice. In March 1875, he took a prominent part in the organization of a public debate in Poona on the religious validity of widow remarriages.

The fact that the verdict of the Hindu Pontiff, the Sankaracharya, went against the reformers was less important than that the reformers had sought scriptural sanction for reform instead of basing it entirely on the rational and humanitarian ethic of the West. Curiously enough, the head-on collision between the champions and opponents of social reform in Maharashtra was provoked not by the reformers, but by a Parsi journalist, Behramji Merwanji Malabari (1853-1912). His famous Notes on ant Marriage and Enforced Widowhood, published in August 1884, suggested, among other things, that child marriages should be denounced in school textbooks, that married students should not be allowed to take university examinations, that preference in government employment should be given to bachelors, that child-widows should be protected by the state against social ill-usage', that priests should be prohibited from excommunicating anyone who assisted in the remarriage of a widow. Malabari's proposals touched off a fierce controversy. British officials in India professed sympathy with his aim, but were loath to meddle in the religious beliefs and superstitions of an alien race. A resolution of the Government of India in 1886 ruled out official initiative in a matter which required reform from within the Hindu society rather than coercion from without. Frustrated in India, Malabari took his crusade to England. His appeal on behalf of the 'Daughters of India' struck responsive chords in former Viceroys and Governors, the Bench of Bishops, the Roman Catholic Episcopacy, the non-conformists, and the universities. It won the sympathy of Tennyson, the poet-laureate; Herbert Spencer, the most influential philosopher of the time; and of Max Muller, the Indologist.

A largely attended meeting was held in London on 18 July 1890, with Lord Reay in the chair. In the face of the mounting pressure of public opinion in England, the Viceroy, Lord Lansdowne, felt that the Government of India had to do something. 'It seems to me', he wrote on 15 September 1890, 'that the law as it stands does not afford protection to children of tender age." The outcome of the deliberations which followed was the introduction of the Age of Consent Bill in the Governor-General's Legislative Council. The

Age of Consent Bill sought to raise the age for the consummation of marriage from ten years (as fixed by the Act of 1860) to twelve years. It fell short of what Malabari had been asking for, and it did not even touch the problem of enforced widowhood. All it did was to make mating with a girl below twelve years equivalent to rape. It was a conservative, and as it turned out, ineffective measure, but it raised a terrific storm. The press in Bengal thundered against it. A mammoth meeting was held in the Maidan at Calcutta on 25 February 1891 to Protest against the intervention of the Government. Handbills announcing the meeting screamed: 'Brethren! The danger is serious! Total destruction is imminent. Government, without understanding the Hindu religion, are about to interfere with it! The honour of our mothers and wives is about to be destroyed.' This hysterical reaction had its counterpart in Maharashtra where the Age of Consent Bill led to a major collision between the forces of Hindu orthodoxy and the party of social reform.

Tilak headed the orthodox party. He questioned the right of Malabari, a Parsi, to tell the Hindus what was good for them; he disputed the competence of a foreign government to legislate on social and religious issues; he charged the Hindu reformers with ignorance of their scriptures. When R. G. Bhandarkar, the orientalist, affirmed that marriages after puberty did not violate the Hindu religious law, Tilak retorted: 'If you don't know how to interpret the Shastras correctly, then at least try to remain silent.' Bhandarkar and Ranade were not ignorant of their religious heritage; they were well-versed in Hindu law; they knew how the ancient texts had been twisted in thepast by an unscrupulous priesthood. They claimed 'not to revolutionize, but only to lop off the diseased overgrowth and excrescences'. As Ranade explained, state intervention was not necessarily an evil. 'The State in its collective capacity represents the power, the wisdom, the mercy and charity, of its best citizens." If Hindu society was to free itself from the bondage of the past, it was necessary to withdraw one by one the fetters of the socalled religious injunctions and turn them into civil restraints which were more amenable to change and adaptation. The initiative for reform was almost wholly Indian; all that was sought at the hands of the foreign government was that the reform should be given the force and sanction of law. It is over three-quarters of a century since India was convulsed with the agitation over the Age of Consent Bill. It is not easy to understand the fierce emotions aroused by a measure which seems almost innocuous today. The motives of some of those who participated in this controversy were not as unmixed as they made out at the time.

The Government of India under Lord Lansdowne was not at all eager to jump into the fray. But for Malabari's propaganda in England, they would probably have continued to profess neutrality in social and religious controversies. Malabari's humanitarianism, stimulated as it was by Christian and philanthropic influences of the West, was probably sincere, but he could not have been unaware that his crusade was being exploited by Anglo-Indian apologists, anxious to divert public opinion from political questions. 'The Indian press',, wrote Sir Auckland Colvin, the Finance Member of the Viceroy's Council, 'should confine itself to social reform, the merits of which it thoroughly understands than in wasting itself in barren philippics against English rule and English character.' Malabari's close contacts with high British dignitaries and the scornful tone he adopted in private towards the aspirations and the leaders of the Congress suggest that he was not wholly the disinterested philanthropist he professed to be. In fairness to Malabari, it must, however, be said that among his opponents there were several who had their own axes to grind. A. O. Hume, the founder of the Indian National Congress, observed that Motilal Ghose, the proprietor of the Amrita Bazar Patrika, had been deliberately whipping up opposition to the Age of Consent Bill to gather public support for the conversion of his newspaper from a weekly into a daily. Unfortunately for Maharashtra, the controversy on the Age of Consent Bill became involved in the factional feud in Poona, which had split the Deccan Education Society, and was before long to wreck the Sarvajanik Sabha. Agarkar, one of the leaders of the reform party, alleged that Tilak was deliberately pampering the ignorant masses to win cheap popularity, and leading a crusade in which he did not believe. Tilak denounced the superior, almost supercilious attitude of Agarkar and his fellow-reformers towards the common people.

The battle of words between the Kesari and the Sudharak raged fiercely.

Both Tilak and Agarkar were born journalists and could wield their native Marathi with deadly effect. The reformers were however, at a disadvantage: they were a tiny minority and could be represented as renegade Hindus, guilty of outraging the cherished sentiments of their community. Agarkar had to face a continuous barrage of ridicule and invective: his effigy with an egg in one hand and a bottle of liquor in the other was taken in a procession through the streets of Poona and ceremoniously consigned to flames on the outskirts of the town. Early in 1891, the excitement in Poona reached its peak. To rally its forces, the reform Party summoned a meeting at Kridha Bhawan. The meeting was broken up by local rowdies while the police looked on apathetically. It was only after the arrival of a posse of European constables that the trouble-makers dispersed. Most of them were student-admirers of Tilak, who was present at the meeting. The Kridha Bhawan fiasco was a frustrating experience for the reformers in Poona. They felt powerless between the invective in the local press and the threats of physical violence in the town. Gokhale was not yet senior enough to be counted among the leaders of the party, but he was close to both Ranade and Agarkar, and was editing the English section of the Sudharak, the mouthpiece of social reform in Poona. This was his first introduction to the rough and tumble of politics. What he saw in Kridha Bhawan did not exactly correspond to the image of political life which he had learnt to cherish. He unburdened himself in a letter to Ranade's friend, G. V. Joshi. G.K. Gokhale to G. V. Joshi, 3 March 1891:... The conduct of 'leading men' of Poona which culminated in the disgraceful rowdyism of Wednesday last has fairly sickened me. It has exercised a deciding influence on my wavering mind and I am now most exceedingly anxious to be relieved of the necessity of keeping up any kind of connection with them.... I am longing for the time when I shall have nothing to do directly with these people.... To the young politician, not yet twenty-five, disenchantment had come a little too soon. Gokhale and his friends of the reform party could not see that their opponents had the advantage of riding on the tide of a Hindu revival. The fact that the Age of Consent Bill passed through the Viceroy's Legislative Council with the support of its official majority did not alter this fundamental fact. 'A dozen years ago', wrote the Amrita Bazar Patrika on 14 October 1895, 'when educated men sat together they talked of politics; now, generally speaking, they talk of religion. Oddly enough, it was the nationalist sentiment which fostered a reaction against the West. The symptoms of this reaction were noted by the young Jadunath Sarkar, the future historian: 'Twenty years ago to discredit a reformer with a Hindu audience it was enough to call him a Christian at heart. Now you have to call him a Sahib at heart.' Sarkar noted that leaders of Hindu opinion, who had 'been the men of light and learning' in the 1870s, had reverted to orthodox ways in the 1890s, and the Bengali stage turned the laugh against the reformers by making them ape Europeans on the stage. The reversion to orthodoxy was to some extent a natural reaction against the earlier indiscriminate admiration for everything western' The rationalism and individualism of the early Victorian era had swept many educated Indians off their feet; the Brahmo Samaj and other 'progressive' groups had fallen under the intellectual and cultural spell of the West and declared total war on caste and custom. Christian missionaries heaped ridicule on Hindu beliefs and ritual. Hinduism seemed to be on the defensive, almost defenceless, but, as the century wore on, it showed signs of recovery. The feeling of inferiority vis-a-vis the West was offset by the tributes paid to Indian philosophy, art and religion by western scholars like F. Max Muller.

The emergence of theosophy on the Indian scene stimulated this process: the uncritical enthusiasm of Annie Besant and her friends for Hindu tenets and ritual proved infectious; on the authority of western observers, Hinduism turned out to be not only ancient but scientific. Bankim Chandra Chatterji, one of the foremost Bengali writers of his time, sought a reinterpretation of Hindu theology in the light of 'new rules of literary criticism and scriptural interpretation'. The reconciliation of western-educated intelligentsia to the faith of their forefathers was accelerated by that gentle prophet of the Vedanta, Ramakrishna Paramahansa, and his dynamic disciple, Swami Vivekananda. In north India

Swami Dayananda offered, in the Arya Samaj, a purified, almost puritanic, version of Hinduism, which appealed not it only to the English-educated Hindu's rationalistic ethic, but also to his idealistic image of the pristine purity of the Vedic age, unsullied by the encrustations of later times. The Arya Samaj was the Church Militant; it claimed that India was the chosen land, the Aryans were the chosen people, and the Vedas were the chosen gospel. This religious revival in the closing decades of the century was not merely an urban or middle-class affair. One of its significant manifestations, which caused the government much concern, was the phenomenal growth of the 'cow protection' movement. The Governor of the North-West (the United) Provinces, where the movement was most vigorous, was convinced that it was anti-British as well as anti-Muslim; he urged the Viceroy, Lord Lansdowne, to enact a new law to suppress it. 'I doubt', wrote Lord Lansdowne on 28 December 1893, whether, since the Mutiny, any movement containing in it a greater amount of potential mischief has engaged the attention of the Government of India. The magnitude of the danger arises from this, that the agitation has supplied the whole of the disloyal elements to be found in the Indian community with a popular backing which they could not have obtained from another source ... a common ground has been found upon which the educated Hindus and the ignorant masses can combine their forces. Western India did not remain immune from the religious revival which swept over the rest of the country. The Hindu community was pulsating with a new vitality, confidence, even a new and unwonted aggressiveness. Tilsit sensed the new mood of the community, to which the Bombay riots in August 1893 were a pointer.

The riots were touched off by a minor incident of 'music before a mosque', but the Hindu mill-hands of Bombay, who had heard of rumours of illtreatment of Hindus in the neighbouring Muslim state of Junagadh, were in an angry mood, and struck fiercely. There were heavy casualties; sixty persons were killed and three hundred injured; shops were plundered, places of worship were desecrated; the police lost control of the situation, and British troops had to be called in. Appeals for the restoration of peace emanated from Queen Victoria downwards. The Anglo-Indian papers laid the blame on the Hindu community, and the British officials, led by the Governor, Lord Harris, did not conceal their sympathy for the Muslims. The official reaction to the Bombay riots made Tilsit's blood boil. Writing in the Kesari, he rejected the thesis that the riots were due to the cow protection movement, and the Hindus were the guilty party. He asserted that Muslims had attacked first and Hindus had only acted in self-defence: 'They [the Hindus] waited for a day; they could not get protection from the police, and then they had to resort to retaliation for self-protection.' It was at this juncture when the Hindus in Poona were excited over the riots in Bombay that Tilak gave a new complexion to the Ganapati festival, the annual celebration of the 'elephant-headed god' which had long been a gay family affair. From 1893, under his inspiration, the festival acquired a congregational aspect: the numerous little processions for the immersion of the image of Ganapati were coordinated and combined for a common massive celebration.

In 1894, Tilak commented upon the success of the festival he had inspired: 'the excellent arrangements for the melas [music and singing parties] ... the attractive dresses . . ., the parties marching in measured steps, the delightful voice of the singers, the songs full of devotion, the notes of songs full of praise for our religion, and the enthusiasm of the heroic zeal of our Maratha brethren'. The tenday Ganapati festival, argued Tilak, simply sought to unite the Hindus on a platform of religious piety and innocent gaiety. This was not how it struck British officials and Muslim critics, whose worst suspicions were confirmed by the riots which broke out in Poona on 13 September 1894. On that day, a meld (singing party) led by Sardar Tatya Sahib Natu, an orthodox leader of Poona, marched past a mosque near Daruwalla's bridge with his musicians. There was a clash which left a trail of tension and bad blood not only in Poona, but in other towns of Maharashtra. The government was inclined to blame the majority community for these disturbances.

The social reformers, who took their inspiration from Ranade, were anxious to play down the riots and to avoid any provocation to the government and the minority community. Ranade did not like the congregational twist to the Ganapati festival, which weaned the Hindus from their traditional participation in the Muharram festival and aroused the fears and suspicions of the Muslim community. To Tilak the attitude of the government seemed partisan, that of Ranade and his friends pusillanimous. 'When Ranade opposed the proposal to hold a meeting of the Hindus of Poona to discuss the communal riots in Bombay, Tilak taunted: 'As Rao Bahadur [Ranade] has been bound by silver chains [as ;a government servant], we cannot say that his opinions on political matters must always be to our good.' Ranade and his friends feared that the Ganapati festival by sharpening the communal consciousness of the Hindus was bound to provoke a reaction from the Muslim community. Tilak was not impressed by this argument. He protested that the government was not holding the scales even between the two communities on such contentious questions as processions in public places, music before mosques, and cow-slaughter. He did not see the logic of the Hindus being asked to throw away their legitimate rights simply because they were in a majority. He did not see why congregational worship should be barred to Hindus, when Muslims and Christians were free to practise it. Tilak did not give up his interest in the organization of the Ganapati festival; indeed, he developed another great celebration, the Shivaji festival. The initial impulse for the renovation of Shivaji's Samadhi had come from an Englishman, James Douglas, who in A Book of Bombay (1883) pointed out: 'Over all those wide domains, which once owned him Lord and Master... not one man now contributes a rupee to keep or repair the tomb of the founder of the Mahratta Empire.'

In 1885, Ranade supported a fund-raising campaign for Shivaji's memorial, but it was Tilak who focused the limelight on Shivaji. It was under Tilak's inspiration that on 5 April 1896 the first Shivaji festival was organized at Raigarh, a place consecrated by Shivaji's coronation and death. The following year, the festival was celebrated in June on the anniversary of Shivaji's coronation. His heroic struggle against the Muslim rulers of the Deccan and the Mughal empire, and his success in carving a Maratha kingdom were recalled to inspire the people of Maharashtra with a new pride and enthusiasm. The festival had the usual features of a Hindu religious celebration: songs, dances, readings from the scriptures and distribution of sweets. Ballads exalting Shivaji's heroic deeds were sung, and lectures on Maratha history delivered. Huge portraits of Shivaji were carried in procession to the accompaniment of devotional hymns and shouts of 'Shivaji Maharaj ki jai'. Tilak was criticized for playing on the emotions of the masses. He retorted that there was 'no greater folly than the educated people thinking themselves to be a different class from the rest of the society.... The educated people can achieve through these national festivals results which would be impossible for the Congress to achieve.'

The festivals 'could carry political activities to the humblest cottages in the villages'. Tilak did not consider English education a sine qua non for political capacity, and looked forward to the day when the telis (oil vendors) and tambolis (betel leaf sellers) would understand political questions. Ranade's cautious, pragmatic and rational approach to political questions clashed with Tilak's emotional and bold stance. The Age of Consent Bill, the Ganapati and Shivaji festivals, and the communal riots revealed the basic differences between the rival parties in Poona which looked up to Ranade and Tilak. So strained were the relations between them that almost any issue could become a casus belli. The final breach came on an issue which should really have united them: the decision to hold the Congress session in Poona in December 1895. Ranade was well aware of the factional and personal rivalries in Poona, and had, therefore, supported Tilak's appointment as a joint secretary of the committee which was to raise funds and make arrangements for the Congress session. The two parties could not, however, work together on the committee. A fierce controversy broke out over the propriety of holding the National Social Conference in the Congress pavilion. The National Social Conference, of which Ranade was the founder, had, ever since its inception in 1887, held its annual session after the conclusion of the Congress session at the same place and in the same pavilion in which the Congress held its deliberations. The two organizations were of course entirely distinct; the resolutions of one did not commit the other. But the practice of holding the Indian National Congress and Social Conference meetings at the same place and around the same time had the merit of saving trouble and expense to scores of delegates who were interested in both the organizations.

This was not how Tilak and his friends viewed the problem; they saw the social 'reformers' pitted against the vast majority of their countrymen. To use the Congress pavilion for the Social Conference was, therefore, unjust to those Congressmen who did not subscribe to the policies of the Social Conference. 'The use of the Congress pavilion for ventilating social grievances', wrote Tilak's paper, the Mahratta (8 December 1895), 'is very likely to make Congress itself unpopular.' Social reform was an explosive subject in Poona; it revived something of the deep emotions of 1890-1 over the Age of Consent Bill. A local firebrand, S. V. Date, threatened that it would be 'murderous' if the 'Sudharaks' (reformers) were permitted to hold the Social Conference in the Congress pavilion. The reformers saw that efforts were being made to cow them down by press attacks and public demonstrations. They felt that on the issue of the use of the Congress pavilion for the Social Conference, justice and precedent were on their side; why could Poona not do what other principal towns in India (which played host to the Indian National Congress) had done for seven successive years ? The reformers suspected that the pavilion controversy was merely another stick with which their opponents sought to beat them out of the political life of Poona. The very existence of the reform party seemed at stake. Gokhale's friends remonstrated with him for not hitting back at Tilak. The contest, however, was not really between Tilak and Gokhale, but between Tilak and Ranade. 'We do not desire the struggle', Ranade confided to K. Subba Rao on 16 October 1895, 'but it can't be helped... the small band of workers [of the Social Reform Party] scattered in every town... are being cried down and abused by the other side....' The reformers sought to resolve the problem by seeking the views of the Provincial Congress Committees. Of the replies received, almost two-thirds supported Ranade's stand, but they urged that a split in the Congress must be avoided. Even Ranade's supporters did not desire a show-down with the orthodox party in Poona which could jeopardize the success of the Congress session. He decided to hold the Social Conference in a separate pavilion. This was Tilak's victory but it was a pyrrhic one.

By driving Ranade to the wall, he alienated the Pherozeshah Mehta-Dinshaw Wacha group in the Bombay Congress, which controlled the party organization. This group turned on Tilak and hamstrung him by appointing additional secretaries to the Reception Committee of the Poona Congress; one of these secretaries was Gokhale. Tilak did not take the affront lying down. He resigned from the Reception Committee. Tilak was present and even spoke at the Poona Congress in December 1895. But it was Gokhale who was in the centre of the political stage; it fell to him to read the welcome address to the Congress delegates on behalf of Moreshwar Bhide, the chairman of the Reception Committee, who was too old and feeble to perform this duty. The controversy on the use of the Congress pavilion for the Social Conference in Poona was complicated by another development which undermined the position of Ranade's adherents. For nearly a quarter of a century the Sarvajanik Sabha had functioned under his direction. For the last five years Gokhale had been its secretary and the editor of its quarterly journal. The Sabha had acquired a certain standing not only with the people, but with the authorities; it was one of the foremost political associations in India. Its statements and representations, thanks to their association with Ranade, carried weight. But Ranade's influence over the Sabha came to a sudden end on 14 July 1895, after the annual general meeting of the Sabha. His adherents found themselves for the first time in a minority in the Sabha. Tilak and his friends had enrolled new members just before the meeting and outvoted their opponents. The new managing committee of thirty-four members included ten of the outgoing committee and Gokhale was elected one of the secretaries. But there was no doubt that the control of the committee had passed to Tilak. The complexion of Poona politics changed overnight. Well might Tilak and his friends say that what had happened was the perfectly constitutional process of 'converting minorities into majorities'.

To Gokhale, and other members of the Ranade group, all this was specious reasoning; the truth was that Tilak and his friends had effected a coup d'etat. The majority of the members of the new managing committee were opponents of social reform; one of them, Krishnarao Bapu Mande, who was appointed assistant secretary, had even tried to get Ranade into trouble with the government. Gokhale did not wish to continue as secretary of the

Sabha when its managing committee was dominated by the rival party. However, he was prevailed upon by Pherozeshah Mehta and Ranade not to press his resignation till the Poona Congress session was over. Gokhale himself had no doubt that the 'revolution' in the affairs of the Sarvajanik Sabha was directed against Ranade. In a letter to Dadabhai Macron, he explained its implications: G. K Gokhale to Dadabhai Macron, 3 September 1896: Developments of a distressing character have already taken place in the political life of this city. God's curse seems to be resting on this country, else how should it always be that directly some good and useful work is begun, dissensions arise to undo it!

The Sarvajanik Sabha a child of Mr Justice Ranade's for which he has worked so nobly now for a quarter of a century, has been taken out of his hands and for a whole year the Sabha has done absolutely no work. The whole attempt here is to drive out of public life all workers who sympathize with the cause of social reform by discrediting them with the masses by all manner of means.... These events revived Gokhale's disgust with Politics in his home town. 'I have grown', he wrote to G. V. Joshi on 8 February 1896,,absolutely sick of public life in Poona. Recent events have opened my eyes very wide indeed.... I wish now to wash my hands of all Political work in Poona. There is so much that is selfish and ignoble here that I would fly from it to the furthest extremities of the world, if I could.' Gokhale's pessimism was evidently not shared by Ranade, who took the initiative in starting a new political body in Poona. At Ranade's instance, a meeting was called in the historic Kiba Wada in Poona. Attended by 101 prominent citizens it decided to found the Deccan Sabha. The manifesto of the new organization, drafted by Ranade, emphasized that it would represent moderate and liberal public opinion....

The spirit of liberalism implies a freedom from race and creed prejudices and a steady devotion to all that seeks to do justice between man and man, giving to the rulers the loyalty that is due to the law they are bound to administer, but securing at the same time to the ruled the equality which is their right under the law. Moderation imposes the condition of never vainly aspiring after the impossible, or after too remote ideals, but striving each day to take the next step in the order of natural growth by doing the work that lies nearest to our hands in a spirit of compromise and fairness. The foundation of the Deccan Sabha brought the conflict between the two parties in Poona to a head. Tilak was furious. What did Ranade mean by professing to be the embodiment of moderation and liberalism? Did he imply that Tilak and his friends were immoderate and illiberal ? Was not such a stance an invitation to the government to visit official displeasure on the Sarvajanik Sabha under its new management? The Kesari denounced Ranade, labelled him a Kautilya and even the 'meanest of men'. 'Is it dotage or puerility asked Tilak in the Kesari in an article which, in the words of N. C. Kelkar, would 'go down in the history of Marathi journalism as a classical example of invective'. This bitterness boded ill for nationalist politics in Poona. Without the guiding hand of Ranade and the tireless industry of Gokhale, the Sarvajanik Sabha could not maintain its position for long. Its relations with the government, even during the last few months of Gokhale's secretaryship, had been strained. Local officials were probably waiting to pounce on the Sabha; its new management easily provided an opportunity. One of the agents of the Sabha was accused of making unverified statements in the countryside about the remission of land revenue.

The Bombay Government called for an explanation, and after the exchange of a few letters, curtly informed the Sabha that its representations would no longer be entertained. For a political body which was founded to 'mediate between the rulers and the ruled', and functioned only constitutionally, this act of de-recognition was a crippling blow. No wonder Dadabhai Naoroji, writing from England, remonstrated with Tilak for destroying an institution built up with infinite patience and dedicated labour over several decades. The Sarvajanik Sabha lost its effectiveness. The Deccan Sabha did not prove a reasonable substitute, or alternative; its politics were much too tame. Tilak's description of it 'as a pinjrapole [stable] of Rao Bahadurs' in his characteristic satirical vein was not altogether unjust. So long as Ranade lived the Deccan Sabha could muster strength for sporadic fits of activity, but after his death it was practically dormant. Gokhale made an attempt to give it another lease of life in 1908 but failed. The events in Poona during 1895-6 seemed catastrophic not only for the causes for which Gokhale stood, but for his own political future. He and his friends had been outwitted and outmanoeuvred. He had lost control of the Sarvajanik Sabha, and its quarterly journal. When the first issue of the journal under the new management announced that Gokhale had resigned, and proposed to devote all his time to his duties as a teacher, his political opponents were serving a notice on him that he would henceforth be on the shelf. Things looked pretty bleak for Gokhale in 1896. Luckily for him, however, events were conspiring to bring him back into the limelight not only of local, but national politics.

3

Gokhale with Gandhi in South Africa

Mahatma Gandhi had started movement in South Africa, Gokhale also played a significant role with him. 'Gokhale's interest in South Africa brought him closer to Gandhiji who hailed Gokhale as his political guru and in turn slowly and gently fashioned Gandhiji for his ultimate role in history.' Gokhale taught Gandhiji that the dream of every Indian who claimed to love his country, should be not to glorify the country in language but to spiritualize its political life and institutions. Gandhiji learnt from Gokhale that political life must be an echo of our private life. There could not be any divorce between the two.

South Africa : Its Political Perspective

South Africa was first settled by Europeans-the Dutch, the French and the British in the seventeenth century. The descendents of the Dutch and French were called Boers. They established their first republic in Natal' in 1893. The British annexed the Cape' by the same time. They also acquired Natal in the middle of the nineteenth century. The Boers created republics in the Transvaal' and Orange Free State" which were later recognized by the British. The discovery of diamonds and gold led to rivalry between the British and the Boers. This resulted in a series of wars between 1880 and 1902. The eventual outcome was the passing by the British Parliament, in 1909 of the South Africa Act, which established a new British dominion called the Union of South Africa. The Union consisted of four former colonies of the Orange River, Transvaal, the Cape and Natal. The Union came into being in 1910 with Louis Botha', the Boer leader as the first Prime Minister of the new state.

Gandhiji went to study law in London. Gandhiji practiced law in Bombay until 1893, when an Indian firm in South Africa sent for him to help in a law suit. He was distressed to see the oppression of the Indian settlers by the white people. He stayed there to fight the cause of Indians for the next 21 years. He was imprisoned many times by the Government.

One occasion was in 1913, when he led more than 2,000 Indians across the border between the Transvaal and Natal in defiance of a South African Law which forbade Indians to move from one province to another. It was in South Africa that Gandhiji developed his technique of Satyagraha which he later tried in India. He was much impressed by the writings of Ruskin' and Tolstoy and had intimate correspondence with the later. Gandhiji kept contact with Indian leaders about the developments in South Africa. He sought their help in the cause of South African Indians. At while all the leaders sympathised with the cause, Gokhale took an active interest from 1896 till his death.

Gandhiji met Gokhale for the first time in 1896, at Fergusson College, Poona. Gokhale gave him an affectionate welcome. Gokhale's manner immediately won Gandhiji's heart. Gandhiji felt that he was renewing an old friendship. He gave his impressions of Sir Pherozeshah Mehta, Lokmanya Tilak and Gokhale in the following words:

> "Sir Pherozeshah had seemed to me like the Himalaya the Lokmanya like the Ocean. But Gokhale was as the Ganges. One would have a refreshing bath in the holy river. The Himalaya was unscaleable, and one could not easily launch forth on the sea, but the Ganges invited

one to its bosom. It was a joy to be on it with a boat and an oar."

Gokhale examined Gandhiji closely as a school master would examine a candidate seeking admission to a school. He told Gandhiji whom to approach and how to approach them. Gokhale showed him over the Fergusson College and assured him all help. In June, 1897 Gokhale published an article on British Indians in South Africa in The India, the National Congress organ published in London. The condition of Indians in South Africa was that of slaves. It was idle on our part to expect justice from the Englishmen. Where it did not suit their interests.

The Indians in Natal were robbed, assaulted and treated like beasts. They were unable to obtain redress. Gokhale commented extensively on the pamphlet written by Gandhiji on the grievances of the British Indians in South Africa. He praised the courage and manliness of Gandhiji in spite of grave provocations." In 1901 Gandhiji was in Calcutta to attend the annual session of the Congress. With the help of Gokhale he was able to pilot his resolution on the plight of Indians in South Africa. Gokhale invited Gandhiji to stay with him. Gandhiji spent one month under the roof of Gokhale. Gokhale made Gandhiji completely at home. He treated Gandhiji as though he were his younger brother. Gokhale was deeply impressed with Gandhiji's habit of funding for himself, his personal cleanness, perseverance and regularity. Gokhale introduced Gandhiji to all the important people who called on him. To see Gokhale at work was a joy and an education. His private relations and friendships were all for public good. At a public meeting held in Calcutta on 19 January, 1902 Gokhale spoke on the Indian problem in South Africa and paid a tribute to Gandhiji. He said that Gandhiji was made of the stuff of which heroes were made. If Mr. Gandhi settled in India it was the duty of all earnest workers to place Gandhiji at their head.

Gokhale on 2 November, 1905 delivered a lecture to the Lambeth Radical Club in England. He spoke on the problem of Indians in South Africa. The lecture made a deep impression on George Godfrey, a close associate of Gandhiji.

- Public Meeting in Bombay (9th September, 1909)
- public meeting was conversed by the leading citizens of Bombay on 9th September, 1909 to consider the question of the treatment of Indians in the Transvaal. Gokhale proposed a resolution on the subject. Indians in Transvaal were facing humiliation on account of the combined operation of the Registration Act and the Immigration Act in that colony. The colony had 6,000 Indians. The burnt of the persecution was being borne by a brave band of about five hundred Indians led by the indomitable Gandhi, a man of tremendous spiritual power. Gokhale called Gandhi a man who was made of the stuff of which great heroes and martyrs were made. Gokhale recalled the principal facts of the situation. He told the audience that under the Old Boer Government of the Transvaal a law was in existence which required all Asiatics who entered the Transvaal after 1880 to register themselves and to pay a registration fee of $3. There was no limit to the number that might so enter and the Indian population in the Transvaal before the war was estimated at 15,000 males, leaving women and children out of account. The Boer war ended in 1902, resulting in the annexation of the Transvaal to the British empire. The substitution of the British Government for the Boer made the position of Indians worse. The cry was started that the Indians were flooding the Colony and it was necessary to stop the flux. In reality the population of Indians in the Colony had gone down. In July, 1907 when the first stage the passive resistance began there were about 9,000 Indians in the Colony.

It had come down to 6,000 in 1909. The real object of the white colonists was to get rid of the Indian element altogether. The South African Government introduced in the Legislative Council in 1906 an ordinance called the Asiatic Law Amendment Ordinance, which provided for a fresh compulsory registration of all Asiatics entitled to be in the Colony under very humiliating conditions, The Asiatics protested against the Ordinance but it was passed by the Legislative Council. Gandhiji headed a delegation to England to explain the position of the Indians but it could serve no purpose. In March, 1907 the Transvaal Parliament passed an amendment entitled the Asiatic Law Amendment Act.. The regulations framed under the Act required the Indians to register themselves by the end of October, 1907, to give their finger prints and other details for the purposes of identification.

The Indians declined to submit to the regulations. A sharp conflict between the Transvaal Government and the passive resisters followed. In January, 1908, a compromise was arrived at between Gandhiji and general Smuts. The terms of the compromise were not implemented by the government. The Indians re-opened their struggle. Explaining the concept of passive resistance. Gokhale said:

> "Passive resistance to an unjust law or an oppressive measure is a refusal to acquiesce in that law or measure and a readiness to suffer the penalty instead which may be prescribed as an alternative. If we strongly and clearly and conscientiously feel the grave injustice of a law and there is no other way to obtain redress, I think to refusal to acquiesce in it, taking the consequences of such refusal as the only course left to those who place conscience and self-respect above their material or immediate interests."

The passive resistance movement had been splendidly managed in South Africa. Hindus, Mohammedans and Parsis, all held together us one man. Surely a man who could achieve this represented a great moral force. Gokhale appealed to the Imperial Government and the Imperial Parliament to use their influence and close the bitter question in a satisfactory manner. He also called upon the Government of India to stop the recruitment of Indian labour for South Africa."

Resolution on Passive Resistance

Gokhale moved a resolution about passive resistance in South Africa at the annual session of the Indian National Congress held at Lahore in December, 1909. Gokhale divided the whole period of the struggle in South Africa into three parts—the period of the Boer Governments, the period of the Crown Government, and the present period of self-government for the Transvaal. During the time of the Boer government the position of Indians was not very satisfactory. But emigration into the colony was unrestricted. Any Indian who chose to go there could go there. All that was required of him was a payment of three pounds as registration fee. When the Boer War broke out, there were in the colony fifteen thousand male Indians. During the Crown Government the position of Indians became worse.

There was a cry of dishonest influx of Indians into the colony. The white colonists were determined to prevent Indians from entering Transvaal. They passed the Asiatic Law Amendment Ordinance. The object of the Ordinance was to confine entry into the Transvaal to pre-war residents and to compel all Indians in Transvaal to register themselves under humiliating conditions. Indians held a protest meeting and decided to send a deputation to England under the leadership of Gandhiji. Recalling the immortal role of Gandhiji in the South African struggle. Gokhale said:

> "It is one of the privileges of my life that I know Mr. Gandhi intimately, and I can tell you that a purer, a nobler, a trover and a more exalted spirit has never moved on this earth. Mr. Gandhi is one of those men, who living an austerely simple life themselves and devoted to all the highest principles of love to their fellow beings and to truth and justice, touch the eyes of their weaker brethren as with magic and give them a new vision. He is a man who may be well described as a man among men, a herd among heroes, a patriot among patriots, and we may well say that in him Indian humanity at the present time has really reached its high water mark."

The British Government granted self-government to the colony The new Colonial Parliament passed the Asiatic Law Amendment Act. Its objects were to keep out of the Colony all

Indians that might seek to enter there unless they were pre-war residents, and to compel resident Indians there to register themselves.

The regulations framed under the law required the Indians to register under the most humiliating circumstances. Indians under the leadership of Gandhiji, took steps to resist there regulations. The South African Government entered into a compromise with Gandhiji but general Smuts broke the faith. Gandhiji started his passive resistance. There were arrests and imprisonments. About 2.500 people were put behind bar mostly with hard labour. Gokhale underlined four facts in connection with the struggle:

(1) The condition of the Indians had deteriorated steadily from the time of the Boer Government to the present time.

(2) Our cause was right and just.

(3) Our countrymen have done nothing unjust.

(4) Our countrymen are struggling for the honour of India."

Gokhale made a fervent appeal to Imperial Parliament, Indian Government and Indian people to understand the problem of Indian settlers in South Africa and find its just solution.

Resolution on the Indentured Labour

On 25th February, 1910, Lord Minto, the Viceroy presiding, Gokhale moved a resolution about indentured labour for Natal. It recommended that the Governor-General in Council should be empowered to prohibit the recruitment of indentured labour in British India for the Colony of Natal. In moving the resolution Gokhale stated that the indentured labour was near-slavery. Gokhale observed that the time had come not only for making representations but for resorting to retaliation. The government accepted the resolution.

In 1911 a ban was imposed on recruitment of indentured labour for Natal". In 1916 it was extended to labour for all overseas colonies." Gandhi had been requesting Gokhale and other leaders to go to South Africa and to study the condition of the Indian settlers there. Gokhale was in England in 1911. He had been a student of the struggle in South Africa. He had initiated debates in the Legislative Council of India and moved a resolution in favour of prohibiting the recruitment of indentured labour for Natal which was carried. Gandhiji had been in communication with him all along. Gokhale conferred with the Secretary of State for India and informed him of his intention to proceed to South Africa and acquaint himself with the facts of the case at first hand. The Minister approved of Gokhale's mission. Gandhiji made elaborate arrangements for his visit and determined to accord him a reception which even princes might envy." The Secretary of State for India informed the Union Government of South Africa of Gokhale's high rank and his position in the Empire. A comfortable Cabin was reserved for him and he had a happy and peaceful voyage to South Africa. The South African Government offered Gokhale their hospitality during his stay at Pretoria and placed the state railway saloon at his disposal." Gokhale landed at Cape Town on October 22, 1912. Gandhiji acted as his secretary throughout the tour. Gandhiji organised a big meeting to welcome Gokhale. Gokhale made a firm and courteous speech which pleased the Indians and fascinated the Europeans. From Cape Town Gokhale went to Johannesburg. He was received at the railway platform. The Mayor of Johannesburg. The Mayor of Johannesburg placed his car at the disposal of Gokhale.

An address was presented to him on the station itself. He was put up in a fine house belonging to Mr. Kallenbach, a colleague of Gandhiji. The house was perched on a hill-top five miles from Johannesburg. Gokhale liked the place immensely. A special office was hired in the city for Gokhale to receive all visitors. He was taken to make private calls upon some distinguished men in the city. A private meeting of leading Europeans was organized so as to give Gokhale a thorough understanding of their standpoint. A banquet was organised in his honour in which were invited 400 persons including about 150 Europeans. It was a novel experience for the Europeans of South Africa to sit at dinner with so many Indians on the same table. To this gathering Gokhale addressed his longest and most important speech in South Africa. This happened on October 31, 1912. Gokhale in his address referred to the European fears of being swamped.

The European Community had established itself in that vast country in the midst of a very large indigenous population. The indigenous population was alien to it in race and on an entirely different plane of civilization. This had given rise to problems social, political, economic and moral. These problems filled the thoughtful men of European Community with serious concern for its future. In addition to this the members of a third race were going to South Africa. The numbers of this third race were small but there was a steady influx going on. Further, there was undoubtedly the colour prejudice. The total population of Indians in South Africa was 1,50,000. Out of that number, nearly 1,20,000 were ex-indentured people or their descendants. The bulk of that population consisted of men who had been brought into the country to the British Government, in the interests of a section of the white population of that country. The remaining 30,000 had wake of those indentured men. Indentured labour was introduced in Natal in 1860.

The Imperial Government had made the most solemn promises to the Government of India that the people who were brought to Natal would be treated with every possible consideration. After their indentured they would be allowed to settle in the land. Every facility would be given to them so that they might prosper in the country. For the first few years the attitude of the European Community in Natal towards the indentured men was helpful. A change took place in the attitude of the European community towards the eighties. They imposed a tax of $3 per year on every man and women if they continued to reside in the colony after having completed their indentures."

Behind the Indians an South Africa stood India, and behind India was the Empire. Gokhale emphasised the need for a practical solution. He was in favour of giving responsible assurance to Europeans. In his view, Indians should also be allowed under equal laws with themselves. Gokhale advised that moderate men on both sides should join hands and insist that some such solution should be adopted in the interests of both sides. Gokhale paid a handsome tribute to Gandhiji. Gandhiji was a great and illustrious son of India.

Men of all races and creeds recognized in him one of the most remarkable personalities of their time. Gandhi would break but never bend in a just or righteous cause. Appreciation of Gandhi was not confined to the Indian Community alone. He was held in universal esteem by the European Community also." In Johannesburg Gandhiji arranged a mass meetings of Indians only. He pursued Gokhale to speak in Marathi and he himself translated it into Hindustani for the benefit of Gujarati and North Indian members of the audience. Gokhale visited Tolstoy Farm during his sojourn in South Africa. He walked about a milk and a half from the station to the Farm. The hardship was too much for him to bear and he caught a chill. Gandhi and his associates slept on the floor. Gokhale was offered a cot which he refused. Gandhiji ironed the scarf of Gokhale which was a gift from Ranade. After Johannesburg Gokhale visited Natal and then proceeded to Pretoria. He was put up by the Union Government at the Transvaal Hotel. He met General Botha and General Smuts. The interview lasted for about two hours. Gokhale told Gandhiji that everything had been settled. He advised Gandhiji to return to India within a year." A reception was organised in Gokhale's honour by the Indian community of Pretoria on November 14, 1912. In reply to the speeches of welcome Gokhale made a speech expressing his sense of relief and gratitude.

This was his last public utterance in South Africa. He pleaded for just and equitable treatment of Indians, and urged for sympathetic administration of immigration laws." During his visit to Natal Gokhale came in contact with many Europeans in Durban, Maitzburg and other places. He left South Africa on November 17, 1912. Gandhiji and Mr. Kallenbach accompanied him as far as Zanjibar. On the steamer Gokhale analysed for Gandhiji the characters of all the leaders in India."

Gokhale returned to Bombay from South Africa on December 13, 1912. On the following day he addressed a largely attended public meeting in the Town Hall at Bombay. He described his South African Impressions and smooth progress of his visit. Paying his tribute to Gandhiji he said:

> "From the moment I landed at Cape Town to the moment I left South Africa and even afterwards during nearly the whole of my visit to East Africa, Mr. Gandhi was with me and we were together nearly every moment of our waking hours. He had taken upon himself the duties of my private secretary, but he was in reality my guide, philosopher and friend."

Gokhale stated that Gandhiji was made of the stuff of which heroes and martyrs were made. He had in him the marvellous spiritual power to turn ordinary men around him into heroes and martyrs. During the recent passive resistance struggle in Transvaal twenty seven hundred people courted imprisonment under Gandhiji. Some of the men were humble poor individuals. The Indian cause in South Africa was really built up by Gandhiji. Without self and without stain, he fought his great fight. India owed an immense debt gratitude to him. He had sacrificed himself utterly in the service of the cause.

One most striking fact about him was that though he had waged his great struggle so ceaselessly his mind was absolutely free from all bitterness against the Europeans. Gokhale analysed the latest position in South Africa. He informed that four-fifths of the entire Indian population in South Africa represented indentured labourers, ex-indentured labourers and their descendants. There was no educated class among the Indians in South Africa. There was hardly any provision for the education of India Children. Gokhale referred to the position of the European Community in South Africa. They were about a million and a quarter in all in the midst of a vast indigenous population. The present number of Indians in South Africa was only a lakh and a half against twelve and half lakhs of Europeans. The Europeans felt that there were 300 millions of people in India. They could go there and could make South Africa another India. In addition to this, there was tremendous colour prejudice in South Africa.

Congress South African Report

The Indian National Congress held its 1912 session at Bankipore in Bihar, on December 27 and the following two days. It gave special consideration to the problem of Indians in the colonies generally and that of those in South Africa in particular Gokhale was requested to propose the resolution on the subject." Gokhale in his address clarified that he had not given any assurances to the South African Government and to the European Community there in the name of India. He had not surrendered India's rights in the matter of immigration. Indians in South Africa wanted equal citizenship rights. They wanted an end of the various social and legal disabilities to which they were subjected. They should be allowed to acquire property. There should be no ban on Indian trade. Provision should be made for the education of Indian children. The monstrous $3 poll tax should be abolished. Government service should be opened for Indians. They should get political franchises.

Resuming of Satyagraha

The Government of South Africa did not carry out their assurances given to Gokhale. Gandhiji resumed his Satyagraha. The South African Government adopted a policy of "blood and iron". Gandhiji was sentenced to nine months rigorous imprisonment. Gokhale was deeply pained. In spite of his poor health, he toured the country and raised funds for South African Satyagraha.

The Viceroy Lord Hardinge expressed his deep sympathy for the cause of Indians in South Africa. He sent Mr. Benjamin Robertson as his envoy to that country. C.F. Andrews, a young English missionary and teacher at St. Stephen's College Delhi along with his friend W.W. Pearson reached Durban in January 1914. General Bothe and Smuts were impressed with Gandhiji's sincerity and Gandhi-Smuts Agreement was reached in January, 1914.

At the conclusion of the Satyagraha struggle in 1914. Gandhiji received Gokhale's instructions to return India via

London. In July he sailed for London. He suffered from pleurisy and Dr. Jairaj Mehta treated him. Gokhale left for India in October, 1914. Gandhiji reached Bombay towards the end of 1914. He called on the governor of Bombay on the advise of Gokhale. After this he went to Poona and met the members of the Servants of India Society.

Gokhale was keen that Gandhiji should join the Society. Gandhiji was also willing to do so. But the members felt that there was a great difference between their ideas and methods of work. Gandhiji did not join the Society but Gokhale continued to shower his affection on him. From Poona Gandhiji went to Shantiniketan. When he was there Gokhale passed away on 19 February, 1915.

Gandhiji wrote and spoke on Gokhale from time to time after his death. He sent a message on February 19, 1916. The first anniversary of the death of Gopal Krishna Gokhale. In the message he said:

> "Gokhale's life was that of a man of religion. Everything he did was done in the spirit of a devotee... Gokhale once called himself an agnostic. He observed that he had not, but wished he had, Ranade's faith. Even so I could discern a religious strain in his work. It would not be improper to say that his very doubt was inspired by religion. A man who leads a dedicated life, who is simple in habits, who is the very image of truth, who is full of humanity, who calls nothing his own-such a man is a man of religion whether he himself is or is not conscious of it. Such was Gokhale as it. Such was Gokhale as I could see during the twenty years of my friendship with him."

Gokhale always identified himself with the work in hard. His tour of South Africa, and the subsequent agitation he started in India demonstrate this quality in a remarkable manner. Testifying this quality of Gokhale, Gandhiji says:

> "As soon as he entered Cape Town he immediately began a special study of the South African Question. In fact

he had acquired a good general knowledge of the subject, even before he set foot in Cape Town. But it was not enough according to his standards. During his four week's stay in South Africa he had made such a deep and comprehensive study of the problem facing the Indian residents of South Africa that all those who had met and discussed the question with him were surprised at the depth of his knowledge and his grasp of the question. When the time to meet general Botha and General Smuts arrived he asked us to prepare so many notes for his use that I at one time thought that it was hardly necessary for him to put himself to so much trouble. His health was very delicate all through the period and required great cave. But in spite of it, he would work late, upto twelve in the night and would be up again by four or even two and ask for his papers.'

Gandhiji felt that Gokhale was well-acquainted with the inner spirit of religion. He never pretended to observe any religious practice that his life was full of the true spirit of religion.

Gokhale believed that political activities could lead to salvation and freedom only if they were based on religion or in other words spiritualized. So be placed this great ideal before his servants of India society and before the whole nation. Elaborating this point Gandhiji says: "Any Indian who aspired to lead his people in the way of pure religion could hardly afford to remain aloof from politics. In other words, one who aspires to true religious life could not but undertake service of his people as his mission, and we are today so far involved in the political system that obtains in our land that service of the people is impossible without taking part in politics. The peasants of our country who used to remain indifferent as to who the political ruler of the country was and could yet lead their simple lives without any danger are not today in the same state of aloofness from the working of the state. If our sadhus, rishis, munis, maulvis and padris realized the bearing of politics on the condition of our peasants 'we would have servants of India Societies in every village, the spirit of religion would assume such vast all-pervading proportions that the political system which has become odious would reform itself, India would again have its empire of religion as we know it had in the past, the bonds which hold India under subjection would be severed in an instant, and the ideal state of peace which an ancient seer had described would come into being where iron would not be used for forging swords but for forging plough shares, and the lion and the lamb would be friends and live together in peace the ideal of Gokhale's life was to work to bring about this state of affairs."

Gandhiji admired Tilak for his indomitable will, his vast learning, his love of country, and above all the purity of his private life and great sacrifice. Of all the men of modern times, he captivated most the imagination of his people. He breathed into us the spirit of Swaraj. No one perhaps realized the evil of existing system of Government as Tilak did. Gandhiji claimed to deliver Tilak's message to the country as truly as the best of his disciples. Pointing out his difference, with Tilak, Gandhiji said: "But I am conscious that my method is not Tilak's method. And that is why I have still difficulty with some of the Maharashtra leaders. But I sincerely believe that Tilak did not disbelieve in my method. I enjoyed the privilege of his confidence. And his last word to me in the presence of several friends was, just a fortnight before his death, that mine was an excellent method if the people could be persuaded to take to it. But he said he had his doubts. I know no other method. I can only hope, that when the final test comes, the country will be proved to have assimilated the method of non-violent non-cooperation. Nor I am I unaware of my other limitations. I can lay no claim to scholarship. I have not his powers of organization, I have no compact disciplined party to lead, and having been an exile for twenty-three years, I can not claim the experience that the Lokmanya had of India. Two things we had in common to the fullest measure love of country and the steady pursuit of Swaraj.'

Gandhi has given his impressions of contemporary Indian leaders like justice Ranade, Dadabhai, Badruddin Tyabji, Pherozeshah Mehta and Dr. Bhandarkar, justice Ranade awed him. He could hardly talk in his presence." Badruddin Tyabji fathered him, and asked him to be guided by Ranade and Pherozeshah'. Pherozeshah became a patron. His will had to be law. He taught Gandhiji to take orders. He did not make him his disciple." When Gandhiji went to see Dr. Bhandarkar, the latter greeted him as a teacher greets his disciple. Gandhiji worshipped the venerable doctor with his wise face. But he could not find for him a place on the throne of his heart.

It was different with Gokhale. Gandhiji met him at his quarters on the college ground. About his first meeting with Gokhale Gandhi says: "It was like meeting an old friend, or better still a mother after a long separation. His gentle face put me at ease in a moment. His minute enquiries about myself and my doings in South Africa at once enshrined him in my heart. And as I parted from his, I said to myself, 'you are my man.' And from that moment Gokhale never lost sight of me' Gokhale was concerned about how Gandhiji spoke, dressed, walked and ate. His mother was not more solicitious about him than Gokhale. There was no reserve between them. It was really a case of love at first sight. Gokhale seemed to Gandhiji all he wanted as a political worker-pure as crystal, gentle as a lamb, brave as a lion and chivalrous to a fault. He was the most perfect man on the political field." It is indeed rose for a disciple to find a true teacher. It is also rare for a teacher to find a true disciple. When it happens, it leads to the fulfilment of both the disciple and the teacher. This was the case with Gandhi and Gokhale. In Kathopanishada Yama found a disciple after his own heart in Nachiketa. He exclaimed: "Wonderful is the teacher, and equally eleven the pupil. Wonderful indeed is he who comprehends it when taught by an able preceptor. Nachiketa, may we often get inquirers like then."

4

GOKHALE ON PATH OF POLITICS

In 1889 the British Committee of the Indian National Congress came into being with Sir William Wedderburn as its chairman. For the next thirty years the British Committee was the pivot of Congress propaganda in Britain. Sir William Wedderburn was its moving spirit, and the journal India its mouthpiece. Dadabhai Naoroji and Wedderburn, who were elected to Parliament in 1892 and 1893 respectively, formed the 'Indian Parliamentary Committee'. The Indian Parliamentary Committee was an amorphous body, its size fluctuating with the fortunes of the Liberal Party from which it drew almost all its members. Most of them had only a superficial acquaintance with Indian affairs, but the Committee had a small dedicated core, which functioned as a pressure group on behalf of the Indian National Congress. This group at first met with a quick and astonishing series of successes. In 1893 it carried through the House of Commons a resolution in favour of holding the I.C.S. examination simultaneously in India and England.

The following year it pressed for a parliamentary inquiry into Indian expenditure, and an equitable redistribution of financial burdens between India and Britain. A parliamentary enquiry had long been demanded by Indian leaders, and resisted by the Anglo-Indian officials, who felt safer with a Royal Commission than with a parliamentary inquisition into Indian affairs. Sir Henry Fowler, the Secretary of State, had promised a Select Committee, but was persuaded in favour of a Royal Commission. The Royal Commission on Indian Expenditure, which was announced in 1895, was headed by the sixty-three yearold Lord Welby, a former Permanent Secretary of the British Treasury. The thirteen members of the Commission included M.P.s as well as veterans of the civil and military services in India. From the Indian point of view, the most heartening aspect of the Royal Commission was that Dadabhai Naoroji and two of his closest colleagues in England, William Wedderburn and W. S. Caine,' were appointed to it. Their appointment was hailed in India as a promise of better things to come. The pro-Indian trio knew that there was no cause for immediate rejoicing. Not only was the Commission heavily weighted with British officials, but its terms of reference enjoined it only to go 'into the administration and management of the military and civil expenditure of India and into the apportionment of charges between the Governments of the United Kingdom and of India'.

The scope of the inquiry was thus circumscribed so as to exclude matters of high policy. But could the line between finance and administration be rigidly drawn? Were financial inequalities not really the result of economic policies? Could economic ills be cured without administrative and political remedies? The fact that an enquiry had been conceded at all was in itself an achievement. It was obvious that the Indian nationalists' case needed to be put forward by the ablest Indians available, the more so because the Government of India, the India office and the British Treasury were likely to marshal a formidable array of witnesses on behalf of the 'Establishment'. 'A supreme effort is to be made now in this Commission', wrote Dadabhai Naoroji to D. E. Wacha; 'we may not get another opportunity of the kind for a generation.' He pleaded with Ranade to come to England and appear before the Commission. 'Dear Ranade,' he wrote on 18 June 1896, 'you have an opportunity-now to do the greatest service you can to our poor country that you will have in your lifetime. Come and support me in your own able way....' Ranade was willing to go, and Lord Welby, the Chairman of the Commission, was ready to invite him, but the Government of India blocked the way.' The Viceroy's advisers argued that Ranade was,an unfortunate selection', that as a judge he was supposed to be above politics, that he was unacceptable to Europeans in India, and that he was 'a puller of strings'.

'In the event, D. E. Wacha was selected as a representative of the Bombay Presidency Association, G. Subramania Iyer on behalf of the Mahajan Sabha, Madras, and, Surendranath Banerjee on behalf of the Indian Association, Calcutta. Himself thwarted, Ranade decided to depute Gokhale as a representative of the Deccan Sabha. He arranged for funds from the rulers of Baroda and Kolhapur. Gokhale took the assignment earnestly; he spent ten days at Sholapur discussing economic and financial matters with G. V. Joshi, and before embarking from Bombay received a final briefing from Ranade himself. While Gokhale was on the high seas, Ranade commended his young disciple to the care of his friend Sir William Wedderburn. Ranade to William Wedderburn, 19 March 1897:... Prof. Gokhale is a young man who has been very useful as Honorary Secretary to the Poona Sarvajanik Sabha.... He has been acting under my advice for the last ten years and I have found that he possesses a very high order of natural talents and scholarship. He is a Professor of English and History in the Fergusson College, being one of the life-members. He is also one of the few 'good speakers we have on this side of India.... Prof. Gokhale goes fully equipped on the points on which he gives evidence. He is, however, a young man and you, Mr Caine and Prof. Dadabhoy shall have to do your best to see that his examination is conducted in a spirit of fairness.... As he is a good speaker, I would very much like that some arrangement be made to enable him to visit the chief towns where he might speak with great freedom on general questions.... The encounter between Gokhale and Wedderburn was fateful for its effect on them and on Indo-British relations. It was the beginning of a lifelong friendship between two men belonging to different races and generations, but sharing a common purpose. From this moment it is impossible to understand the course of Gokhale's political career without understanding the personality and politics of William Wedderburn. The Wedderburns of the Scottish border were a family of great antiquity, but since the beginning of the nineteenth century they had served in India's Civil Service. 'I can say', Sir William Wedderburn wrote, 'that I always regarded this [I.C.S.] a profession, which was also a profession of my choice, the noblest career open to youthful talent.' His father, Sir John Wedderburn (1789-1862), retired as Accountant-General, Bombay.

Sir William's elder brother, John, was the Magistrate and Collector of Hissar in the Punjab and lost his life in the Mutiny of 1857. Sir William's career in the I.C.S. began in 1860 when, at the age of 23, he landed in Bombay. He held a number of administrative and judicial appointments, officiating as Secretary to the Government of India, Judicial Commissioner Sind, Judge of the Bombay High Court, and Member of the Governor's Council. William Wedderburn did not wholly fit in the official grooves. He was no selfconscious sahib. He worked out schemes for rural credit, and interested himself in education, particularly girls' education. The Poona meeting which resolved upon the formation of the Deccan Education Society in 1885 was presided over by him. Unlike most of his colleagues in the Indian Civil Service, he did not give the leaders of educated India a wide berth. Early on, he helped Pherozeshah Mehta become a Justice of the Peace. In Poona, he made friends with Ranade, and in Bombay, with Dadabhai Naoroji. He was present at the first meeting of the Indian National Congress held in the Gokuldas Tejpal Sanskrit College, Bombay, in 1885. The following year when he officiated as the Chief Secretary to the Government of Bombay, an Indian paper wrote: 'Sir William Wedderburn's presence in the secretariat will be a guarantee that the popular side of the question will not be unrepresented.' Such a close association with Indian opinion was not calculated to make him a favourite of the government.

In November 1885, Lord Randolph Churchill, the Secretary of State for India, told the Viceroy that Sir William Wedderburn could not be given a permanent seat on the bench of the Bombay

High Court, because 'he was crotchety and also to a great degree a political incendiary. He... never loses an opportunity of associating himself with native political movements.' Wedderburn's promotion was thus blocked; this, coupled with the fact that the Indian climate did not agree with his wife, led him to seek premature retirement. When Wedderburn returned to England in 1887 he was only fifty. He could have led a quiet life. He loved gardening; he was fond of travel; he had a baronetcy and could well have hoped for a seat in Parliament. The twenty-seven years he had spent in India did not, however, allow him rest. He had seen something of the poverty of the country; he had also seen from the inside the working of the efficient but unfeeling bureaucratic machine. His ingrained liberalism, his sympathy with the Indian educated classes, his impatience with the ruling caste in India-so confident, so smug and so superior made it impossible for him to live the life of a retired English gentleman. He decided to back up the efforts of his friend A. O. Hume in India. He threw himself into the work of the British Committee of the Congress and its journal India.

In December 1889, two years after his retirement, he had the honour of being invited to preside over the fifth session of the Indian National Congress. 'I have been in the service of the people of India', he said in the course of his presidential speech, 'and have eaten their salt. And I hope to devote to their service what still remains to me of active life.' During the years 1890-2, when the reform of the Indian councils was on the parliamentary anvil, Wedderburn was continually in touch with Bradlaugh, Ripon and other Liberal statesmen. In 1893, he was elected to the House of Commons and took the lead in organizing the Indian Parliamentary Committee. From the first he assumed the role of a fearless critic of the 'Simla Clique', as he called the Indian administration. He affirmed that the interests of the British officials in India ('repression at home and aggression abroad') were at odds with those of the Indian tax-payers. He pleaded for the employment of Indians in senior posts in the interests of efficiency as well as economy. He denounced military expeditions beyond the Indian frontier for the burdens they imposed on an already impoverished country. He pleaded for a parliamentary enquiry into Indian affairs. 'I affirm', he told the House of Commons in 1893, 'that every good thing done for the people of India has arisen out of an inquiry in this House for reform." These criticisms did not endear Wedderburn to his former colleagues in the Indian Civil Service or to the British non-officials in India. He was called a faddist, a crank, and even a traitor. His presidential address at the Bombay Congress was described by the British-owned Pioneer of Allahabad as a piece of sophistical impertinence rarely equalled and never surpassed in the annals of political clap-trap. Sir William Wedderburn's speech in short was a simple appeal to the cupidity and vanity of his audience. There are those who may wonder at an Englishman hinting to an assembly of natives that the English army of occupation is a pure element of turbulence far more costly than it is worth; and that all the work of the Government could be done as well and more cheaply than it is at present by native machinery; but then to be at once a professional agitator and an Englishman is undoubtedly hard. No-one could be less like a professional agitator than Sir William Wedderburn.

The epithet was belied by his benign face, his modest, almost shy demeanour, his habit of balancing the rights and wrongs of every situation, his ingrained caution and deep consideration for others. Long years in the civil service had taught him to look at the practical rather than the ideological aspect of public affairs; he was incessantly engaged in tackling specific issues: finding funds for a girls' school in Poona, improving the clauses of a measure for legislative reform, extending famine relief in an Indian district, or softening the rigour of a discriminatory law against Indian immigrants in Natal. He had seen the Indian bureaucratic apparatus; he knew how difficult it was to change its direction. But as a civil servant he had also learnt the value of tenacity and was not discouraged by rebuffs, nor daunted by obstacles. Pragmatic, patient, plodding, tireless, incorrigibly optimistic, he was an epitome of moderation, conciliation, and compromise. In 1897 his chief interest was the Welby Commission of which he was a member. It was for this Commission that his friend Ranade had sent Gokhale to England. Gokhale does not seem to have enjoyed his first voyage to England. From the familiar routine in Poona, the cosmopolitan atmosphere on a modern steamer was a tremendous change; English dress and manners did not sit easy on him, and his vegetarianism was an additional embarrassment. To the amusement of his senior and welltravelled companion, Wacha, Gokhale nervously scanned the menu card at each meal to make sure that he did not order anything that contained eggs or meat. He was also worried about the important assignment at hand. Would he be able to acquit himself well? It was difficult for him to take his mind off the ordeal that awaited him in London; like a student preparing for a stiff test, he pored over the Blue Books he had brought with him and Puzzled out the problems of Indian finance.

As ill-luck would have it, he received a serious injury in the P and O train between London and Calais when a door struck against his chest. He arrived in London in great pain, but such was the reverential awe in which he held his host, Dadabhai Naoroji, that he did not breathe a word of his suffering to him or to anyone else. It was only when the pain became unbearable that Gokhale took Wacha into confidence. A doctor was summoned at once, and it was found that he had suffered a severe concussion of the heart which could have proved fatal. He was ordered complete rest in bed, and slowly nursed back to health by a friend of Dadabhai's, Mrs Congreve, 'a highly polished lady... exceedingly sympathetic and full of humanity'. Testimony to her devoted nursing has been left by Wacha: 'No sister could have nursed better. And none could have kept Mr Gokhale so cheerful and bright all through that serious illness. In a way it was a fortuitous circumstance that the friendship of Mrs Congreve dispelled to a considerable extent his shyness....' As he lay convalescing, Gokhale was visited by his former pupil, R. P. Paranjpye, who was a student at Cambridge. Gokhale dictated to him part of his evidence for the Welby Commission. Fortunately, he felt well enough to appear before the Commission on 12 and 13 April. His written statement was a sober and effective presentation of the nationalist case on the financial and economic grievances of India. That the distribution of burdens between Britain and India was inequitable, that there was discrimination in favour of British and against Indian industries, that there was a heavy 'drain' from India in the interest of the British garrison and capital. This was a familiar charge-sheet against British rule; it was embodied in Congress resolutions, and was the recurrent theme of Congress publicists such as Dadabhai Naoroji, R. C. Dutt and William Digby. Gokhale made use of the 'drain' theory' in his criticisms of British economic policies, but he did not make it the main plank of his argument. Nor did he confine himself only to financial issues. Subtly and effectively, he built into his evidence a reasoned denunciation not only of the economic, but the social and political policies of the Government of India as well. His lucid arguments were supported by facts and figures, drawn for greater effect from official publications.

Only occasionally did his passionate nationalism break the self-imposed restraint of the scholar: 'For years past we have been treated as a vassal dependency bound to render services to the suzerain power and to place our resources, whenever required, at its disposal. As a result, millions upon millions have been spent on objects which have not advanced the welfare of the Indian people so much as by an inch even the empty sense of glory, which is a kind of barren compensation to self-governing nations for such a large expenditure of money, is not available to us as a consolation.' Gokhale went on to voice a grievance which rankled in the breasts of three generations of educated Indians from Naoroji to Nehru: 'We must live all the days of our life in an atmosphere of inferiority, and the tallest of us must bend, in order that the exigencies of the existing system must be satisfied.... Our administrative and military talents must gradually disappear owing to sheer disuse, till at last our lot as hewers of wood and drawers of water in our country is stereotyped.' It is important to remember that these words were addressed in London in 1897 by a young Indian to a Royal Commission. Lord Welby and his British colleagues could not of course be expected to let Gokhale get away with this massive indictment. Besides the Chairman, he was cross-examined by a former Bombay civilian, the sixtyseven year-old Sir James B. Peile, who had served as the Director of Public Instruction, Bombay, Political Agent, member of the Famine Commission, Vice-Chancellor of the Bombay University, and member in turn of the executive councils of the Governor and the Viceroy. 'Was it not a fact', asked Lord Welby, 'that the working expenses of the Indian railways were the lowest in the world and that as a Government speculation, it was a beneficial one?' 'I do not think so, my Lord,' replied Gokhale, 'our wages are very low and therefore the working expenses must be low. If the Indian Railways on the whole are a profitable undertaking, why do English investors, with all their enterprise, almost invariably insist on a Government guarantee of interest in one form or another?' The Indian people felt, Gokhale added, that railway construction was undertaken principally in the interests of the English commercial and moneyed classes.

Gokhale on the explosive issue of Indian poverty and famines, clashed head-on with Sir James Peile, who cited the import of bullion into India as evidence of increased prosperity in India.

Sir James Peile:... You accept those facts, I think? Gokhale: I accept the figures from you.

Sir James: Are not these facts that I have mentioned signs of decreasing rather than of increasing poverty?

Gokhale: I do not think so.

Sir James: You do not; can you tell us why?

Gokhale: It all depends on what classes all these things go to... you must also be able to show that these increased imports of precious metals found their way into the pockets of the agriculturists into the pockets of these poor people....

Chairman: Perhaps you hesitate to accept proofs of prosperity?

Gokhale: I am quite open to correction, but I do not quite see clearly how the mere fact of the imports of gold and silver being so and so can mean that the country is increasing in prosperity. This is a fallacy of the mercantile system long regarded as exploded.

Sir James Peile suggested that famines, such as the one in the Deccan which Gokhale had seen at first-hand before embarking for England, were a mere adjunct of an agricultural economy, largely attributable to the vagaries of the monsoon and the follies of a thriftless peasantry.

Sir James Peile: Well if you take farm labourers and mill-hands in England, supposing that a great calamity fell upon England and the food supplies were suddenly stopped, do you think that the farm labourers and weavers and mill-hands and so on, would have resources which would enable them to live over the period of high prices which would result?

Gokhale: That is a very hypothetical case, because such a calamity never seems to come to England.

The fact that the peasants had sold their gold and silver ornaments was, according to Sir James, a sign that they had a resource to draw upon. 'Is it not then a resource?' asked Sir James. 'It is a resource,' retorted Gokhale, 'but it is a very cruel resource to use.' Lord Welby, the Chairman, intervened to suggest that the import of gold into India showed 'the great taste of the Indian people for ornaments which is a. form of luxury'. 'Just in the same way', replied Gokhale, 'they [Indians] have to spend large amounts on funerals. They groan under the system and have to go to the money-lender, but they must do it, it is the social life of the people.' Lord Welby had no more success than Sir James Peile in brow-beating the young politician from Poona. When reminded that he was no military expert to comment on military expenditure in the Indian budget, Gokhale replied, 'I admit that, but it is not our fault... we are non-official critics and all the information that is available to us, we utilize.' One of the tensest moments in the cross-examination came when Lord Welby suggested that it could be an advantage to a country to borrow capital cheaply in another country to help the development of its resources.

This provoked Gokhale into an outburst which could have been echoed many years later by young radicals of a later generation. 'If I had a vast property myself, I would rather allow that property to remain as it is with the consciousness that I may make full use of it when I have the means, rather than allow somebody else to come and use it and give me only a pittance, the outsider getting all the rest.' Gokhale's cross-examination continued for two days, 12 and 13 April. 'You have done most splendidly', Wedderburn assured him. 'Your evidence will be much the best on our side.' Caine, Wedderburn's colleague on the Royal Commission, described Gokhale's evidence 'as the most masterly exposition of the views of an educated Indian reformer on all the subjects dealt with'.

These compliments pleased Gokhale, but he hastened to acknowledge his debt to Ranade and G. V. Joshi, who had briefed him before he left India. His role, he wrote to Joshi, was 'no more than that of a conduit pipe and Edison's phonograph'. This was becoming modesty in a young man, but it underrated his own contribution to the final result. His mentors had supplied him with Blue Books, statistical tables and much useful advice. But it was Gokhale who had drafted the memorandum of his evidence, which won such high praise, after his arrival in England. What distinguished Gokhale's evidence was its skilful presentation and lucid exposition. More important than his memorandum was the oral examination which gave Gokhale's performance the quality of a triumph. To be crossexamined by old India hands like Sir James Peile was no trifling matter. Backed by the massive resources of their archives and their lifelong experience of Indian administration, the British officials were eager to explode what they considered the myths of Congress propaganda. When the Government of India were considering the selection of Indian witnesses for the Royal Commission, Lord Elgin was told by his Finance Member that he 'thought it might be an instructive lesson if a man like Mr [Pherozeshah] Mehta could be subjected to the cross-examination of a Royal Commission'.' It was to Gokhale's credit that he succeeded not only in parrying the thrusts of Lord Welby and his colleagues, but even in hitting back at them. A new confidence and militancy surged in Gokhale as he faced the Commission, which was sitting in judgement I on the affairs of his country. There was probably no-one in England whom Gokhale's performance pleased more than Sir William Wedderburn. For ten long years Sir William had been trying to educate English opinion on Indian affairs. In this task he had been assisted by the Congress veterans Dadabhai and W. C. Bonnerjee. But these veterans were getting on in years. Sir William saw in Gokhale a new ally for the British Committee of the Congress; able, urbane, earnest and with a gift for exposition, which made him equally at home in the committee room and on the public platform. Sir William invited Gokhale to his house in Meredith, Gloucestershire, initiated him into the mysteries of British politics, and introduced him to prominent British politicians and Anglo-Indian officials.

Gokhale was touched by the kindness of Sir William, who was his senior by thirty years, but he was not awed by him as he had been by Ranade and Dadabhai Naoroji. From the first Gokhale treated Sir William more like an elder colleague than as a mentor. Ranade had suggested to Sir William that Gokhale be given a chance to address meetings in Britain. A lecture tour had in fact been organized by the British Committee for the Indian witnesses before the Welby Commission. Gokhale spoke at Lambeth on 13 May, at Hastings on 26 May, at Dublin on 4 June, at Gloucester on 16 June and at Acton on 20 June. The summer months were not the ideal period for public meetings.

Gokhale noted that the people were more attracted by cricket and the preparations for Queen Victoria's Diamond Jubilee than by the affairs of a distant dependency. Nevertheless he made the most of his opportunity. Speaking at Hastings on 26 May, he referred to the partnership between India and Britain as that 'of the giant and the dwarf, where everything went to the giant and what was left went to the dwarf'. On 16 June, when he addressed a meeting at Gloucester, he was in his native dress. He acknowledged the efforts being made by the Government of India to relieve famine, but pointed out that the famine had been brought on by its own mistakes: the government, he argued, by merely palliating the efforts of their unsympathetic administration, did not get rid of their responsibility in the matter'. 'No people', said Gokhale, 'could be so well governed as by men who knew them well... but the Indian people were living under a despotic and perfectly irresponsible government by... Officials, whose interests were to take care of their own positions.... who... did not care to know the language and did not mix with the people." The Charter Act of 1833 had promised equality to the people of India with the other subjects of the British Empire, but even after sixty years the promise remained unrealized and the people of India were 'merely hewers of wood and drawers of water. In questions of legislation and taxation they had practically no voice. Their laws were made for them by officials.' It is difficult to gauge the effects of this lecture tour on British public opinion, but there is evidence that it nettled the authorities. A letter written by Lord George Hamilton, the Secretary of State for India, appeared in the Standard (24 May 1897) criticizing the Indian speakers and warning 'that to introduce a system of representative government would be fatal to the external safety of the country and the maintenance of order internally... it is useless to eulogize in the abstract the blessings of the British rule in India and then propose to destroy that which alone makes British rule possible and beneficent.' The intervals between lectures enabled Gokhale to do some sightseeing and to visit some educational institutions. His initial self-consciousness and diffidence had worn off; he had shed the courtly manners which had at first amused his companion, Wacha. He was learning to move freely in English society. He took lessons in French, frequented the theatre, and on one occasion, pulled his fellowdelegate Surendranath Banerjee out of his bed to show him Sir Henry Irving play the part of Napoleon. Gokhale made a good impression in England as a speaker. He was invited to a garden party by the Countess of Warren where he spoke on 'Female Education in India'.

At the annual general meeting of the Indian National Association he was present on the platform. In the National Liberal Club, he was introduced to a number of leading politicians, including T. P. O'Connor. He met Sir William Hunter to discuss educational problems. He visited Eton, Cambridge, Dulwich College and the Bedford College for Women. At the Educational Congress in the

Women's Section of the Victorian Era Exhibition, he read a paper in which he lamented the 'enforced ignorance and over done religion which had made India's women willing victims and of custom and formidable opponents of reform'. It was only natural that as a teacher Gokhale should have been interested in educational problems, but his heart really lay in politics. He was pleased at the notice which Hume, Naoroji and Caine took of him. Wedderburn missed no chance of paying a compliment to Gokhale and of improving his knowledge of English politics. He gave him letters of introduction to the leading politicians and officials who mattered in Indo-British relations. It was at Wedderburn's instance that Gokhale went to see John Morley, the distinguished writer and a prominent member of the Liberal Party. Gokhale to Morley, 9 May 1897: 1 beg to send herewith a letter of introduction which Sir William Wedderburn has kindly given me... your teachings next after John Stuart Mill have been for years past largely moulding the thought of New India, and there are, I believe, many young men like my humble self in my country who are greatly indebted for the main inspiration of their life. Under the circumstances I thought it as much a duty as a privilege not to leave this country without paying my respects to you.... The meeting took place on 12 May 1897 and lasted half an hour. Morley's reactions are not known, but Gokhale returned to his lodgings, 'overjoyed like a grown-up schoolboy who had gratified the inmost desire of his heart'.

Gokhale wrote home that Morley had been very kind and sympathetic, and expressed a wish that I should see him again before leaving England. My object in going to him was to enlist his sympathy on the side of our aspirations to which he has been unaccountably cold. He spoke to me very frankly on the subject and said that somehow or other he had an impression that a terrible catastrophe was in store for England in connection with India.... It was merely a vague instinctive presentiment. In May 1897 neither Gokhale nor Morley could have foreseen the chain of events which was to bring them together again nine years later in critical discussions on India's constitutional future. 'Overjoyed like a grown-up schoolboy' was a pardonable hyperbole of Wacha's, but there is no doubt that Gokhale was in high spirits in the summer of 1897. His evidence before the Welby Commission had raised his political stock; compliments were showered upon him. 'Our rising man' was Ranade's description of him. One of Gokhale's friends, more enthusiastic than the rest, compared his performance before the Welby Commission with Benjamin Franklin's deposition before the House of Commons: 'You have made a name for yourself in the history of India when words instead of swords are to be wielded. Gokhale could not but notice the extremely favourable impression he had made on Naoroji, Hume and Wedderburn whom he had so far dared to admire only from a distance. As he attended the meetings of the British Committee, addressed English audiences, talked to well-known English politicians, heard debates in the House of Commons, and paced its corridors, the flame of his political ambition which had been flickering under the wet blanket of Poona's factional politics began to burn brightly. Was it too much to hope that the mantle of Dadabhai Naoroji would fall on him? The words 'G. K. Gokhale, M.P.' had a pleasant ring. New vistas were suddenly unfolded to him. He saw himself pleading for his country from a seat in the House of Commons. Little did he know that six thousand miles away in his home town there were rumblings of a storm which would wreck all these fancies.

Gokhale had been elected president of the Benares Congress only a few days before he sailed for England. 'The Presidential speech', he wrote to N. A. Dravid from S. S. Caledonia on 26 September 1905, 'is fermenting in the head and some of the ideas are already taking a definite shape. But the thought of the responsibility is oppressive and God alone knows how it will be discharged in the end." How oppressive the responsibility was to be was mercifully hidden from him at that time. During the next three months, while he campaigned on behalf of the Congress in England, the Indian political scene underwent a radical transformation. The transformation was caused by Curzon's persistence in enforcing the partition of Bengal in the teeth of popular opposition. Criticism in newspapers, protest meetings, petitions and deputations failed to deflect him from the 'collision course' on which he had embarked. The Bengali bhadralok felt (in the words of Surendranath Banerjee) that they had been 'insulted, humiliated and tricked'. The sixteenth of October 1905, when the partition actually took effect, was observed as a day of mourning; in Calcutta thousands abstained from food, suspended business and walked barefoot to the banks of the Ganges for a dip in the holy river amidst deafening cries of 'Bande Mataram'. The same day Anand Mohan Bose, the veteran Bengali nationalist, was carried in an invalid's chair to a moving ceremony for laying the foundation-stone of the 'Federation Hall', which was to symbolize the indissoluble bond between the two parts of Bengal. The official reaction to the agitation was characteristic; efforts were made to silence the critics and particularly to curb students, who were in the vanguard of the agitation. Repressive measures had, however, just the opposite effect. With the rising crescendo of popular indignation, the anti-partition agitation became more vehement. The boycott of British manufactures and the use of 'swadeshi' (India made goods) were advocated to bring the government to heel.

Traditional Congress policies seemed ineffective in the new political context, and there was a clamour for new methods and a new leadership. The older Congress leaders like Surendranath Banerjee at first tried to keep pace with popular feeling, but soon found that they were being led by, instead of leading, public opinion and that the reins of the movement were slipping from their hands. The new mood of Bengal was reflected in an 'open letter' to the leaders of the Indian National Congress published in the Amrita Bazar Patrika. It affirmed that: the country in general has grown almost impatient of your tinkering Congress politics. It seems to have realized that the most successful of your Congresses cannot secure permanent good for the country simply by a policy of what is called begging.... The Congress must ... adapt itself to the changed conditions of life.... Places in Government service, shadowy representation in the Legislative Councils, this or that makeshift in the policy of the Government are not exactly the things the people want at present. True self-government... is the new creed .... The feeling that old methods would not do was also voiced by Lala Lajpat Rai, Gokhale's fellow-delegate to England in 1905. 'What Bengal has done', wrote Lajpat Rai, 'should be done by every province in ventilating its grievances.' He proposed a monster demonstration against the policies of Lord Curzon by a hundred thousand men in Benares to coincide with the Congress session. Such a demonstration, Lajpat Rai told Babu Ganga Prasad Varma, a prominent Congress leader of the North-West (later, United) Provinces, will carry more weight and will impress the people in England more than any number of your Congresses.... People are just now fairly well-excited and you should not fail to take advantage of this. Unless you are prepared to change the nature of your movement in this direction, you are not likely to make any progress towards political freedom at all, and I am sure that if the Congress will not take the initiative in this matter, some other movement may have to be set up to do the same and the Congress will dwindle into insignificance. Lajpat Rai may have been in tune with the new spirit in Indian politics, but unlike Gokhale, he was not in the inner counsels of the Congress leaders in Bombay or in the confidence of the British committee in London, who between themselves determined the Congress strategy.

Pherozeshah Mehta and his adherents in Bombay did not like much that was being said and done in Bengal in the wake of the partition. Wedderburn, Hume and Dadabhai Naoroji were critical of Curzon's decision to partition Bengal, but they saw it only as the crowning blunder of a reactionary Tory regime which was on the way out. By the end of the year Curzon had left India, and a Liberal ministry was in office in England. 'I think', wrote Dadabhai Naoroji to Gokhale on 26 November 1905, 'our day of emancipation is much nearer than many of us imagine' Wedderburn was More explicit. He wanted the Benares Congress 'to take full advantage of the great upheaval in this country [Britain] which has suddenly placed in power the friends (and some very advanced ones) of progress and popular aspirations', and expressed the hope that the Benares Congress would be guided by Gokhale.

Gokhale's task as president of the Congress was more difficult than Wedderburn and Dadabhai Naoroji knew. The aftermath of the partition had strengthened the hands of extremist elements in the Bengal Congress. These elements found allies in like-minded men in Maharashtra and the Punjab, who had been chafing under the inaction of the Congress leadership. The anti-British upsurge in Bengal had given a temporary spurt to 'swadeshi' and the boycott of British goods, and there was even talk of passive resistance. Gokhale saw that it was not going to be easy to keep the Congress at Benares in the grooves within which it had moved for twenty years. He looked around for allies. If only he could persuade Pherozeshah Mehta to go to Benares, all might be well. Pherozeshah knew how to handle dissidents and rebels; he had silenced his critics in 1903 at the Madras Congress, and deftly managed the Bombay Congress the following year; he could be relied upon to ensure a smooth session at Benares. But Pherozeshah declined to attend the session with a single peremptory sentence: 'We shall not go to Benares.' It was not only his sore throat which held him back. In recent months, Pherozeshah had not been able to see eye to eye with Gokhale on several matters. He had a lurking feeling that Gokhale had not been ruthless enough in his criticism of the Universities Bill. Pherozeshah did not like the way he had been pushed by the British Committee into sanctioning Gokhale's departure for England in September 1905. Some of the radical stuff in Gokhale's speeches in England also seems to have jarred on Pherozeshah. It seemed to him that Ramada's disciple was going off the track. Even the foundation of the Servants of India Society had struck Pherozeshah as a presumptuous if not futile exercise. Would not Gokhale's 'political missionaries' with their emphasis on renunciation develop a supercilious attitude towards their colleagues in the Congress?" The fact that, on his return from England, Gokhale had been taken out in a huge procession in Poona (in which Tilak's adherents had enthusiastically joined) and that he had even spent an hour at Tilak's house in Gaikwad Wada struck Pherozeshah as odd. Indeed, the Kesari and the Mahratta were already hinting at an estrangement between Pherozeshah and Gokhale, commending Gokhale's views on the partition of Bengal and the boycott, and denouncing Pherozeshah as the major reactionary influence in the Congress. The editor of the Gujarati, who was close to Pherozeshah and also a friend of Gokhale, thought it prudent to warn Gokhale of the pitfalls which awaited him at Benares. N. V. Gokhale to G. K. Gokhale, 22 December 1905: Please do not get offended, because I can mean no offence to you. But Sir P.M.M. [Pherozeshah M. Mehta] thinks that you are, in spite of yourself, about to play into hands of men, who until recently persecuted and denounced you, and who, you declared, were not gentlemen to be argued were irreconcilable. This was said to a few select friends who have a high regard for both of you.

The situation is very delicate and difficult, and I only hope everything may pass off successfully. The choice of Benares as the venue for the annual Congress session had struck some observers as a 'daring' one. The ancient city of Benares was the principal seat of Sanskrit learning and a stronghold of Hindu orthodoxy, but its citizens were not much concerned with politics. Nevertheless, during the Christmas week of 1905 Benares was agog with excitement. Besides the Congress session, an industrial conference was being held for the first time to coincide with the industrial exhibition. There was a 'Ladies Conference', besides 'caste' gatherings of Gaur Brahmans, the 'Rajput Sabha' and the 'Kalwar Sabha', in addition to a meeting of scholars presided over by R. Cc. Dutt to consider the question of a uniform script for the whole of India. The citizens of Benares gave a splendid welcome to Gokhale. He was taken in a huge procession from the railway station to the venue of the Congress and was deeply moved by the popular enthusiasm. At the plenary session on the afternoon of 27 December, Gokhale's name was formally proposed for the presidency by Pandit Bishambhar Nath, one of the oldest Congressmen of U.P. and seconded by R. C. Dutt and G. Subramania Iyer. Bishambhar Nath, in traditional Congress oratory, described the Congress as 'the crowning triumph of Pax Britannica with its untold numerous blessings'. Munshi Madholal, the Chairman of the Reception Committee also repeated the old cliches about the Congress being 'the intellectual product of British rule and English education'. Earlier, in a telegram to the Viceroy, the Munshi had 'respectfully' pleaded for an alteration in the Prince of Wales' tour programme, enabling him to see the industrial exhibition organized by 'the Indian National Congress, a loyal body representing all sections of His Majesty's Indian subjects'.

The sedate tone of these speeches was to some extent a part of the ritual at Congress sessions, but it was also a reminder that the North-West (United) Provinces continued to be a political backwater, barely ruffled by the storm of the partition of Bengal. Gokhale had a keen sense of political realities; he perceived the beginning of the process of polarization in the Congress; and the belligerent mood of Bengal had struck sympathetic chords in the Central Provinces, Berar, Maharashtra and the Punjab. These provinces accounted for more than half of the delegates present at the session and two-thirds of the delegates from outside the United Provinces. It was obvious that an inter-provincial group, visibly impatient with old leaders and old slogans, was emerging at Benares, informally evolving a common approach to controversial issues, and trying to push forward the Congress in opposition to the government. This group by and large admired and respected Gokhale, who himself took care not to gratuitously offend it. Indeed, in his presidential address, which usually set the tone for the Congress session, Ghokhale shrewdly took a position half-way between the Congress Establishment and the new radicals. Gokhale's presidential address included an appraisal of the political situation at the end of 1905, a historical retrospect and a forecast of the future. It also contained a reiteration of his own political faith and a restatement of the ideals and policies of the Indian National Congress. He recalled the days when the Congress had first met at Bombay in 1885, when 'hope was warm and faith shone bright', and the founders of the Congress believed that they would secure a steady advance 'in the direction of the political emancipation of the people'. Twenty years had elapsed and much had happened to chill that hope and dim that faith. It was true the Congress had succeeded in making only meagre political gains and latterly stagnation, even reaction, had set in.

Nevertheless, the Congress was resolved to attain its goal 'that India should be governed in the interest of the Indians themselves, and that in course of time a form of Government should be attained in this country similar to what exists in selfgoverning colonies of the British Empire'. The advance to such a goal could only be gradual, for it was a 'reasonable proposition, that the sense of responsibility required for the proper exercise of the political institutions of the West can be acquired by an Eastern people through practical training and experiment only'. To admit this was not to question the fitness of the Indian people for selfgovernment. Had not Mr Gladstone 'in words of profound wisdom' pointed out that 'it is liberty alone which fits men for liberty'? Gokhale made a scathing attack on the monopoly of power by the British bureaucracy in India. The gulf separating British officials from educated Indians had widened; the bureaucracy was growing 'frankly selfish' and 'openly hostile' to the national aspirations of India. The domination of one race over another inflicted great injury on a subject race, which faced not merely demoralization, but also impoverishment.

For a century or more, India had been for the British 'a country where fortunes were to be made to be taken out and spent elsewhere'. As in Ireland, the evil of absentee landlordism had in the past aggravated the racial domination of the English over the Irish, so in India, 'absentee capitalism has been added to the racial ascendancy of Englishmen'. Self-government was the only real and permanent remedy for the evils from which India suffered. The time had come for the British bureaucracy in India to part with some of its powers in favour of the educated classes. The argument that the educated classes were as yet a very small fraction of the community was unconvincing. At the end of the eighteenth century, not one man in ten or one woman in twenty knew how to read and write in England, and yet there was a House of Commons. In India about fifteen million could read and write, and a million of them had come under the influence of some kind of English education. It was true that the educated class was still small in size, but in the circumstances prevailing in India, they were the natural leaders of the people. They controlled the vernacular press which reached the masses; in a hundred ways they had access to the latter's minds, and 'what the educated Indians think today, the rest of India thinks tomorrow'. Gokhale called for a beginning, even a modest beginning in administrative and constitutional reforms: the enlargement of the size, elective element and powers of the legislative councils, the appointment of Indians to the councils of the Secretary of State, the Viceroy and the provincial Governors, the formation of advisory boards at the district level, the separation of the judicial from the executive functions, the reduction of military expenditure, and the expansion of primary, technical and industrial education. These demands, many of which were embodied in Congress resolutions from year to year, may not sound revolutionary today, but in 1905 few Britons (or even Indians) considered them immediately attainable. What lent special significance to the reiteration of these demands in 1905 was the exit of the Tory Government in England. 'For the first time since the Congress movement began', said Gokhale, 'the liberal and radical party will come into real power.' He described the Liberal Prime Minister, Sir Henry Campbell-Bannerman, as 'a tried and trusted friend of freedom', and referred to John Morley, the new Secretary of State for India, as 'the reverent student of Burke, the disciple of Mill, the friend and biographer of Gladstone', to whom large numbers of educated men in India felt 'as towards a Master and the heart hopes and yet it trembles as it had never hoped or trembled before'. 'A more gratifying combination of circumstances', declared Gokhale, 'could not be conceived and it now rests with us to turn it to the best advantage we can for our motherland.' Though he ended on a note of cautious optimism, he had earlier in his address bluntly analysed the great ferment caused by the partition of Bengal.

> The partition was a cruel wrong inflicted on our Bengali brethren... a complete illustration of the worst features of bureaucratic rule in India, its utter contempt for public opinion, its arrogant pretensions to superior wisdom, its reckless disregard of the most cherished feelings of the people... and its cool preference

of Service interests to those of the governed. Gokhale's tribute to 'Bengal's heroic stand', his support for swadeshi and even for boycott as a political weapon in extreme cases were not merely sops to Bengali delegates at the Benares Congress. There was hardly anything in his address which he had not expressed a few weeks before in England in even stronger language. Khaparde, an associate of Tilak, grudgingly confided to his diary on 27 December 1905: 'Mr Gokhale's speech as president was not quite in the ultra moderate style and was cheered in its stronger parts.' F. J. Bennett of the Times of India regretted that Gokhale had ceased to be 'a steadying force' on public feeling. 'The Mr Gokhale who presided over the Benares Congress yesterday', wrote the Times of India on 28 December 1905, 'will seem to many readers of his inaugural address to be a different person from the Mr Gokhale whom they knew some years ago as a sober and dispassionate critic of the acts and policy of the Government.' It seemed to this Anglo-Indian paper that Gokhale had fallen into 'the wild ways of the perfervid orators and writers of the Deccan who, in the days when he was much more restrained in utterance than he is now, seemed to move him to remonstrance'. The presidential speech was a great occasion at the annual Congress session, but the crucial decisions which determined its success or failure were taken in the meetings of the Subjects Committee.

The Subjects Committee, which met after the presidential speech on the evening of 27 December, got bogged down on the very first resolution, one welcoming the Prince of Wales (later King George V) to India. Lajpat Rai raised objections to the resolution on the ground that the country, suffering from famine and the after-effects of Curzon's repressive policies, was in no mood to stage pageantry for the royal couple. The Prince had been invited to Benares, but had not responded. In fact, the Congress could express its regret that the Prince had not found it possible to see the Congress session and the exhibition. Tilak supported Lajpat Rai, but the original resolution was passed by a majority. A threat was then held out by Lajpat Rai and his supporters that they would oppose the resolution in the plenary session. The Congress leaders had so far scrupulously kept the royal family above politics; the debate on the Prince of Wales was inadvisable, an ill-chosen phrase could do much harm by tarnishing the image of the Congress in England just when the Liberal Government had come into office. There was much excitement in the Congress camp on the night of 27 December, and Munshi Madholal and his friends in the Reception Committee even feared a riot. Gokhale did not, however, lose his nerve; he preferred quiet diplomacy to an acrimonious public debate. Just before the Congress session was scheduled to begin on 28 December, he sent for Lajpat Rai and made a 'personal appeal' to him not to oppose the resolution on the Prince of Wales and sought his assistance in persuading Tilak and the Bengali extremists to exercise similar restraint. While the controversial resolution was debated in the plenary session, the opponents of the resolution stayed out of the Congress pavilion; some of the Bengali delegates had to be forcibly kept out by Lajpat Rai and S. B. Bapat, an adherent of Tilak. On his part Gokhale was sporting enough to agree that the Congress records would not show the resolution as having been passed unanimously. The other resolution which caused some anxious moments at the Benares session was on the boycott of foreign goods 'as a last protest, and perhaps the only constitutional and effective means left to them [the people] of drawing the attention of the British public' to the iniquity of the partition of Bengal. The remaining twenty resolutions, such as those on the expansion of the Councils, the public service question, military expenditure, police and land revenue reforms, were hardy annuals. One of the resolutions recorded the appreciation of the work done by Gokhale in England; another enjoined him to visit England again 'to urge the more pressing proposals of the Congress on the attention of the authorities'. To have emerged unscathed from the Benares Congress was no mean achievement for Gokhale. The tensions released by the partition of Bengal had fortunately been contained within the Subjects Committee, and not allowed to spill into the plenary session. The battle lines between the Congress Old Guard led by the adherents of Pherozeshah Mehta and the emerging Bengali-Maharashtra-Punjab alliance had been drawn, but a clash had been avoided, thanks to Gokhale's acumen, patience, and tact. In his presidential address he succeeded in treading the tight rope between the old Congress orthodoxy and the new radicalism. The absence of Pherozeshah Mehta, whose sledge-hammer tactics could crush, but also incite opposition, Gokhale's personal equation with Lajpat Rai, and the latter's influence over Tilak had helped to stave off a show-down at Benares and to maintain the facade of Congress unity. This unity was essential if Gokhale was to plead for a new deal for his country under the new regime in India and England.

5

Gokhale's Plans and Programmes for the Congress

Gokhale during the welcome address as the Congress session held at Poona in 1895, put forward the plan for an enduring work for the Congress. He emphatically declared that the watchword of the Congressmen in Indians first and communities of various regions afterwards. He claimed that our whole nature has to be purified and elevated by constant struggles. Such struggles, he opined, were inevitable and people who were put out by the first signs of such differences were not the men from whom we could expect success in such high tasks. His elevation to the highest chair in the Congress party was a tribute of the highest degree to the selfless services performed by Gopal Krishna Gokhale. He delivered a forceful speech during the course of which he dwelt upon several issues and problems facing India in the first decade of the twentieth century. He talked about the visit to India of the Prince and Princess of Wales, the new Viceroy, Lord Minto after Lord Curzon, Curzon's administration, partition of Bengal, the Swadeshi Movement, the aims and objects and aspirations of the people of India, our immediate demands along with several resolutions on council reforms, excise, larger representation, parliamentary enquiries, Indians in public service, surplus revenues, military expenditure, condition of Indians in the colonies abroad, separation of judicial and executive functions, police commission, partition of Bengal, repression in Bengal, system of education, famine, Muslim pilgrims and support for Dadabhai Naoroji.

Gokhale Welcome Address as President of Congress

Brother Delegates, Ladies and Gentlemen,

On behalf of the Reception Committee and the general public of this Presidency, I offer to you all a most cordial welcome to this ancient and historical city, where we have now met under this roof to inaugurate the sittings of the 11th session of the Indian National Congress. There is a peculiar propriety in our meeting together here on this occasion. Such of you, as have been privileged to labour in this great national cause for the last 10 years and more, know full well that it was in Poona that our General Secretary first discussed the scheme of the National Congress with his native friends, and it was in this city that its first sitting was to have taken place in December 1885. Untoward circumstances, however, interfered with that arrangement, and at the eleventh hour the meeting had to be transferred to Bombay. After having completed its first cycle of ten years' existence, the Congress now enters upon a fresh cycle of another ten years of useful activity, as a great instrument of political education, welding together all the various races and creeds of India into a great and glorious whole, destined under Providence to take its rank among the foremost nations of the world. The welding process is always a work of time, and implies a long course of heating and hammering and this process of heating and hammering has to be repeated times out of number, before the union is completed.

The hammering is done for us under Providence by great extraneous agencies, represented by the supremacy of a militant civilisation and literature which will allow us no rest and no seclusion from the outside world, but will force us to take our place in the race of material improvement, in which it deservedly occupies the foremost position. Not all the hammering in 'the world, however, can accomplish the full results of the welding process, unless it is accompanied by a responsive generation of internal heat, without which the outside forces would only splinter us to pieces, as has been unfortunately the case in many other parts of the world, where old civilisations have crumbled down and never learnt to raise their head again. Even in our own days, in these last years of the 19th century, we have before us the spectacle of a great Mohammedan power in Europe and a great Mongolian power in Asia unable to retain their places from sheer inability to generate the heat, without which the outside influences can never work to any good account. A hundred years ago, the city, where we now meet, was the centre of a Native confederacy of powers, which held together the whole continent of India from the foot of the Himalayas to Cape Comorin, and from Dwarka in the West to Cuttack in the East. And appeared at one time well able to dispute on equal terms the place of supremacy with the great European power which had established itself in the lower Gangetic Valley and on the Coromandel Coast. You all know what change a hundred years have effected.

The moral union among even the stronger races that inhabit India was of such a loose and unorganised character that it gave way, at all points when the struggle commenced in right earnest. If after a hundred years we had stood in no better position than we did than in regard to these moral forces which tend to union and strength in union, our condition would be hopeless indeed. Fortunately for us, our affairs have been entrusted to the safe keeping of a power which has won a world-wide reputation as the mother of great nations and the liberator of mankind. Brought up under such a discipline, which, while it strikes gently and lends its helping hand to all who aspire to, rise again, we have benefited by the education that we receive, and by the material civilisation which annihilates time and distance, and brings us together to feel a common interest in our own elevation under the vivifying influence of a literature, and a history, the like of which the world has not known in the past for its triumphs in the emancipation of mankind. The meetings of this Congress represent the highest triumph of the influences that have been at work for fifty years and more and it is for us to respond to this noble call in a way worthy of the place we occupy in the world's history. I know there are those among our critics who dispute the truth of this position and proclaim with an air of superior wisdom that India is but a geographical expression and that there is no Indian nation as such, but only a congeries of nations, races and creeds, who have no cohesion in them and are only prevented from throttling each other by the fear of the Pax Britannica which rules over us all. At times indeed we do present in our internal quarrels about trifles a humiliating spectacle which provokes this scorn and ridicule of nations better circumstanced than ourselves.

But I feel that with the magnificent spectacle we now see before us, you will agree with me in thinking that these temporary aberrations do not represent our true condition, and that the races and creeds in India have learnt to love and respect each other, and to work together for their common elevation. Here in this gathering we have representatives from the most distant provinces, Bengal, Assam, Punjab, N.W. Provinces, Rajputana, Sindh, Gujarat, Maharashtra, Carnatic, Telangana, and the Dravid country. Nobody forces us to come together from all these distant places, and nothing but a common spark of heavenly fire could animate so many of the best and noblest of the land to sacrifice time, money and convenience and testify by their presence in these gatherings from year to year that they are determined to forget all their differences and do all that is in their power to build up the great Indian Nation, which has been their aspiration by day and dream by night, and which, if not fulfilled before their eyes, will certainly be accomplished in the near future. All the elements which go to make a common united nation are now present with us; a common political citizenship, a common loyalty to the Queen-Empress, a community of interests, under the influence of which no part can thrive of suffer without the whole sharing in the prosperity or misfortune, and a common language and literature which binds us morally and spiritually together and connects us with the wider world outside.

Differences of race and creed there still exist, but they are getting more and more tolerant of each other, and less angular every day, and it is the function of the National Congress, its chief and most glorious function, to induce in all the electric current of enlightenment, which will hasten the union and make it strong to bear the strain which time may place upon it. The watchword of the Congressmen is Indians first, Hindus, Muslims, Parsees, Christians, Panjabees, Mahrattas, Bengalees, and Madrasees afterwards. It is for us by the moderation and business-like character of our deliberations, by our mutual toleration of each other's feelings and prejudices, to justify in act and word the hopes and aspirations of those, who, in the not distant future, seek to realise the dream of a united and federated India, resting secure in its loyal dependence on the great British Nation and able to lead the nations of Asia in the path of progressive advancement in all directions of human activity. I have said that the welding process is a process of hard hammering and heating. We should not delude ourselves with the thought that things will be made easy for us and that, we could enter upon this new inheritance until we are regenerated, and our sins in the past have been washed out in the tears that burn with repentance. Our whole nature has to be purified and elevated by constant struggles with injustice in ourselves and others. Many people among us do not sufficiently realise how hard this struggle is naturally bound to be. They seem to imagine that we can pass from the old world to the new, pass from the dominion of custom and status to one of individual freedom and responsibility, from a fond clinging to the past to an earnest confidence in the future, from obedience to force to an appreciation of self-imposed law, in fact from a narrow castiron type of life to a freer and more liberalised form of existence, without budging an inch or sacrificing anything.

The sooner they abandon visions such as these, the better will it be for them and for us all. There will be struggles, our consciences, accusing and excusing night and day, castes and creeds in conflict with one another in endless directions. Such struggles are inevitable and people who are put out by the first signs. Of such differences are not the men from whom we can expect success in such high tasks. The process of fusion always requires and develops a great amount of heat. The heat of controversy is only a form of such struggle for self-improvement. Already the struggle has commenced in earnest, and though it is a most unpleasant experience to those who have to take part in it, we have to reconcile ourselves to its inevitable necessity. Compromises and adjustments are practical lessons which can only be learnt usefully and become parts of our second nature-habit when we are earnestly engaged in a war of principle. As the Chairman of the Reception Committee, it is not for me to enter more into the history of our recent experiences in Poona. I can, however, assure you, brother delegates, that if the struggle was keener here than elsewhere, it was due to the fact that on both sides there was an earnest desire to make this Congress gathering as great a success as any that preceded it. How far we have succeeded in giving you all a cordial welcome, and providing for your comforts and conveniences is more than I can say at present with confidence. This much is certain that this gathering of delegates is one of the largest that have hitherto taken place. We see assembled here the representatives of all the races, classes and creeds that inhabit this vast country. They come from all provinces and I can only hope that our actual success in the arrangements adopted here will not fall far short of what we desire.

The last Congress gave a commission to the Poona Committee to frame a draft constitution, which will give some stability to our organisation and provide for its permanence. The Committee have accordingly prepared such a draft. I trust it will receive due consideration at the hands of this Congress. The necessity for some written code like this is becoming every day more and more apparent and it is hoped that our labours in this respect will commend themselves to you all. Our Mohammedan friends in this town have, as in some other places, held aloof, but it is a matter of great satisfaction to us to find that this organised attempt to stand aloof is entirely confined to this city, and that the Mohammedans of other places have more or less cordially cooperated with their Hindu brethren in this national work.

Even our local Mohammedan friends, who have held aloof, have found it necessary to formulate their reasons for so doing. This is a welcome change, as it makes the question not one of feeling but one of reasonableness, with which argument is possible, and further discussion may lead to a change of conviction. It is urged by our Poona Mohammedan friends that the Congress does not represent adequately all the races of India. This statement is itself a great concession, because the fact of representation is not denied, but the question is narrowed to a consideration of its adequacy. The proportions are not certainly adequate in regard to the population test, but judged by the test of the spread of English education, the adequacy will not seem to be very far from the true numbers. Besides what defect exists in this respect will be most satisfactorily removed by Mohammedans sending more representatives to the Congress. The second reason assigned is difficult to deal with. Even the bitterest enemies of the Congress do not now venture to question the honesty of the motives which lead so many men from all provinces to cast in their lot with its success. Its wisdom has been questioned. Its practical usefulness might be improved, but there is only one opinion now that it is an honest, spontaneous, native Indian effort to cooperate loyally with the British rulers of the land, by setting forth the non-official view on all the great questions of the day which engage public attention. Great British statesmen have always been anxious to see such an organization spring up in the land. Lord Ripon paved the way for it by his local and municipal reforms. Lord Landsdowne assigned a distinct constitutional function to the Congress. It is not necessary, therefore, to dwell further on this reason which has been assigned by our Mohammedan friends in justification of their position. The third reason has more force in it. But every year the Congress programme of work has shown improvement on its practical side, and the leading Bombay organs have especially noted this feature, as a hopeful characteristic of this year's work. The note and the resolutions issued by the Reception Committee will be the best answer to this charge that we can give for the present. The fourth reason assigned is that the Congress is not important enough to deal satisfactorily with the subjects it takes up. This is, however, a defect for which the responsibility is on other shoulders. It rests with the Government to utilise this vast force of public opinion, and I feel sure a day will come when such a recognition will be cordially extended to it.

The rulers in the land have recognized its value by undertaking some of the reforms which it has striven for. They no doubt are waiting to see that it strikes its roots deeper in the soil, and when they recognize it as a part of their deliberative machinery, the Congress will naturally be enabled to claim the full measure of the importance to which its title at present may, to some, appear inadequate. The fifth reason assigned is one, which, in our opinion, calls for no answer. The Congress meets and deliberates from a faith in the capacity and willingness of Government to do all that it can to promote the material prosperity, and raise the general conditions of the people of India. If this were not its faith, it would not meet from year to year. If it meets as it has been doing, it is because it wishes to co-operate with Government in this work. The question is not what Government is doing, but how we respond to the call it makes on us. If Government errs, it errs from ignorance, from want of touch with the people, from differences of language, race and creed, from variation in its stand-point, which cannot be the stand-point of the millions under its rule. It is to supply this want that it becomes the duty of the people to organise themselves and give voice to public opinion.

The last argument of an appeal to the Koran is an argument which begs the whole question at issue and the Mohammedans of other parts have shown by their attendance here that they do not desire to transfer their responsibility for inaction in the matter to their scriptures. These explanations, it is hoped, will satisfy our Musalman friends in Poona that their position in untenable, and will secure more sympathetic action on their part in future.'

Gokhale's Address as President

Fellow-Delegates, Ladies and Gentlemen,

I thank you from the bottom of my heart for the great, the signal honour, which you have conferred upon me by electing me to preside over your deliberations this year. As has been said by more than one of my predecessors, the Presidentship of the Congress is the highest distinction, which it is in the power of our countrymen to bestow upon anyone; and proud indeed is that moment in an Indian's life, when he receives at your hands this most conspicuous mark of your confidence and your favour. As 1, however, stand before you today, it is not so much the honour of the position, great as that is, as the responsibility, which it imposes upon me, that occupies my thoughts. When I was first invited nearly four months ago to accept this office, we were able to see on the horizon only the small cloud-no bigger than a man's hand. Since then the sky has been overcast and for sometime a storm has been raging; and it is with rocks ahead and angry waves beating around that I am called upon to take charge of the vessel of the Congress. Even the stoutest heart among us may well own to a feeling of anxiety in such a situation. Let us, however humbly trust that in this holy city of Benares, the Divine guidance, on which we may securely throw ourselves, will not fail us, and that the united wisdom and patriotism of the delegates assembled will enable the Congress to emerge from the present crisis with unimpaired and even enhanced prestige and usefulness.

Royal Highnesses

Gentlemen, our first duty today is to offer our most loyal and dutiful welcome to Their Royal Highnesses the Prince and Princess of Wales on the occasion of this their first visit to India. The Throne in England is above all parties-beyond all controversies. It is the permanent seat of the majesty, the honour and the beneficence of the British Empire. And in offering our homage to its illustrious occupants and their heirs and representatives, we not only perform a loyal duty, but also express the gratitude of our hearts for all that is noble and high-minded in England's connection with India. The late Queen-Empress, again, was known, within the limits of her constitutional position, to, exercise during her reign her vast influence in favour of a policy of justice and sympathy towards the Indian people. We can never forget that the great Proclamation of 1858, on which we, take our stand so largely in our constitutional struggle, was not only in spirit but also in substance her own declaration of the principles, on which India was to be governed.

The present King-Emperor has announced his resolve to walk in the foot-, steps of his mother, and we have no doubt that the Prince of Wales is animated by the same desire to see a policy of righteousness pursued towards India. We rejoice that His Royal Highness, and his noble consort have come out amongst us to acquaint themselves personally with the ancient civilization of this country and its present condition. The Congress earnestly and respectfully wishes their Royal Highnesses a most successful tour through India, and it humbly trusts that the knowledge they will acquire and the recollections they will carry back with them will constitute a fresh bond of sympathy and attachment between the Royal Family in England the Princess and People of this country. The Congress also offers a most cordial and respectful welcome to Their Excellencies Lord and Lady Minto. The new Viceroy assumes the responsibilities of his office at a critical, juncture. The temper of the people, so sorely tried during the last three years, calls for the exercise of wise and statesmanlike conciliation on the part of those who are in authority, if further estrangement between the rulers and the ruled is to be prevented. I earnestly trust that such conciliation will be forthcoming. Meanwhile a special responsibility rests upon all to see to it that the immediate task that confronts His Excellency is not made more difficult than it already is. The difficulties of the situation are not of Lord Minto's creating, and has right to expect the cooperation of both the officials and the public in his endeavours to terminate a state of tension, which has already produced deplorable results and which cannot be prolonged without serious detriment to the best interests of the country. Gentlemen, how true it is that to everything there is an end! Thus, even the Viceroyalty of Lord Curzon has come to a close! For seven long years, all eyes had constantly to turn to one masterful figure in the land—now in administration, now in astonishment, more often in anger and in pain, till at last it has become difficult to realize that a change has really come. For a parallel to such an administration, we must, I think, go back to the times of Aurangzeb in the history of our own country.

There we find the same attempt at a rule excessively centralized and intensely personal, the same strenuous purpose, the same overpowering consciousness of duty, the same marvellous capacity for work, the same sense of loneliness, the same persistence in a policy of distrust and repression, resulting in better exasperation all round. I think even the most devoted admirer of Lord Curzon cannot claim that he has strengthened the foundations of British Rule in India. In some respects, his Lordship will always be recognized as one of the greatest Englishmen that ever came out to this country. His wonderful intellectual gifts, his brilliant powers of expression, his phenomenal energy, his boundless enthusiasm for work—these will ever be a theme of just and unstinted praise.

But the gods are jealous, and amidst such lavish endowments, they withheld from him a sympathetic imagination, without which no man can ever understand an alien people; and it is a sad truth that to the end of his administration Lord Curzon did not really understand the people of India. This was at the root of his many inconsistencies and made him a perpetual puzzle to most men. And thus the man, who professed in all sincerity, before he assumed the reins of office, his great anxiety to show the utmost deference to the feelings and even the prejudices of those over whom he was set to rule, ended by denouncing in unmeasured terms not only the present generation of Indians but also their remote ancestors and even the ideals of their race, which they cherish above everything else; he, who in the early part of his administration, publicly warned the official classes that "official wisdom is not so transcendent as to be superior to the stimulus and guidance" of public opinion and who declared that in the present state of India, "the opinion of the educated classes is one which it is not statesmanship to ignore or to despise," ended by trampling more systematically upon that opinion than any of his predecessors, and claiming for his own judgment and that of his official colleagues a virtual character of infallibility.

The fact is that Lord Curzon came to India with certain fixed ideas. To him India was a country, where the Englishman was to monopolize for all time all power and talk all the while of duty. The Indians only business was to be governed and it was a sacrilege on his part to have any other aspiration. In his scheme of things there was no room for the educated classes of the country; and having failed to amuse them for any length of time by an empty show of taking them into his confidence, he proceeded in the end to repress them. Even in his last farewell speech at the Byculla Club in Bombay, India exists only as a scene of his Englishmen's labours, with the toiling millions of the country-eighty per cent of the population in the back ground. The remaining twenty per cent, for aught they are worth, might as well be gently swept into the sea! Had Lord Curzon been less self-centred, had he had more humility in his nature, he might perhaps have discovered his mistake before it was too late. This would probably have enabled him to avoid giving so much offence and causing so much pain as he unhappily did during the last two years, but I doubt if the main current of his administration would even then have flowed in another channel. Lord Curzon's highest ideal of statesmanship in efficiency of administration. He does not believe in what Mr. Gladstone used to call the principle of liberty as a factor of human progress. He has no sympathy with popular aspirations, and when he finds them among a subjects people, he thinks he is rendering their country a service by trying to put them down.

Thus, in his Byculla Club speech he actually stated that he had not offered political concessions to the people of India, because he "did not regard it as wisdom or statesmanship in the interests of India itself to do so!" Taking Lord Curzon at his highest, we find him engaged in a herculean attempt to strengthen Englishman's monopoly of power in India and stem the tide of popular agitation and discontent rousing the members of the bureaucracy to a sense of duty similar to his own and raising the standard of administrative efficiency all round. The attempt has failed, as it was bound to fail. Never was discontent in India more acute and widespread than when the late Viceroy laid down the reins of office; and as regards the bureaucratic monopoly of power, I think we are sensibly nearer the time when it will be successfully assailed. One claim Lord Curzon advanced in his farewell speech at Bombay, which it is necessary to examine a little. He told his hearers, as he had done once before-on the occasion of the last Budget-that even if he had incurred the hostility of educated

Indians, the masses would be grateful to him for what he had done for them. This attempt to distinguish between the interests of the educated classes and those of the bulk of their countrymen is a favourite device with those who seek to repress the legitimate aspirations of our people. It is significant that Lord Curzon had never resorted to it till he had finally broken with the educated classes. We know of course that the distinction is unreal and ridiculous and we know also that most of those who use it as a convenient means to disparage the educated-classes cannot themselves really believe in it. Lord Curzon mentions the reduction or the salt-duty, the writing off of famine areas, the increased grants to primary education and to irrigation, the attempt at Police Reform as measures on which he bases his claim.

The suggestion here is that he adopted these measures for the good of the masses in spite of the opposition-at any rate, the indifference of the educated classes when the plain fact is that it was the Congress that had been urging these measures year after year on the attention of Government and that it was only after year of persistent agitation that it was able to move the Government in the desired direction. Four years ago, when with a surplus of seven crores or nearly five millions sterling in hand, the Government of India did not remit any taxation, and I ventured to complain of this in Council and to urge an immediate reduction of the salt-duty; I well remember how Lord Curzon sneered at those who "talked glibly" of the burdens of the masses and of the necessity of lowering the salt-tax as a measure of relief. Lord Curzon was fortunate in coming to India when the currency legislation of Lord Lansdowne and Sir David Barbour had succeeded in artificially raising the rupee to its present level, thereby enabling the Government of India to save about four millions sterling a year on its Home remittances.

This, with the recovery of the opium revenue, placed huge surpluses at Lord Curzon's disposal throughout his administration, and he never knew a moment of that financial stress and anxiety, which his predecessors had to face for a series of years. Considering how large these surpluses have been, I do not think the relief given by Lord Curzon to the tax-payers of the country has by any means been liberal. He himself estimated last March the total amount of this relief at 7 millions sterling. He did not mention that during the same time he had taken from the taxpayers 33 millions sterling over and above the requirements of the Government. Again how paltry is the relief given by the reduction of the salt-duty and the writing off of famine arrears, compared with the enormous injury done to the mass of our people by the artificial raising of the value of the rupee, which led to a heavy immediate depreciation of their small savings in silver and which makes a grievous addition to their permanent burdens by indirectly enhancing their assessments and increasing their debts to the money-lender, as prices adjust themselves to the new Rupee! Much has been made of Lord Curzon's increased grants to primary education.

Considering how little the State does in India for the education of the masses, it would have been astonishing, if with such surplus Lord Curzon had not made any addition to the educational expenditure of the country. But if he has given a quarter of a million more to education, he has given five millions a year more to the Army; and with reckless profusion he has increased the salaries of European officials in my departments and has created several new posts for them. "A spirit of expenditure," to use an expression of Mr. Gladstone's has been abroad in all directions 'during his time, and he has never practised the old-fashioned virtue of economy, with which the real interests of the people are bound up. Of course a ruler cannot labour as devotedly as Lord Curzon has done for seven years for increased efficiency without removing or mitigating important administrative evils; but that it quite different from a claim to champion the special interests of the masses, as against their natural leaders and spokesmen, the educated classes of the community. Gentlemen, the question that is uppermost in the minds of us all at this moment is the Partition of Bengal. A cruel wrong has been inflicted on our Bengali brethren and the whole country has been the case before.

The scheme of partition, concocted in the dark and carried out in the face of the fiercest opposition that any Government measure has encountered during the last half a century, will always stand as a complete illustration of the worst features of the present system of bureaucratic rule-its utter contempt for public opinion, its arrogant pretensions to superior wisdom, its reckless disregard of the most cherished feelings of the people, the mockery of an appeal to its sense of justice, its cool preference of Service interests to those of the governed. Lord Curzon and his advisers-if he ever had any advisers-could never allege that they had no means of judging of the depth of public feeling in the matter. All that could possibly have been done by way of a respectful representation of the views of the people had been done. As soon as it was known that a partition of some sort was contemplated meeting after meeting of protest was held, till over five hundred public meetings in all parts of the Province and proclaimed in no uncertain voice that the attempt to dismember a compact and homogenous province, to which the people were passionately attached and of which they were justly proud, was deeply resented and would be resisted to the uttermost. Memorials to the same effect poured in upon the Viceroy of India. The Secretary of State for India was implored to withhold his sanction to the proposed measure. The intervention of the House of Commons was sought first by a monster petition, signed by sixty-thousand people, and later by means of a debts on the subject raised in the House by our ever-watchful friend, Mr. Herbert Roberts. All proved unavailing. The Viceroy bad made up his mind. The officials under him bad expressed approval. What business had the people to have an opinion of their own and to stand in the way?

To add insult to injury, Lord Curzon described the opposition to his measure as "manufactured"—an opposition in which all classes of Indians, high and low, uneducated and educated, Hindus and Mohammedans bad joined, an opposition than which nothing more intense, nothing more widespread, nothing more spontaneous had been seen in this country in the whole course of our political agitation! Let it be remembered that when the late Viceroy cast this sigma on those who were ranged against his proposal, not a single public pronouncement in favour of those proposals bad been made by any section of the community; and that among foremost opponents of the measure were men like Sir Jolindra Mohan Tagore and Sir Gurudas Banerji, Raja Peary Mohan Mukerji and Dr. Rash Behary Ghose, the Maharajas of Myrnensing and Kassimbazar—men who keep themselves aloof from ordinary political agitation and never say a word calculated in anyway to embrass the authorities, and who came forward to oppose publicly the Partition project only from an overpowering sense of the necessity of their doing what they could to avert a dreaded calamity. If the opinions of even such men, are to be brushed aside with contempt, if all Indians are to be treated as no better than dumb, driven cattle, if men, whom any other country would delight to honour, are to be thus made to realize the utter humiliation and helplessness of their position in their own, then all I can say is "Goodbye to all hope of cooperating in any way with the bureaucracy in the interests of the people;" I can conceive of no raver indictment of British rule than that such a state of things should be possible after a hundred years. Of that rule. Gentlemen, I have carefully gone through all the papers which have been published by the Government, on this subject of Partition. Three things have struck me forcibly—determination to dismember Bengal at all costs, an anxiety to promote the interests of Assam at the expense of Bengal and a desire to suit everything to the interests and convenience of the Civil Service. It is not merely that a number of new prizes have been thrown into the lap of that service-one Lieutenant Governorship two Memberships of the Board of Revenue, one Commissionership of a Division, several Secretaryships and Under-Secretaryships—but alternative schemes of readjustment have been rejected on the express ground that their adoption would be unpopular with members of the Service. Thus, even if a reduction of the charge of the Lieutenant Governor of Bengal had really become inevitable—a contention, which the greatest living authority on the subject, Sir Henry Cotton, who was Secretary to the Bengal Government under seven Lieutenant-Governors, does not admit-one would have though that the most natural course to take was to separate Behar, Orissa and Chota Nagpur from Bengal and from them into a separate Province. This would have made the Western Province one of 30 millions in place of the Eastern. But this, says the Government of India "would take from Bengal all its best districts and would make the Province universally popular." This was of course a fatal objection, for compared with the displeasure of the Civil Service, the trampling under foot of public opinion and the outraging of the deepest feelings of a whole people was a small matter! But one can see that administrative considerations were really only secondary in the determination of this question.

The dismemberment of Bengal had become necessary, because in the view of the Government of India," it cannot be for the lasting good of any country or any people that public opinion or what passes for it should be manufactured by a comparatively small number of people at a single centre and should be disseminated thence for universal adoption, all other view, being discouraged or suppressed." "From every point of view," the Government further states "it appears to us desirable to encourage the growth centres of independent opinion, local aspirations, local ideals and to preserve the growing intelligence and enterprise of Bengal from being cramped and stunted by the process of forcing it prematurely into a mould of rigid and sterile uniformity." You will see that this is only a paraphrase, in Lord Curzon's most approved style of the complaint of the people of Bengal that their fair Province has been dismembered to destroy their growing solidarity, check their national aspirations and weaken their power of cooperating for national ends, lessen the influence of their educated classes with their countrymen, and reduce the political importance of Calcutta. After this let no apologist of the late Viceroy pretend that the object of the partition was administrative convenience and not political repression! Gentlemen, it is difficult to speak in terms of due restraint of Lord Curzon's conduct throughout this affair. Having published his earlier and smaller scheme for public criticism, it was his clear duty to publish similarly the later and larger scheme, which he afterwards substituted for it. But in consequence of the opposition which the first scheme encountered, he abandoned the idea of taking the public any more into his confidence and proceeded to work in the matter in the dark.

For more than a year nothing further was heard of his intentions, and while he was silently elaborating the details of his measure, he allowed the impression to prevail that the Government had abandoned the Partition project. And in the end, when he had succeeded in securing the Secretary of State's sanction to the scheme, it was from Simla, where he and his official colleagues were beyond the reach of public opinion that he sprang the final orders of Government upon an unprepared people. Then suddenly came his resignation. And the people permitted themselves for a while to hope that it would bring them at least a brief respite, especially as Mr. Brodrick had promised shortly before to present further papers on the subject to Parliament and that was understood to mean that the scheme would not be brought into operation till Parliament reassembled at the beginning of next year.

Of course, after Lord Curzon's resignation, the only proper, the only dignified course for him was to take no step, which it was difficult to, revoke and the consequence of which would have to be faced, not by him, but by his successor; he owed it to Lord Minto to, give him an opportunity to examine the question for himself, he owed it to the Royal visitors not to plunge the largest Province of India into violent agitation and grief on the eve of their visit to it. But Lord Curzon was determined to partition of Bengal before he left India and so he rushed the necessary legislation through the Legislative Council at Simla, which only the official members could attend, and enforced his orders on 16th October last—a day observed as one of universal mourning by all classes of people in Bengal. And now, while he himself has gone from India; what a sea of troubles he has bequeathed to his successor!

Fortunately, there are grounds to believe that Lord Minto will deal with the situation with tact, firmness, and sympathy, and it seems he has already pulled up to some extent Lord Curzon's favourite Lieutenant, the A ruler of the new Eastern Province. Mr. Fuller has evidently cast to the winds all prudence, all restraint, all sense of responsibility. Even if a fraction of what the papers have been reporting be true, his extraordinary doings must receive the attention of the new Secretary of State for India and the House of Commons. There is no surer method of goading a docile people into a state of dangerous despair than the kind of hectoring and repression he has been attempting. But, gentlemen, as has been well said, even in things evil there is a soul of goodness, and the dark times, through which Bengal has passed and is passing, have not been without a message of bright hope for the future. The tremendous upheavel of popular feeling, which has taken place in Bengal inconsequence of the partition, will constitute a landmark in the history of our national progress. For the first time since British rule began, all sections of the Indian Community, without distinction of caste or creed, have been moved by a common impulse and without the stimulus of external pressure to act together in offering resistance to a common wrong. A wave of true national consciousness has swept over the Province, and at its touch old barriers have, for the time at any rate, been thrown down, personal jealousies have vanished, other controversies have been hushed! Bengal's heroic stand against the oppression of a harsh and uncontrolled bureaucracy has astonished and gratified all India, and her sufferings have not been endured in vain, when they have helped to draw closer all parts of the country in sympathy and in aspiration.

A great rush and uprising of the waters, such as has been recently witnessed in Bengal, cannot take place without a little inundation over the banks here and there. These little excesses are inevitable, when large masses of men move spontaneously especially when the movement is from darkness into light, from bondage towards freedom—and they must not be allowed to disconcert us too much. The most outstanding fact of the situation is that the public life of this country has received an accession of strength of great importance, and for this all India owes a deep debt of gratitude to Bengal. Of course, the difficulties which confront the leaders of Bengal are enormous and perhaps they have only just begun. But I know there is no disposition to shrink from any responsibilities and I have no doubt that whatever sacrifices are necessary will be cheerfully made. All India is at their back and they will receive in their work that lies before them the cordial sympathy and assistance of the other Provinces.

And discredit, that is allowed to fall on them, affects us all. They on their side must not forget that the honour of all India is at present in their keeping. Gentlemen, I will now say a few words on a movement, which has spread so rapidly and has been hailed with so much enthusiasm all over the country during the last few months the Swadeshi movement. It is necessary at the outset to distinguish it from another movement, started in Bengal, which has really given it such immense impetus-the boycott of British goods. We all know that when our Bengali brethren found that nothing would turn the late Viceroy from his purpose of partitioning Bengal, that all their protests in the Press and on the platform, all their memorials to him, to the Secretary of State and to Parliament were unavailing, that the Government exercised its despotic strength to trample on their most cherished feelings and injure their dearest interests and that no protection against this of any kind was forthcoming from any quarter, they, in their extremity, resolved to have recourse to this boycott movement. This they did with a two fold object first a demonstration of their deep resentment at the treatment they were receiving, and secondly to attract the attention of the people in England to their grievances, so that those who were in a position to call the Government of India to account might understand what was taking place in India. It was thus as a political weapon, used for a definite political purpose, that they had recourse to the boycott; and in the circumstances of their position they had every justification for the step they took. And I can tell you from personal experience that their action has proved immensely effective in drawing the attention of English people to the state of things in our country.

But a weapon like this must be reserved only for extreme occasions. There are obvious risks involved in its failure and it cannot be used with sufficient effectiveness, unless there is an extraordinary upheaval of popular feeling behind it. It is bound to rouse angry passions on the other side, and no true well-wisher of his country will be responsible for provoking such passions, except under an overpowering sense of necessity. On an extreme occasion, of course, a boycotting demonstration is perfectly legitimate, but that occasion must be one to drive all classes, as in Bengal, to act with one impulse, and make all leaders sink their personal differences in the presence of a common danger. It is well to remember that the term "boycott" owing to its origin, has got unsavoury associations, and it conveys to the mind before everything else a vindictive desire to injure another. Such a desire on our part, as a normal feature of our relations with England, is of course out of the question. Moreover, if the boycott is confined to British goods only, it leaves us free to purchase the goods of other foreign countries and this does not help the Swadeshi movement in any way. The devotion to motherland, which is enshrined in the highest Swadeshi, is an influence so profound and so passionate that its very thought thrills and its actual touch lifts one out of one self. India needs today above everything else that the gospel of this devotion should be preached to high and low, to, prince and to peasant, in town and in hamlet, till the service of motherland becomes with us as overmastering a passion as it is in Japan.

The Swadeshi movement, as it is ordinarily understood, presents one part of this gospel to the mass of our people in a form, which brings it within their comprehension. It turns their thoughts to their country, accustoms them to the idea of voluntarily making some sacrifice for her sake, enables them to take an intelligent interest in her economic development and teaches them the important laws of cooperating with one another for a national end. All this is most valuable work and those who undertake it are entitled to feel that they are engaged in a highly patriotic mission. But the movement on its material side is an economic one; and though self-denying ordinances, extensively entered into, must serve a valuable economic, purpose, namely, to ensure a ready consumption of such articles as are produced in the country and to furnish a perpetual stimulus to production by keeping the demand for indigenous things largely in excess of the supply, the difficulties that surround the question economically are so great that they require the cooperation of every available agency to surmount them. The problem is indeed one of the first magnitude. Twelve years ago, the late Mr. Ranade remarked at an Industrial Conference held at Poona: "The political domination of one country by another attracts for more attention than the more formidable, though unfit domination, which the capital, enterprise and skill of one country exercise over the trade and manufactures of another. This latter domination has an insidious influence, which paralyzes the springs of all the varied activities, which together make up the life of a nation." The question of production is a question of capital enterprise and skill, and in all these factors, our deficiency at present is very great. Whoever can help in any one of these fields is, therefore, a worker in the Swadeshi cause and should be welcomed as such. Not by methods of exclusion but by those of comprehension, not by insisting on every one working in the same part of the field but by learning each one free to select his own corner, by attracting to the cause all who are likely to help us, are the difficulties of the problem likely to be overcome. Above all, let us see to it that there are no fresh divisions in the country in the name of Swadeshism. No greater perversion of its true spirit could be imagined than that. Take the question of cotton piece-goods, of which we import at present over 22 millions sterling worth a year. This is by far the heaviest item among our imports and our present Swadeshi agitation is directed mainly towards producing as much of these goods in our own country as possible. I have consulted three of the best experts available in India on this subject, Mr. Bezanji of Nagpur, the right hand man of the late Mr. Tata in mill matters, Hon. Mr. Vithaldas Damodardas, who has kindly placed a copy of his article at my disposal, and our friend Mr. Wacha. They are all agreed about the requirements and the difficulties of the situation.

So far as cotton fabrics are concerned, even strict Free Traders should have nothing to say against the encouragement, which the Swadeshi movement seeks to give to their manufacture in India. In the first place, many of the usual objections that may be urged against a system of State protection do not apply to helpful voluntary action on the part of consumers, such as the Swadeshi movement endeavours to promote. Moreover, the essence of Free Trade is that a commodity should be produced where the comparative cost of its production is the least and that it should be consumed where its relative value is the highest; and if accidental circumstances have thwarted such an adjustment in a given case, any agency which seeks to overcome the impediments, works in the end in the interest of true Free Trade. Now everyone will admit that with cheap labour and cotton at her own door, India enjoys exceptional advantages for the manufacture of cotton goods; and if the Swadeshi movement helps her to regain her natural position in this respect—a position which she once occupied but out of which she has been driven by an extraordinary combination of circumstances-the movement works not against but in furtherance of true Free Trade.

Even at present the Cotton Industry in India is an important one. It is the largest industry after agriculture in the country; it is also the only one agriculture excepted in which the Indians themselves have a substantial share. It is represented by a paid-up capital of about 17 crores of rupees or a little over 11 millions sterling, the number of mills being about 200, with five millions spindles and fifty thousand powerlooms. In addition to this, there are, according to the Census of 1901, about a quarter of a million persons engaged in handloom weaving in the country. Our mills consume nearly 60 per cent of the cotton produce of India and produce 58 crores lbs of yarn. Of this quantify, Mr. Vithaldas tells us, about 23.5 crore lbs is exported to China and other foreign countries, about 13.5 crore lbs is used in our weaving mills, and about 19 crores is woven by hand loom weavers, the remaining 2 crores going to the manufacture of rope and twine. In addition to this, 3 crore lbs of yarn is imported from the United Kingdom, and is consumed by handlooms. The hand loom industry of the country thus absorbs, in spite of its hard struggles, about 22 crore lbs of yam, or nearly double the quantity woven by powerlooms, and this is a most interesting and significant fact. The yarn used by the weaving mills produces about 55 crores of yards of cloth of which about 14 crore yards is exported to foreign countries and about 41 crores is left for consumption in the country. If we put down the production of the handlooms at about 90 crore yards, we have about 130 crore yards as the quantity of Swadeshi cloth consumed at present in India. The quantity of piece-goods imported from the United Kingdom and retained for use in the country is about 205 crore yards a year. Of a total cloth consumed, therefore, over one-third is at present Swadeshi. This is an encouraging feature of the situation. But the imported cloth is almost all superior in quantity. "While our mills," Mr. Vithaldas says, "produce the coarser cloth, say from yarn up to 30s count and in a few cases up to 40s, the bulk of the imported cloth is of the finer quality, using yarn over 30s count. The Indian weaving mills are obliged to restrict themselves for the most part to weaving coarser cloth owing to the inferior quality of cotton now grown in the country." It may be noted that even from existing cotton, handlooms can owing to their greater delicacy of handling the yarn, produce finer cloth than tile power-looms.

Fortunately owing to the exertions of the Agricultural Department of Bombay Government-exertions for which it is entitled to the best thanks of the whole country-Egyptian cotton has just been successfully introduced into Sind, and this year a thousand bales of a quality equal to very good Egyptian have been produced. A much heavier crop is expected next year and there is no doubt that its cultivation will rapidly extend. The main difficulty in the way of our manufacturing the quality of cloth that is at present imported is one of capital. Mr. Wacha estimates that if the whole quantity of 205 crore yards is to be produced by mills, the Industry requires an additional capital of about 30 crores of rupees. Even if we propose to spread this over ten years, we should require an addition of 3 crores of rupees every year. Now if we turn to the Statistical Abstract of British India, we shall find that the total increase in the capital invested in cotton mills during the last ten years has been only about 3 crores—an amount that Mr. Wacha wants every year for ten years.

The normal development of the mill industry is thus plainly unequal to the requirements of the situation. Moreover it is well to remember what Mr. Bezanji says-that the present mill-owners must not be expected to be very keen about the production of finer cloth, because its manufacture is much less paying than that of the coarser cloth. This is due to various causes, the principal one among them being that English capital, similarly invested, is satisfied with a smaller range of profits. Capital from other quarters must, therefore, be induced to come forward and undertake this business. If we again turn we shall find that our people hold Government Securities and about to the Statistical Abstract, about 50 crores of rupees in 11 crores in Postal Savings. Banks, the private deposits stand at about 33 crores of rupees, but there are no means of ascertaining how much of the amount, is held by Indians. Considering the extent of the country and the numbers of the population, these resources are, of course,' extremely meagre. Still they might furnish some part of the capital needed. In this connection may I say that a special responsibility now rests in the matter on the Aristocracy of Bengal! And this not merely because the Swadeshi movement is being so vigorously advocated in their Province, but also because owning to the Permanent Settlement of Bengal they are enabled to enjoy resources, which in other parts of India, are swept into the coffers of the State. If sufficient amount of capital is forthcoming Mr. Bazanji's patriotism may, I am sure, be relied on to secure for the undertaking whatever assistance his great capacity and unrivalled, knowledge can give. It must, however, be admitted that capital will come forward only cautiously for this branch of the business. But the handlooms are likely to prove of greater immediate service. Mr. Vithaldas looks forward to a great revival of the handloom industry in the country, and I cannot do better, than quote what he says on this point in his paper. "This village industry," he says, "gives means of livelihood not only to an immense number of the weaver class but afford means of supplementing their income to agriculturists-the backbone of India—who usually employ themselves on handlooms, when field-work is unnecessary and also when, owing to famine, drought or excessive rains, agricultural operations are not possible. Now the apparatus with which they work is nearly two centuries behind the times. Mr. Havell, Principal of Calcutta School of Art, Mr. Chatterton of the Madras Schools of Art, and Mr. Churchill of Bangalore, along with many others, are doing yeoman's, service by taking keen interest in the question of supplying economical and improved apparatus to the handloom weavers, Mr. Havell has pointed out that in preparing the work our handloom weavers are incapable of winding more than two threads at a time, though the simplest mechanical device would enable them to treat 50 or

100 threads simultaneously. The latest European handloom, which successively competes with the powerloom in, Cairo and in many places in Europe, can turn out a maximum of 48 yards of common cloth in a day. Mr. Havell is satisfied that the greater portion of the imported cotton cloth can be made in the Indian land-looms with great profits to the whole community.

The question of the immediate revival of the handloom weaving industry on a commercial basis demands the most earnest attention of every well-wisher of India and evidence gives promise of a successful issue to efforts put forward in this direction. "The outlook here in thus hopeful and cheering; only we must not fail to realize that the cooperation of all who can help-including the Government is needed to overcome the difficulties that lie in the path. Gentlemen, this the twenty-first session of the Indian National Congress. Last year, since 1885, we have been assembling in these gatherings to give voice to our aspirations and to formulate our wants. When the movement was first inaugurated, we were under the influence of that remarkable outburst of enthusiasm for British Rule, which had been evoked in the country by the great Viceroyalty of the Marquis of Ripon. The best beloved of India's Viceroys was not content to offer mere liphomage to the principle that righteousness alone exalted a nation. He had dared to act on it in practice and he had braved persecution at the bands of his own countrymen for its sake. Lord Ripon's noblest service to this country was that he greatly quickened the processes by which the consciousness of a national purpose comes to establish itself in the minds of a people. The Congress movement was the direct and immediate outcome of this realization. It was started to focus and organize the patriotic forces that were working independently of one another in different parts of the country so as to invest their work with a national character and to increase their general effectiveness. Hope at that time was warm and faith shone bright largely as a result of Lord Ripon's Viceroyalty, and those who started the Congress believed that by offering their criticism and urging their demands from a national platform, where they could speak in the name of all India, they would be able to secure a continuous improvement of the administration and a steady advance in the direction of the political emancipation of the people. Twenty long years have since elapsed and during the time much has happened to chill that hope and dim that faith, but there can be no doubt that work of great value in our national life has already been accomplished.

The minds of the people have been familiarized with the idea of a united India working for her salvation; a national public opinion has been created; close bonds of sympathy now knit together the different Provinces; caste and creed separations hamper less and less the pursuit of common aim; the dignity of a consciousness of national existence has spread over the whole land. Our record of political concessions won is, no doubt, very meagre, but those that have been secured are of considerable value; some retrogression haand been prevented; and if latterly we have been unable to stem the tide of reaction, the resistance we have offered though it has failed of its avowed purpose, has substantially strengthened our public life. Our deliberations have extended over a very wide range of problems; public opinion in the country is, in consequence, better informed and the Press is steadily growing in authority and usefulness. Above all, there is a general perception now of the goal towards which we have to strive and a wide recognition of the arduous character of tile struggle and the immense sacrifices it requires. The goal of the Congress is that India should be governed in the interests of the Indians themselves, and that in course of time a form of Government should be attained in this country similar to what exists in the self-governing Colonies of the British Empire. For better, or worse, our destinies are now linked with those of England and the Congress recognizes that whatever advance we seek must be within the Empire itself. That advance, moreover, can only be gradual, as at each stage of the progress it may be necessary for us to pass through a brief course of apprenticeship before we are enabled to go to the next one; for it is a reasonable proposition that the sense of responsibility, required for the proper exercise of the political institutions of the West, can be acquired, by an Eastern people through practical training and experiment only.

To admit this is not to express any agreement with those who usually oppose all attempts at reform on the plea that the people are not ready for it. "It is liberty alone," says Mr. Gladstone in words of profound wisdom, "which fits men for liberty." This proposition, like every other in politics, has its bounds; but it is far safer than the counter doctrine, "wait till they are fit." While, therefore, we are prepared to allow that an advance towards our goal may be only by reasonably cautious steps, what we emphatically insist on is that the resources of the country should be primarily devoted to the work of qualifying the people by means of education and in other ways, for such advance. Even the most bigoted champion of the existing system of administration will not pretend that this is in any degree the case at present. Our net revenue is about 44 millions sterling. Of this very nearly one-half is now eaten up by the Army. The Home Charges, exclusive of their military portion absorb nearly one-third. These two, between them, account for about 34 millions out of 44. Then over three millions are paid to European officials in civil employ. The leave only about 7 millions at the disposal of the Government to be applied to other purposes. Can anyone, who realizes what this means, wonder that the Government spends only a miserable three-quarters of a million out of State funds on the education of the people-primary, secondary and higher, all put together! Japan came under the influence of Western ideas only forty years ago, and yet already she is in a line with the most advanced nations of the West in matters of mass education, the State finding funds for the education of every child of school-going age. We have now been a hundred years under England's rule, and yet today four villages out of every five are without a school house and seven children, out of eight are allowed to grow up in ignorance and in darkness! Militarism, Service interests and the interest of the English capitalists-all take precedence today of the true interest of the Indian people in the administration of the country. Things cannot be otherwise for it is the Government of the people of one country by the people of another, and this, as Mill points out, is bound to produce great evils. Now the Congress wants that all this should change and that India should be governed, first and foremost, in the interests of the Indians themselves.

This result will be achieved only in proportion as we obtain more and more voice in the government of our country. We are prepared to bear-and bear cheerfully our fair share of the burdens of the Empire, of which we are not a part, but we want to participate in the privileges also, and we object most strongly to being sacrified, as at present, in order that others may prosper. Then the Congress asks for a redemption of those promises for the equal treatment of Indians and Englishmen in the Government of this country, which have been solemnly given us by the Sovereigns and the Parliament of England. It is now three-quarters of a century since the Parliament passed an Act, which, the Court of Directors pointed out, meant that there was to be no governing caste in India. The governing caste, however, is still as vigorous, as exclusive as ever. Twenty-five years later, the late Queen-Empress addressed a most memorable Proclamation to the Princess and people of India. The circumstances, connected with the issue of that Proclamation, and its noble contents will always bear witness to the true greatness of that great sovereign and will never cease to shed lustre on the English name.

The Proclamation repeats the pledges contained in the Charter Act of 1833, and though an astounding attempt was made less than two years ago by the late Viceroy to explain away its solemn import, the plain meaning of the royal message cannot be altered without attributing what is nothing less than an unworthy subterfuge to a Sovereign, the deep reverence for whose memory is an asset of the Empire. That the Charter Act of 1833 and the Queen's Proclamation of 1858 have created in the eyes of reactionary rulers a most inconvenient situation is clear from a blunt declaration, which another Viceroy of India, the late Lord Lytton, made in a confidential document, which has since seen the light of day. Speaking of our claims and expectations based on the pledges of the Sovereign and the Parliament of England, he wrote: "We all know that these claims and expectations never can or will be fulfilled. We have had to choose between prohibiting them (the Natives of India) and cheating them, and we have chosen the least straight-forward course... Since I am writing confidentially, I do not hesitate to say that both the Government of England and of India, appear to me upto the present moment, unable to answer satisfactorily the charge of having taken every means in their power of breaking to the heart the words of promise they had uttered to the ear." We' accept Lord Lytton as an unimpeachable authority on the conduct of the Government in evading the fulfilment of the pledges. We deny his claim to Jay down that our "claims and expectations never can or will be fulfilled." Our whole future, it is needless to say, is bound up with this question. Of the relative position of the two races in this country. The domination of one race over another-specially when there is no great disparity between their intellectual endowments or their general civilization-inflicts great injury on the subject race in a thousand insidious ways. On the moral side, the present situation is steadily destroying our capacity for initiative and dwarfing us as men of action. On the material side, it has resulted in a fearful impoverishment of the people for a hundred years and more now India has been for members of the dominant race, a country where fortunes were to be made to be taken out and spent elsewhere.

As in Ireland, the evil of absentee landlordism, has in the past aggravated the racial domination of the English over the Irish, so in India what may be called absentee capitalism has been added to the racial ascendancy of Englishmen. A great and ruinous drain of wealth from the country has gone on for many years, the not excess of exports over imports (including treasure) during, the last forty years amounting to no less than a thousand millions sterling. The steady rise in the death rate of the country-from 24 per thousand, the average for 1882-84, to, 30 per thousand, the average for 1892-94, and 34 per thousand, the present average—is a terrible and conclusive proof of continuous impoverishment of the mass of our people. India's vast interests-material and moral-no less than the honour of England, demand that the policy of equality for the two races promised by the Sovereign and the Parliament should be faithfully and courageously carried out. Gentlemen, as I have already observed, the manner in which the Partition, of Bengal has been carried out furnishes striking illustration of the worst features of the present system of bureaucratic rule. Happily these features are not always so conspicuously in evidence. No one also denies that a large proportion of the members of the bureaucracy bring to their work a, high level of ability, a keen sense of duty and a conscientious desire, within the limits of the restricted opportunities permitted, by the predominance of other interests, to do what good they can to the people. It is the system that is really at fault—a system which relegates the interests of the people to a very subordinate place and which, by putting too much power into the hands of these men, impairs their sense of responsibility and develops in them a spirit of intolerance of criticism.

I know many of these men are on their side constantly smarting under a sense of unfair condemnation by our countrymen. They fail to realize that if the criticism that is passed on their actions is sometimes ill informed and even unjust this is largely due to the veil of secrecy which carefully hides official proceedings from the view of the people in India. Moreover theirs are at present all the privileges of position and they must bear without impatience or bitterness its few disadvantages. I have already said that our advance towards our goal can only be gradual. Meanwhile, there is a great deal of work to be done for the country in which officials and non-officials could join hands. A considerable part of the way we could both go together, but it can be only on terms consistent with the self-respect of either side. In old times, British rule was new and its higher standards and its more vigorous purposes excited general admiration, the Englishmen's claim to a privileged position, even outside the sphere of official duties, we allowed to pass unchallenged. That is now no longer possible and those officials, who expect the Indians to approach them with bated breath and whispering humbleness and the type is not confined to the new Eastern Province, do more harm to their own class than they imagine. In one respect the gulf between the official and educated classes of the country is bound to widen more and more every day.

The latter now clearly see that the bureaucracy is growing frankly selfish and openly hostile to their national aspirations. It was not so in the past. In a most remarkable letter which I had the honour to receive, while in England, two months ago, from Mr. Hodgson Pratt—a great and venerated name among all lovers of peace, he tells us with what object Western education was introduced into this country. "Fifty years ago," writes Mr. Pratt, who in those days was a member of the Bengal Civil Service, "while India was still under the government of the East India Company, it was considered both just and wise to introduce measures for national education on a liberal scale, with adequate provision of schools, colleges, and universities. This event was hailed with lively satisfaction by the native population as heralding a new era of social progress, and aand satisfying the active intelligence of the Hindus. Now it must be observed that the character of the teaching thus inaugurated by Englishmen would necessarily reflect the ideals which have for centuries prevailed among them. In other words, Indian Youths would be brought up to admire our doctrines of political liberty, popular rights, and national independence; nor it could ever have been supposed that these lessons would fall upon deaf ears and cold hearts. On the contrary, the inevitable result of such teaching was clearly perceived by the Government of those days, and was regarded in a generous spirit. In support of this assertion I may mention that at the time of the inauguration of these measures I accompanied the then Lieutenant Governor of Bengal (Sir Frederick Halliday) on one of his winter tours through the province.

Naturally, he called the attention of these who attended the public meetings held by him to the new education policy, and he always took occasion to declare that the schools would promote one of the leading purposes of British rule, which was to prepare the people for self-government. It certainly was not supposed that at any subsequent time a policy would be adopted which would disappoint the legitimate hopes thus created." Now, however, that the time has come for the bureaucracy to part with some of its power in favour of the educated classes, all kinds of excuses are brought forward to postpone what is no doubt regarded as yet only a very small fraction of the community. The hollowness of this plea was well exposed by the late Mr. George Yule in his address as President of our National Congress in 1888. Quoting Prof. Tharold Rogers, he pointed out that a hundred years ago, not one man in ten or one women in twenty knew how to read and write in England. Going another century or two back, he added, the people of England, man and boy, high and low, with the exception of a mere handful, were steeped in the grossest ignorance and yet there was a House of Commons. We have now in this country about 15 million people who can read and write, and about a million of these have come under the influence of some kind of English education. Moreover, what we ask for at present is a voice in the Government of the country, not for the whole population, but for such portion of it as has been qualified by education to discharge properly the responsibilities of such association. Another argument brought forward in favour of maintaining the present bureaucratic monopoly of power is that though the educated classes make a grievance of it, the mass of the, people are quite indifferent in the matter. Now in the first place, this is not true. However, it may suit the interests of the officials to deny the fact, the educated classes are in the present circumstances of India the natural leaders of the people. There is the Vernacular Press, the contents of which do not fail to reach the mass of our population; in a hundred ways they have access to the minds of the latter; and what the educated Indian thinks today, the rest of India thinks tomorrow.

Moreover do the officials realize how their contention condemns their rule out of their own month? For it means that only as long as the people of India are kept in ignorance and their faculties are forced to lie dormant that they do not raise any objection to the present system of administration. The moment education quickens those faculties and clears their vision, they range themselves against a continuance of the system! Gentlemen, a number of important questions will, come up, before you for discussion during the next two days, and following the practice of previous Congressmen, you will no doubt record after due deliberation, your views on them in the form of resolutions. This is of course necessary; but may I suggest that for purposes of effective agitation in the immediate future, we should now concentrate our main energies on certain selected portions of our programme? Speaking broadly most of the reforms that we have been advocating may be grouped under four heads: (1) those which aim at securing for our people a larger and larger share in the administration and control of our affairs; these include a reform of our Legislative Councils, the appointment of Indians to the Secretary of State'and Council and the Executive Councils, in India, and a steady substitution of the Indian for the European agency in the public service of the country; (2) those which seek to improve the methods of administration, such as the separation of Judicial from Executive functions, Police Reform, and so forth; (3) those which propose a readjustment of financial arrangements with the object of securing a reduction of the burdens of the tax; payers and a more efficient application of our resources; under this head come a reduction of military charges, the moderating of land assessments and so forth; and (4) those which urge the adoption of vigorous extension of primary education, facilities for industrial and technical instruction grants for improved sanitation and a real attempt to deal with the alarming indebtedness of the peasantry. Now what I would most earnestly and respectfully suggest is that we would select from each group such reforms as may be immediately urged with the greatest effect and press them forward in this country and in England with all the energy we can command. In my humble opinion our immediate demands should be: (1) A reform of our Legislative Councils, raising the proportion of elected members to one-half, requiring the budgets to be formally passed by the Councils and empowering the members to bring forward amendments, with safeguards for bringing the debates to a close in a reasonable time. The Presidents of the Councils should have the power of veto. The Viceroy's Legislative Council consists at present of 25 members of whom only 5 are elected, one by the Chamber of Commerce of Calcutta—a body of Europeans and the other four by four provinces. We must ask for the proportion of elected members to be raised to 12.

Of this number, two seats may be given one to commerce and one to certain industries, and the remaining ten should be assigned to different provinces, two to each of the three older provinces and one each to the remaining. And, to begin with the right of members to move amendments may be confined to one amendment each."

(a) The two members for Commerce and Industries will generally be Europeans and they will ordinarily vote with Government. Thus, even if all the ten provincial members voted together they will be only 10 out of 25. Ordinarily, they will not be able to carry a motion against the Government, but On exceptional occasions they may obtain the support of two or three men from the other side and then the moral effect of the situation will be considerable. In the Provincial Legislative Councils, we must have an increase in the members, each district of a province being empowered, to send a member. The objection that these bodies will in that case be somewhat unwieldy is not entitled to much weight.

(b) The appointment of at least three Indians to the Secretary of State's Council to be returned one each by the three older provinces.

(c) The creation of Advisory Boards in all Districts throughout India, whom the heads of districts should be bound to consult in important matters of administration concerning the public before taking action. For the present their function 'should be only advisory, the Collector or District Magistrate being at liberty to set aside their advise at their discretion. Half the members of a Board should be elected representatives of the different Talukas or sub-divisions of the district and the other half should consist of the principal District officers and such non-official gentlemen as the head of the district may appoint. These Boards must not be confounded with what are known as District Local Boards. There is at present too much of what may be called Secretariat, with an excessive multiplication of central departments. District administration must be largely freed from this and responsible opportunities afforded to the people concerned to influence its course before final decisions are arrived at. If such Boards are created we may in course of time expect them to be entrusted with some real measure of control over the district administration. The late Mr. Ranade used to urge the importance of such Boards very strongly. If ever we are to have real local government in matters of general administration the creation of these Boards will pave the way for it. One great evil of the present system of administration is its secrecy. This will be materially reduced, so far as district administration is concerned, by the step proposed.

(d) The recruitment of the Judicial Branch of the India Civil Service from the legal profession in India.

(e) The separation of Judicial and Executive Functions.

(f) A reduction of military expenditure.

(g) A large extension of primary education.

(h) Facilities for industrial and technical education.

(i) An experimental measure to deal with the indebtedness of the peasantry over a selected area.

I think, Gentlemen, if we now concentrate all our energies on some such programme we may, within a reasonable time, see result which will not be altogether disappointing. One thing is clear. The present is a specially favourable juncture for such an effort. In our own country, there is sure to be a great rebound of public opinion after the repression to which it has been subjected during the last three years. And in England for the first time since the Congress movement began, the Liberal and radical party will come into real power. My recent visit to England, during which I enjoyed somewhat exceptional opportunities to judge the situation, has satisfied me that a strong current has already set in there against that narrow and aggressive imperialism which only the other day seemed to be: carrying everything before it. The new Prime Minister is a tried and trusted friend of freedom. And as regards the new Secretary of State for India, what shall I say? Large number of educated men in this country feel towards Mr. Morley as towards a master and the heart hopes and yet trembles as it had never hoped or trembled before. He, the reverent student of Burke, the disciple of Mill, the friend and biographer of Gladstone-will he courageously apply their principles and his, own to the government of this country, or will be, too, succumb, to the influence of the India office around him and thus cast a cruel blight on hopes which his own writings have done so much to foster? We shall see; but in any case his appointment as Secretary of State for India indicates how strongly favourable to our cause the attitude of the new Ministry is. Mr. Ellis, the new Under-Secretary of State for India, is openly known to be a friend of our aspirations. A more gratifying combination of circumstances could not be conceived, and it now rests with us to turn it to the best advantage we can for our Motherland. Gentlemen, one word more and I have done. I have no wish to underrate the difficulties that lie in our path, but I am convinced more than ever that they are not insuperable. Moreover, the real moral interest of a struggle such as we are engaged in lies not so much in the particular—re-adjustments of present institutions which we may succeed in securing, as in the strength that the conflict brings us to be a permanent part of ourselves. The whole life of a people, which is broader and deeper than what is touched by purely political institutions, is enriched even by failures, provided the effort has been all what it should be. For such enrichment the present struggle is invaluable. The true end of our work," said Mr. Ranade nine years ago, "is to renovate, to purify, and also to perfect the whole man by liberating his intellect, elevating his standard of duty, and developing to the fault all his powers.

Till so renovated, purified and perfected, we can never hope to be what our ancestors once were—a chosen people, to whom great tasks were allotted and by whom great deeds were performed. Where this feeling animates the worker, it is a matter of comparative indifference in what particular direction it asserts itself and in what particular method it proceeds to work. With a liberated manhood, with buoyant hope, with a faith that never shirks duty, with a sense of justice and a love that over leaps all bounds, renovated India will take her proper rank among the nations of the world, and be the master of the situation, and of he-own destiny. This is the goal to be reached-this is the promised land. Happy are they who see it in distant vision, happier those who are permitted to work and clear the way on to it, happiest they who live to see it with their eyes and tread upon the holy soil once more. Famine and pestilence, oppression and sorrow, will then be myths of past, and the goods will then again descend to the earth and associate with men as they did in times which we now call mythical." Gentlemen, I can add nothing that may be worthy of being placed by the side of these beautiful words. I will only call to your minds the words of another great teacher of humanity, who asks us to keep our faith in spite of trying circumstances, and warns us against the presumption of despairing because we do not see the whole future clearly before our eyes:

"Our times are in His hand,
Who saith "A whole I planned,
'Youth shows but half trust God; see all, nor be afraid."

CONGRESS RESOLUTION

Welcome to Royal Highnesses

Resolved that this Congress representing His Majesty's Indian subjects of all races, creeds and communities, most humbly and respectfully offers its royal and dutiful welcome to Their Royal Highnesses, the Prince and Princess of Wales, on the occasion of their visit to India. The Congress is deeply touched by the expression of 'I heir Highnesses' sentiments of cordial goodwill towards the people of India and is confident that the personal knowledge gained during the present tour will stimulate their kindly interest in the welfare of its people; and it expresses the fervent hope that His Royal Highness the Prince of Wales will be graciously pleased to submit to His Majesty the King Emperor its earnest prayer that the principles of the Queen's Proclamation will be given effect to the government of this country.

(a) That the President do submit the above resolution to His Royal Highness by wire.

Larger Representation

Resolved that in the opinion of this Congress the time has arrived when the people of India should be allowed a larger voice in the administration and control of the affairs of their country by

(a) the bestowal on each of the provinces of India of the franchise to return at least two members to the British House of Commons;

(b) the appointment of not less than three Indian gentlemen of proved ability and experience as members of the Secretary of State's Council; and

(c) the appointment of two Indians as members of the Governor-General's Executive Council and of one Indian as a member of the Executive Councils of Bombay and Madras.

Council Reforms

Resolved that in the opinion of this Congress the time has arrived for a further expansion and reform of the Supreme and Provincial Legislative Councils, so that they may become more truly representative of the people, and the non-official members thereof may have a real voice in the government of the country. The Congress recommends an increase in the number of nonofficial and elected members and the grant to them of the right of dividing the Councils in financial matters coming before them the head of the Government concerned possessing the power of veto.

Parliamentary Enquiries

Resolved that this Congress is of opinion that to enable Parliament to discharge more satisfactorily its responsibility in regard to the Government of India, periodical Parliamentary enquiries into the condition of India should be received and the salary of the Secretary of the State for India should be placed on the British estimates.

Excise

(a) Resolved that this Congress, while thanking the Government of India for the appointment of a Committee to inquire into the Excise Administration in the several Provinces of the country, regrets that its composition is exclusively official and that, therefore, it cannot inspire full public confidence.

(b) This Congress, concurring with the opinion of previous Congresses, expresses, its deliberate conviction that the recognition of the principle of local option in practical administration and a large reduction in the number of existing liquor-shops are conditions precedent to any satisfactory reform in Excise Administration.

(c) This Congress respectfully urges on the Government of India the desirability of speedily carrying out the principal proposals contained in Sir Frederick Lely's memorandum of last year on Excise Administration.

(d) That the Congress begs to protest against the virtual shelving by the Government of India in its executive capacity, of the Bengal Excise Bill, which has been welcomed as a sound and progressive piece of temperance legislation.

Indians in Public Service

(a) Resolved that, in the opinion of the Congress, the principles and policy enunciated by the Government of India in their Resolution, dated 24th May, 1904, on the subject of the employment of Indians in the higher grades of the Public Service, are inconsistent with those laid down in the Parliamentary Statute of 1833 and the Proclamation of 1858 by the late Queen-Empress, and this Congress enters its respectful but emphatic protest against an attempt to explain away pledges solemnly given by the Sovereign and Parliament to the people of this country, and to deviate from arrangements deliberately arrived at by the Government after a careful examination of the whole question by a Public Commission.

(b) That this Congress is of opinion that the true remedy for many existing financial and administrative evils lies in the wider employment of Indians in the higher branches of the country's service; and while concurring with previous Congress in urging that immediate effect should be given to the Resolution of the House of Commons of 2nd June, 1893, in favour of holding the competitive examinations for the Civil Services simultaneously in England and in India, this Congress places OD record its firm conviction that the only satisfactory solution of this question is to be found in the reorganization of the Indian Civil Service; which should be reconstituted on a decentralized basis, its judicial functions in the meantime being partly transferred to persons who have been trained in the profession of law.

(c) That this Congress, concurring with the opinion of the last Congress, deplores the abolitions of the competitive test for the Provincial Service. Past experience has amply established the fact that a system of Government nomination degenerates, in the special circumstances of this country, into a system of appointment by official favour, and this, by bringing unfit men into the Service, impairs the efficiency of the administration and in addition, unfairly discredits the fitness of Indians for high office. This Congress, therefore, respectfully urges the Government of India to restore the competitive test for the Provincial Service.

Indians in Colonies

(a) Resolved that this Congress, while expressing its sense of satisfaction at the passing by the Australian House of Representatives of a Bill to amend the law of Immigration so as to avoid hurting the susceptibilities of the people of India, again places on record its sense of deep regret that British Indians should continue to be subjected to harassing and degrading restrictions 'and denied the ordinary rights of British citizenship in His Majesty's Colonies. The Congress particularly protests against the enforcement by the British Government of disabilities on the Indian settlers in the Transvaal and Orange River Crown Colonies, which were not enforced even under the old Boer rule, in spite of declarations by His Majesty's Minister that the treatment of the Indian subjects of the King-Emperor by the Boer Government was one of the causes of the late war.

(b) In view of the important part the Indian settlers have played in the development of the Colonies, their admitted loyalty and peaceful and industrious habits, their useful and self-sacrificing services during the recent war, and, above all, the great constitutional importance of the principle of equal treatment of all citizens of the Empire anywhere in the King's dominions, this Congress respectfully, but strongly, urges the Government of India and His Majesty's Government to insist, by prohibiting, if necessary, the emigration of indentured labour and adopting other retaliatory measures, on the recognition of the status of Indian emigrants as British citizens in all the colonies.

Surplus Revenues

Resolved that this Congress, while appreciating the action of the Government of India in applying a portion of its surplus revenues last March to some of the purposes recommended, by the Congress, is of opinion that the financial relief given by it to the tax-payers of this country during the last three years has been most inadequate, and the Congress regrets that advantage has been taken of recent surpluses to increase largely the military expenditure of the country, raise the salaries of European officials in several departments and create a number of new posts for them. The Congress urges that any surpluses that may arise in the future should in the first place, be utilised for purposes of remission of taxation, and, secondly, be devoted to subjects directly benefiting the people such as imparting scientific, industrial and agricultural education, providing increased facilities of medical relief, and assisting Municipal and Local Boards with grants to undertake urgently needed measure of sanitary reform, and the improvement of means of communication in the interior.

Separation of Judicial And Executive Functions

(a) Resolved that in the opinion of this Congress a complete separation of Judicial from Executive functions must now be carried out without further delay.

(b) That this Congress, concurring with previous Congresses, urges that the Judicial Service in all parts of the country should be recruited from the legal profession more largely than at present, as the system of appointing Civilians without special legal training to high judicial offices does not lead to satisfactory administration of justice in the muffasil.

Military Expenditure

(a) Resolved that this Congress, while recording its emphatic protest against any charge which weakens the supremacy of the Civil control over the Military authorities, is of opinion that the necessary Civil control cannot be adequately exercised until and unless the representatives of the tax-payers are placed in a position to influence such control.

(b) That this Congress earnestly repeats its protest against the continued increase in the Military expenditure, which is necessary, unjust and beyond the capacity of the Indian people.

(c) That this Congress is distinctly of opinion that, as the Military expenditure of this country is determined, not by its own Military needs and requirements alone but also by the exigencies of British supremacy and British policy in the East, it is only fair that a proportionate share of such expenditure should be met out of the British Exchequer and shared by the Empire at large instead of the whole of such expenditure failing on a part of the Empire which is the poorest and the least able to bear it.

(d) That, in view of the changed position of affairs in Asia, due to the recent war between Russia and Japan and the Anglo-Japanese Treaty, this Congress earnestly urges that the large expenditure of ten millions sterling sanctioned last year for the Reorganization scheme be not now incurred, and the money be devoted to an extension of education in all its branches and reduction of the ryots' burdens.

Partition of Bengal

Resolved that this Congress records its emphatic protest against the Partition of Bengal in the face of the strongest opposition on the part of the province.

That having regard to the intense dissatisfaction felt by the entire Bengali community at the dismemberment of their province and their manifest disinclination to accept the Partition as an accomplished fact, this Congress appeals to the Government of India and the Secretary of State to reverse or modify the arrangements made, in such a manner as to conciliate public opinion and allay the excitement and unrest present among all classes of the people.

That this Congress recommends the adoption of some arrangement which would be consistent with administrative efficiency, and would place the entire Bengali community under one undivided administration.

Police Commission

Resolved that this Congress, while noting with satisfaction some useful reforms recommended by the Police Commission regrets that adequate measures have not been adopted to materially improve the efficiency and the honesty of the Police Service.

That this Congress records its conviction:

(1) That competitive examinations for the recruitment of the Police Service in the higher grades should be thrown open to all classes of British subjects instead of being confined to candidates of British birth, and that such examinations should be held simultaneously in England and in India.

(2) That educated Indians should be largely employed in the higher grades in order to secure efficiency in work.

(3) That enlistment in the Provincial Service should be by competitive examinations.

(4) And lastly, that District officers, who are the heads of the police, should be relieved of judicial work and of all control over the Magistracy of the District.

Famine

(a) Resolved that this Congress deplores fresh outbreak of famine in several parts of the country; and, holding that the frequent recurrence of famine is due to the great poverty of the people, which forces large numbers of them to throw themselves on State help at the first touch of scarcity, it again urges the Government of India and the Secretary of State to institute a detailed inquiry into the economic condition of a few typical villages in different parts of India.

(b) This Congress is of opinion that the prosperity of an agricultural country like India cannot be secured without a definite limitation of the State demand on land, such as was proposed by Lord Canning in 1862, or by Lord Ripon in 1882, it regrets that Lord Curzon in his Land Resolution of 1902, failed to recognise any such limitation and declined to accept the suggestions of the Right Hon. Sir Richard Garth and other memorialists in the matter. The Congress holds that a reasonable and definite limitation of the State-demand, and not the restriction on tenants' rights, such as has found favour in recent years, is the true remedy for the growing impoverishment of the agricultural population.

Repression in Bengal

Resolved that this Congress records its earnest and emphatic protest against the repressive measures which have been adopted by the authorities in Bengal after the people there had been compelled to resort to the boycott of foreign goods as a last protest, and perhaps the only constitutional and effective means left to them of drawing the attention of the British public to the action of the Government of India in persisting in their determination to partition of Bengal in utter disregard of the universal prayers and protests of the people.

Education

(a) Resolved that this Congress repeats its protest against the present policy of the Government of India in respect of Higher and Secondary Education, as being one of officialising the governing bodies of the Universities and restricting the spread of education.

(b) That this Congress, while thanking the Government of India for the special grant made this year to Primary and Higher Education, again places on record its firm conviction that the material and moral interests of the country demand a much larger expenditure than at present on all branches of education and a beginning in the direction of the Free Primary Education.

(c) That in the opinion of this Congress the recommendations of the Committee on Industrial Education should be promptly carried out by the Government. The Congress specially urges the Government to order an Industrial Survey as recommended by the Committee (and as suggested by the Government of India itself in its Home Department Resolution No. 199, dated Keith June, 18881 as a necessary preliminary to the introduction of an organized system of Technical Education in the several Provinces.

(d) That at least one central fully equipped Polytechnic Institute should be established in the country, with minor technical schools and colleges in the different provinces

Omnibus Resolution

Resolved that this Congress, concurring with previous Congresses, strongly urges:

(1) The constitution of the Punjab into a Regulation Province;

(2) The expansion and reform of the Punjab Legislative Council in accordance with the Indian Council Act of 1892.

(3) The establishment of a Chartered High Court of Judicature in the Punjab.

(4) The enactment of Legislation for Berar by the Supreme Legislative Council and not by Executive orders of the Governor-General in Council;

(5) The restoration to the people of the Central Provinces of the right to elect their representative on the Supreme Legislative Council instead of his being nominated by the Government; and

(6) The cancellation of the Government of India Notification of 25th June, 1891, in the Foreign Department, gagging the Press in territories under British administration in Native States as being serious infringement of the liberty of the Press in those tracts.

Muslim Pilgrims

Resolved that having regard to the fact that there is ten day's international quarantine already in existence to Camran, this Congress holds that the quarantine of five days imposed at the port of Bombay upon the Musalman pilgrims before embarking for Jeddah, is unnecessary and vexatious, and produces a feeling of deep discontent. This Congress, therefore, prays that the quarantine imposed at Bombay be entirely abolished.

Standing Committee

Resolved that a Standing Committee of the Congress be appointed to promote the objects of the Congress and to take such steps during the year as may be necessary to give effect to the Resolutions of the Congress.

That the following gentlemen be appointed members of the Standing Committee for the year 1906:

Bombay	The Hon. Sir P.M. Mehta K.C.I.E.
	The Hon. Mr. Daji Abaji Khare
	Mr. D.E. Wacha
Madras	G. Subramania Iyer
	The Hon. Nawab Sayyid Muhammad
Calcutta	Surendranath Banerjee
	A. Chowdhri
Burdwan	Maulvi Abdul Kasim
Bankipur	S. Sinha

Allahabad	Pandit Madan Mohan Malaviya
Lucknow	Munshi Ganga Prasad Varma
Lahore	Lala Lajpat Rai
	Lala Harkisen Lal
Amraoti	Rao Bahadur R.N. Mudholkar (as a Secretary of the Committee)
Poona	G.K. Gokhale C.I.E. (as a Secretary of the Committee)

Dadabhai Naoroji

Resolved that this Congress desires to record its most cordial support to the candidature of Dadabhai Naoroji for North Lambeth, and appeals to the electors of that constituency to return him to Parliament.

Gokhale and Lajpat Rai

Resolved that this Congress desires to record its sense of high appreciation of the valuable services recently rendered by the Hon'ble G.K. Gokhale. C.I.E. and Lala Lajpat Rai in England.

Congress Proposals

Resolved that in view of the importance of urging the more pressing proposals of the Congress on the attention of the authorities in England, at the present juncture, this Congress appoints its President, the Hon'ble Gopal Krishna Gokhale, C.I.E. as its delegate, and deputes him to proceed to England for this purpose.

6

GOKHALE : THE GURU OF GANDHI

Ranade read a paper on Indian Foreign Emigration before the third conference of the Industrial Association of Western India. 'Few people are aware', he observed, 'of the comparative magnitude of relief... afforded to our surplus population, and of the magnificent field for extension [of emigration], which is opening before our vision in the possibilities of the future. In this respect the expansion of the British Empire is a direct gain to the mass of the population of this country.' This paper was published in the Quarterly Journal of the Poona Sarvajanik Sabha of which Gokhale was then the editor, but it is doubtful if he gave a second thought to the problem of Indian emigration until 12 October 1896 when M. K. Gandhi, a young barrister practising at Durban, came to Poona and called on him. Their first meeting has been graphically described by Gandhi in his autobiography. Gandhi had approached Gokhale with some diffidence.

Gokhale, only three years older than Gandhi, had already been in nationalist politics for nearly a decade; he had been secretary of the Sarvajanik Sabha and a joint secretary of the Reception Committee of the 1895 (Poona) Congress. He was known to be a protege of the great Ranade. Gokhale took an instant liking to the youthful and modest barrister from South Africa, and treated him with an easy informality. He showed him round the Fergusson College, and promised to help in arranging a meeting in Poona to express sympathy with the Indian immigrants in Natal. The first meeting with Gokhale left Gandhi, to use his own words, 'exultantly happy'. Earlier, Gandhi had been courteously received by Pherozeshah Mehta in Bombay and Bal Gangadhar Tilak in Poona, but he was somewhat awed by them. Pherozeshah reminded him of the Himalayas, and Tilak of the ocean, but Gokhale was 'the Ganges. One could have a refreshing bath in the holy river.

The Himalaya was unscalable, and one could not easily launch forth on the sea, but the Ganges invited one to its bosom. Six days later Gandhi wrote his first letter to Gokhale, urging him to take up the question of the Indians overseas. 'The question affects', he wrote,,not only South African Indians, but Indians in all parts of the world outside India.... I submit that our great men should without delay take up this question. Otherwise, within a very short time there will be an end to Indian enterprise outside India. When he returned to Natal in January 1897, Gandhi was nearly lynched by a European mob in the streets of Durban. This provoked a strongly worded article in India (the journal of the British Committee of the Congress) from Gokhale, unfolding a tale 'which no right-minded Englishman ought to read without a feeling of deep shame and indignation'. It struck him as a curious irony of fate that in 1897, the year of the Diamond Jubilee of Queen Victoria, it had been brought home forcibly to the Indian people that, after all, they were 'only British slaves and not British subjects', and that it was 'idle on our part to expect justice or fair treatment where it does not suit the interests of Englishmen to be just or fair'. The meeting between Gandhi and Gokhale in October 1896 was far too brief to permit an intimate interchange of views. The opportunity for this came five years later, when after the Boer War Gandhi decided to leave Natal and practise law at Bombay. In December 1901, he was in Calcutta to attend the annual Congress session. Once again, he felt overawed by the eminent leaders of the Congress but, thanks to Gokhale's support, he succeeded in piloting his resolution on the plight of 'British Indians' in South Africa through the Subjects Committee and the plenary session of the Calcutta Congress. After the Congress session was over, Gandhi decided to spend some time in Calcutta. The India Club, where he took a room, was Gokhale's favourite haunt for a game of billiards. Noticing that Gandhi was inordinately shy and retiring, Gokhale told him, 'You have to stay in this country, and this sort of reserve will not do. You must get into touch with as many people as possible. I want you to do Congress work.' Gokhale invited him to be his guest, and the month that Gandhi spent under his roof in Calcutta set the seal on what was to be their lifelong friendship. Gokhale himself had not long been in Calcutta; his first budget speech in the Imperial Legislative Council in March 1902, which was to raise his political stock sky-high, had not yet been delivered. But already he enjoyed great prestige as a scholarpolitician.

Gandhi has left a fascinating penpicture of Gokhale: 'To see Gokhale at work was as much a joy as an education. He never wasted a minute. His private relations and friendships were all for public good. All his talks had reference only to the good of the country, and were absolutely free from any trace of untruth or insincerity. India's poverty and subjection were matters of constant and intense concern to him. This admiration was reciprocated in equal measure by Gokhale. At a public meeting held in Albert Hall in Calcutta on the 'Indian problem in South Africa' on 19 January 1902, Gokhale paid a tribute to Gandhi which was remarkably perceptive. Gokhale recalled his first meeting with Gandhi and his impression of Gandhi's 'ability, earnestness and tact and also... his manner, at once so gentle and yet so firm'. Gandhi (Gokhale said) was 'made of the stuff of which heroes were made'. He had proved that the fiercest opposition could be overcome and the bitterest misunderstanding removed, if only they were true to themselves and worked in a correct, selfless, straightforward manner, and did not return insult for insult, abuse for abuse. 'If Mr Gandhi settled in this country', continued Gokhale, 'it was the duty of all earnest workers to place him where he deserved to be, at their head." Gandhi could not help feeling that Gokhale was too lavish in his praise. 'It is my honest opinion—and I yield to no one in my honesty', he protested to Gokhale, 'that you have appraised my services to the country altogether too generously." Gandhi's own attitude to Gokhale had a large element of heroworship.

Indeed, Gandhi felt towards Gokhale as Gokhale had felt towards Ranade. Both Gandhi and Gokhale were, however, too intelligent and honest not to be aware of their intellectual and temperamental differences. Gokhale was amused by Gandhi's food-fads, his enthusiasm for nature-cure, scepticism towards science, technology and western political institutions, his idealization of simple village life, and his insistence on travelling in third class by rail and by trams in Calcutta. The word 'Satyagraha' was not to be coined for another four years, but Gandhi was already talking in terms of conquering hatred by love. Before the year was out, Gandhi had been recalled by his patriots in South Africa to resume the struggle on their behalf. Gandhi and Gokhale were not to meet again for ten years, but the reservoir of mutual respect and affection built up in 1902 never ran dry. Before leaving India Gandhi had implored Gokhale to eye on the Indian keep an on in South Africa. He discovered that the Indian settlers had to free themselves not only from the old chains With which they were shackled in Natal but from the new chains forged for them in the Transvaal by the new Briton-Boer partnership.

The British victory in the Boer War did not improve the lot of the Indians; on the contrary, the anti-Indian laws of the Boer regime were compiled in a handy manual and enforced more thoroughly. Gandhi kept up the campaign of Indian protest against racial discrimination. An essential feature of his strategy was the mobilization of public opinion in India. 'All that is needed', he wrote in the Indian Opinion of 28 September 1907, 'is to focus the energy of different organizations and organs of opinion in India and to bring the weight of this solid influence to bear on Lord Minto; then the Indian question [in South Africa] cannot but be solved in accordance with the principles of justice and humanity.' Gandhi counted on a series of pressures; the pressure of Indian opinion on the Viceroy, the pressure of the Viceroy and the Government of India on the British Government, and the pressure of the British Colonial office and public opinion on the South African colonies. For this strategy, Gandhi could not have a better ally than Gokhale.

Gokhale could stir educated India, and had access to the Viceroy and high British officials; he had influential friends in London through whom he could seek the support of the India office and the Colonial office. From Johannesburg Gandhi continually plied Gokhale with questions and requests. Would Gokhale recommend some promising young Indians prepared to work as teachers in South Africa? Would he contribute articles to the Indian Opinion (which Gandhi himself was editing) or suggest correspondents who would write about events at home? Finally, could he ask questions in the Imperial Legislative Council to focus the limelight on specific problems of the Indians overseas? In the columns of Indian Opinion, Gandhi kept track of Gokhale's tours and speeches in India and England, and hailed him as a model patriot, parliamentarian, educationist and reformer. On his part, Gokhale never failed to spring to the defence of his friend and the cause with which he was so completely identified. On 2 November 1905, for his lecture to the Lambeth Radical Club in England, Gokhale chose the problem of Indians in South Africa. The lecture made a deep impression on George Godfrey, one of Gandhi's close colleagues. 'You cannot imagine the gratitude of the Natal Indian Congress and the British-Indian Association of the Transvaal', wrote Godfrey, 'when I report the-great and good work you are doing for them here in England.' Two years later, when Gandhi launched his satyagraha campaign in the Transvaal, Gokhale cabled his good wishes: 'Following struggle closely, anxious interest, deepest sympathy, admiration. Trust securely Divine Will.' Gandhi proudly published the cable in the Indian Opinion and expressed the hope that it would raise the spirit of every Indian to the highest degree of courage. 'That Prof. Gokhale has sent the cable means that the whole of India will now be roused and will run to our rescue.' Unfortunately, India was not roused deeply enough to come to the rescue of her beleaguered children in South Africa. From 1901 onwards, the Indian National Congress passed a resolution every year denouncing the policies of the governments and Europeans of South Africa, but very little in the way of informed comment or active help was forthcoming. This was partly due to the fact that the politically-conscious classes in India were almost wholly absorbed by the exciting sequel to the partition of Bengal, the antagonism between the Government and educated India, the tug-of-war within the Congress between the Extremists and the Moderates, and the controversies in India and Britain surrounding the passage of the Minto-Morley reforms. By 1909, the internal convulsions within the Congress party were over, the reforms had taken shape, and the political temperature had come down. By 1909 Gandhi's own struggle had reached a critical stage, and he badly needed the support of his countrymen. By 1909 the Indian campaign in South Africa was causing serious anxiety to Gokhale. Of the 8,000 Indian adults resident in the Transvaal, no less than 7,500 had taken part in the satyagraha campaign and more than 2,500 had been imprisoned. The losses suffered by Indian merchants were estimated at five million rupees. Gandhi had given up his legal practice, and spent all his savings on the movement. All these sacrifices did not, however, bring the Indians visibly nearer their goal. The colonial governments and the European minority of South Africa seemed as determined as ever to preserve white domination. The British Government, anxious for a British-Boer accord, was reluctant to intervene.

In 1906 Morley, the Liberal Secretary of State for India, had vainly tried to link the mitigation of the rigours of the Anti-Asiatic ordinance with a loan to the Transvaal. Three years later, when Gandhi called on Morley in London, he was asked if public opinion in India was really concerned about the lot of the Indian immigrants in South Africa. Gandhi realized how vital the mobilization of Indian public opinion for his cause was, and decided to send to India H. S. L. Polak, an English Jew and a barrister, who had long been his friend and colleague in the Transvaal. M K. Gandhi to Gokhale, 23 July 1909 : By the time this reaches you, Mr Polak will have been in India. Our work here is very difficult; this, however, will be no news to you. I merely mention it by way of introduction in order to enable me to ask you if you can spare time to give special attention to it. I am anxious that our leaders should realize the national importance of the struggle.... We will continue to suffer in the Transvaal until justice is granted, but we have a right to expect much more than we have yet received from the Motherland. On 9 September 1909, at a public meeting in Bombay's Town Hall (which was attended by Polak) Gokhale moved a resolution calling upon the British Government and Parliament to prevent continued injustice and ill-treatment of His Majesty's Indian subjects in the Transvaal, and urging the Government of India to stop further recruitment of Indian labour for South Africa. It was at this meeting that Gokhale referred to the 'indomitable Gandhi, a man of tremendous spiritual Power, one who is made of the stuff of which great heroes and martyrs are made'. Gokhale traced the connection between what was happening in South Africa and India: 'The root of our present troubles in the colonies', Gokhale observed, 'really lies in the fact that our status is not what it should be in our own country. Men who have no satisfactory status in their own land cannot expect to have a satisfactory status elsewhere. Our struggle for equal treatment with Englishmen in the Empire must therefore be mainly carried on in India itself.' Gandhi had instructed Polak to place himself entirely under Gokhale's guidance. Gokhale spared no pains to make Polak's visit a success. He took the initiative in organizing an influential committee to raise funds for the hardpressed satyagrahis. He vetted a pamphlet, The Indians of South Africa, written by Polak, and had it published by his friend G. A. Natesan, the Madras publisher. Gokhale and his disciples in the Servants of India Society arranged for Polak to meet influential people in different parts of the country and to address public meetings. These meetings were organized at Delhi, Benares, Faizabad, Lahore and other places.

The Benares meeting was addressed by Annie Besant and the Lahore meeting by the local Anglican Bishop. Ratan J. Tata, the industrialist, contributed Rs. 25,000 to the fund. Gokhale appealed for a lakh of rupees at the Lahore session of the- Indian National Congress in December 1909. 'What is a lakh of rupees', he asked, 'compared to the sufferings that they [the South African Indians] have cheerfully borne for the sake of our country and our honour?... It is your duty to come to the assistance of these people... you are on trial, the whole of our nation is on its trial, our patriotism, public spirit and our sincerity, all of them are on their trial before God and Man in this matter.' In February 1 1910, Gokhale successfully piloted a resolution through the Imperial Legislative Council calling for a ban on recruitment of indentured labour. 'The time has come not merely for making representations,' observed Gokhale; 'the time has come for retaliation." The following year, a ban was imposed on recruitment of indentured labour for Natal; six years later it was extended to labour intended for all overseas colonies. Polak's visit helped to educate the Indian intelligentsia on the struggle of the Indian minority in South Africa, but it also had an unexpected result: Polak's comments on Gandhi's personality and philosophy of life at once fascinated and disturbed Congress leaders. The fact was that hardly any of them except Gokhale knew Gandhi, and even Gokhale had not met him for seven years during which Gandhi's radicalism had become more pronounced. Gandhi was a radical in the true sense of the word, always trying to get to the root of every problem and asking 'awkward' questions. Gandhi's radicalism had found a dramatic expression in 1906 in his campaign of passive resistance, or satyagraha, as he called it. A series of articles in the Gujarati section of the Indian Opinion, later published as a pamphlet entitled Hind Swaraj (Indian Home Rule), revealed that Gandhi was evolving not only a new technique for resolving social and political conflicts, but his own peculiar philosophy of life. Hind Swaraj made nonsense of the assumptions, aspirations and beliefs of the educated middle class and its leaders in India. British rule in India, Gandhi asserted, was due to Indian weakness. 'The English have not taken India; we have given it to them. They are not in India because of their strength, but because we keep them.' English education which the Indian elite had always hailed as a gift from

God appeared to Gandhi in a different light: it had 'enslaved the Indian people'.

Gandhi argued that India had no use for the English language, English civilization, English machinery. Nor did he consider the English political system as worth emulating. He prescribed passive resistance as the panacea for India's ills; as an all-sided sword, it can be used anyhow; it blesses him who uses it and him against whom it is used'. It is not surprising that the Law Member of the Viceroy's Executive Council should have considered Hind Swaraj by M. K. Gandhi of Johannesburg' as 'a most pernicious publication'. The Government of India banned its entry into India 'by sea or land'. Hind Swaraj confirmed British suspicions of Gandhi which long antedated its publication. 'I hear of good grounds for suspecting', Morley had written to Minto on 12 November 1908, 'that Mr. Gandhi really is aiming less at claiming rights in Africa than in finding fresh fuel for the smouldering fires in India.' The insinuation that Gandhi's struggle in South Africa was being fomented and financed by Indian Extremists was, of course, without any foundation. Gandhi's political contacts in India were confined to the Moderate party. Indeed in 1909, when he sent Polak to India, he advised him to keep clear of Extremists, and to take instructions only from Gokhale. Polak brought with him a typed copy of the English translation of Hind Swaraj for Gokhale. Gokhale's immediate reactions are not on record, but he could hardly have appreciated a thesis Which contradicted every single tenet of his own political creed. Hind Swaraj had a, strangely utopian and even idiosyncratic flavour; it bore the mark of Gandhi's personality. It was derived from Gandhi's own philosophy and experience rather than from any clear-cut ideology.

Gokhale was not convinced by Gandhi's logic, but he was not disturbed by it to the same extent as most of his colleagues in the Moderate-led Congress were. This was due partly to Gokhale's feeling that Gandhi's ideas had developed in an alien country in response to an extraordinary situation, and would correct themselves when he returned to India. Gandhi had foreseen that

Hind Swaraj would not meet with Gokhale's approval. 'The opinions expressed by me in the booklet', Gandhi wrote to Gokhale, 'are personal to me. Though they have been matured in the course of the struggle [in South Africa], they have nothing to do with it at all....' In 1909, the crucial issue was that of the survival of the Indian community in South Africa and how much support it could obtain from India. At the Town Hall meeting held in Bombay on 9 September 1909, Gokhale had not only paid a high tribute to Gandhi, but committed what was almost a sacrilege for a Moderate Congressman: he had justified passive resistance as a political weapon. 'I think,' Gokhale said, 'and I say this deliberately, that in the circumstances of the Transvaal, passive resistance such as that organized by Mr Gandhi is not only legitimate, but is a duty resting on all self-respecting citizens. Since 1905 'Passive Resistance' had been a plank in the Extremist programme, and was associated in the minds of the Moderates with the dangerous politics of Tilak, B. C. Pal and Aurobindo Ghose. Few Moderate leaders were prepared to go so far as to legitimize passive resistance. As Polak went round the country explaining Gandhi's views, Congress leaders saw that passive resistance was Gandhi's panacea not only for South Africa but for India as well. Deliberate defiance of 'Constituted authority' and of laws was something which few Moderate Congressmen, most of whom were lawyers, could stomach.

Many of them were ambivalent towards Gandhi: they were attracted by his heroism and sacrifices, but bewildered by his political philosophy. This ambivalence led towards the end of 1911 to an imbroglio which came close to irretrievably damaging Gandhi's cause in. South Africa and his friendship with Gokhale. The annual Congress session for 1911 was to be held in Calcutta and be presided over by Ramsay MacDonald, the British Labour leader. Unfortunately his wife was taken seriously ill, and by September 1911 it was clear that he could not come over to India in December. Satyananda Basu, one of the leaders from Bengal, wrote to Gokhale to enquire if Gandhi should be asked to preside. Gokhale replied that personally he would be happy if the honour was conferred on his friend, but he was not sure that Gandhi would be able to come out or even whether he 'still believed in the Congress programme'.25 In any case, it seemed proper to Gokhale that Gandhi should be consulted before his name was proposed. The Secretary of the Bengal Congress Committee then sent the Natal Congress a cable which was vaguely worded and misled both the Natal Congress and Gandhi into believing that he was being invited to preside over the Congress.

Gandhi cabled his consent, and the Reuter flashed the news. The muddle was complete when a majority of provincial committees voted for R. N. Mudholkar, the Congress leader from Berar, and the Bengal Congress Committee which had originally proposed Gandhi's name changed its preference in favour of Sir Henry Cotton. It is not difficult to see why Gandhi should have found so little support in the provincial Congress Committees or among Moderate Congressmen. 'I am positive', C. Y. Chintamani wrote to Gokhale on 24 October 1911, 'that I should not vote for Mr Gandhi, who may preach or support passive resistance in which, according to Mr. Polak, he profoundly believes. I may. say that the idea of honouring Mr Gandhi was present in our minds last year, but we felt that it would be injudicious to elect him after hearing Mr Polak about his opinions.' Gokhale was convinced that the Bengal Congress had handled the whole affair very clumsily: it should either not have proposed Gandhi's name for the Congress Presidency, or seen it through. If there was a contest, and Gandhi was defeated, it was likely to give a handle to his political opponents and to damage the cause for which he was fighting in South Africa. 'The situation as regards Gandhi', Gokhale wrote to Chintamani, 'is very awkward, but for his sake and for the sake of the cause identified with his name, we must extricate him from it with the best grace we can.' Gokhale advised the Secretary of the Indian National Congress to exclude Gandhi's name from the list of candidates on the ground that he would not be able to come out even if elected. 'I cannot tell you', Gokhale wrote to Gandhi, 'how sorry I am for the whole incident. I feel that your name was unnecessarily dragged into a controversy and left there exposed to unnecessary criticism. However, the one comfort of your friends is that you yourself are too calm in spirit, too selfless and too fully conscious of the real triviality of such things to worry about what has happened. 127 Thanks to Gokhale's candour and Gandhi's magnanimity, this incident was soon forgotten, and did not affect their relationship; on the contrary it was just at about this time that the phase of their closest cooperation began. Gandhi had been pleading with Gokhale for many years to pay a visit to South Africa. The visit was intended to boost the morale of the Indian community fighting for its survival, but also to afford Gokhale a little respite from the unceasing strain of public work in India and England. When Gokhale visited England in the autumn of 1905, Gandhi had urged him to visit South Africa before returning to India via the Cape of Good Hope. This was not possible as Gokhale completed his tour of England just in time to sail for India. In 1909, writing from London, Gandhi repeated the invitation. Gandhi to Gokhale, 11 November 1909: In his last letter Polak tells me that overwork and anxiety have ruined your health and that plainspokenness has endangered your life. I venture to suggest that you should come to the Transvaal and join us.... I have moved very freely among our countrymen here [in London] and I notice extreme bitterness against you.

Most consider that violence is the only method for securing any reform. In the Transvaal we are trying to show that violence is futile and that the proper method is selfsuffering, i.e. passive resistance. If therefore you came to the Transvaal, publicly declaring that it was your intention to share our sorrows, and therefore to cross the Transvaal border as a citizen of the Empire, you would give it a worldwide significance, the struggle will soon end and your countrymen will know you better..... If you would come and if you are left untouched, and I am free, I should deem it a great privilege to nurse you. If you are arrested and imprisoned, I should be delighted.... Gandhi had a penchant for high drama, but it is doubtful if the prospect of imprisonment in a Transvaal prison appealed to Gokhale. It was not until October 1912 that Gokhale was able to pay a visit to South Africa. Early in 1912 the

Government of South Africa was making anxious enquiries about Gokhale's visit. It feared that his presence would stiffèn the Indians' attitude. The Secretary of State for India and the Viceroy had their own anxieties; they were disturbed by the possibility of Gokhale himself being subjected to some of the humiliations against which his countrymen in South Africa were fighting. Crewe wrote to Heroines on 2 August 1912: Some uneasiness is felt in many quarters about the visit of Gokhale to South Africa.

The view taken of a brown man varies in many places; at Capetown there would be no difficulty. But he would very likely be turned out of a tramcar-though not nowadays off the pavement—either at Johannesburg or Durban. I had Sir R. Solomon here, and the principal public men, both British and Dutch, are being written to, asking them to have Gokhale looked after, and given a railway compartment and a carriage to drive in if possible. Gokhale had a foretaste of racial discrimination even before he left for South Africa. He had arranged to sail by the s.s. Saxon from Southampton on 5 October 1912. The Union Castle Company, which owned the ship, insisted that he should pay for a whole cabin, as no white man was likely to travel with him in the same cabin. Gokhale was beside himself with anger. 'I have so far made nine voyages' between this country and India in P and O Company's steamers, he wrote, 'and never has such an insult been offered to me. It is not the extra money demanded that I mind so much as the injustice or humiliation involved in it.' Gokhale's protest, backed by an intervention from Whitehall, led the shipping company to waive the condition. Thanks to the hints thrown by the British Colonial office to the Pretoria government and by some British politicians to their friends in South Africa, Gokhale's visit went off without any unpleasant incident. Among those who greeted him on arrival at Cape Town on 22 October 1912 was an official of the Immigration office with a letter from the Minister of Interior extending 'on behalf of the [South African] Government welcome on your arrival in South Africa'.

The same evening a reception was given in the Cape Town City Hall, with the Mayor in the chair. Gokhale was interviewed by the editor of the Cape Times, and met European politicians of both parties. From Cape Town, Gokhale went to Beaconsfield, Kimberley and Johannesburg, New Castle, Ladysmith, Maritzburg, Durban, Phoenix. The enthusiasm of the Indian community knew no bounds. At Johannesburg the address presented to him was engraved on a heartshaped plate of gold from the Rand mounted on Rhodesian teak, resembling a map of India and Ceylon. A vegetarian banquet was held in his honour; covers were laid for 400 guests, including 150 Europeans, 'a novel experience for so many Europeans to sit at the same table'. The cordiality of the European response was partly due to Gandhi's effort to keep racial rancour out of his struggle, and partly to the impression made by Gokhale on the saner section of the European community. Senator Schreiner, a South African politician, was so impressed that in 1913, while speaking on the second reading of the Immigration Restriction Bill in the South African Parliament, he described Gokhale as 'one of the greatest men of the time'. The South African Government and the bulk of the European community were, however, too hard-headed to be swept off their feet. On 14 November 1912 Gokhale saw Prime Minister Botha, and two other ministers, Smuts and Fischer, at Pretoria, the Union capital. After the interview he told Gandhi: 'Everything has been settled. The Black Act will be repealed.

The racial bar will be removed from the emigration law. The tax will be abolished.' 'I doubt it very much', Gandhi replied. 'You do not know the ministers as I do.' In retrospect it seems that the gulf between the Indian and the European points of view had really not been spanned, or if the bridge existed, it was only in the imagination of well-meaning Europeans and Indians who were eager for some kind of modus vivendi in South Africa.

Lord Ampthill, a former Governor of Madras, and a friend of the Indian cause in South Africa, congratulated Gokhale on achieving results which could 'not have been attained in any other way than by the personal influence which you are so fortunately able to exercise, and certainly not by any number of eloquent despatches or speeches in the several Parliaments concerned'. In fact, the Indian problem in South Africa, with its racial and economic overtones, was far too complex to be solved by gestures of goodwill. Gokhale's trip was important more for the effect it had on Gandhi and the Indian community than on the government and people of South Africa. Gandhi saw Gokhale after eleven years, and was shocked to see the deterioration in his health. The programme drawn up for Gokhale was much too strenuous, but Gandhi was continually in attendance, providing as much relief as was possible in the circumstances. During these three weeks Gandhi's affection and respect for Gokhale grew. He observed with admiration the working of Gokhale's mind like a sensitive and precise instrument, his capacity for taking infinite pains, mastery of facts, his innate courtesy and uncanny flair for striking the right note on every occasion. 'I listened to every speech made by Gokhale', Gandhi wrote later, 'but I do not remember a single occasion when I could have wished that he had not expressed a certain idea or had omitted a certain adjective.' Gokhale paid a great tribute to Gandhi at a gathering of Indians and Europeans at Johannesburg, referring to him as 'the pure and indomitable spirit that dwelt in that frail-looking frame, that glorified what it touched, would break but never bend in a just and righteous cause'. Gokhale did not, however, pretend to appreciate all the bees in his host's bonnet. While visiting Tolstoy Farm, Gokhale, who was weak and tired, was made to walk the one-and-a-half miles from the railway station, and caught a chill. Gandhi prepared some soup for him, but the kitchen was so far off that it was cold by the time it was taken to Gokhale's cottage. Gandhi and his companions slept on the floor at Tolstoy Farm.

A bed was offered to Gokhale, which he refused. 'You all seem to think', he gently rebuked Gandhi,,that you have been born to suffer hardships and discomforts and people like myself have been born to be pampered by you.' When Gandhi offered to iron a scarf given to Gokhale by Ranade, he replied: 'I can trust your capacity as a lawyer, but not as a washerman.' Despite the deep bond of affection between the two men, Gokhale was sometimes puzzled by the romantic ideas of his host, but he felt confident that contact with the realities of fife in his homeland would bring him down to earth. Of one remarkable trait of Gandhi, Gokhale saw further evidence: he could evoke intense loyalty for public causes from a great variety of people. That he should have won the devotion of H. S. L. Polak, Hermann Kaltenbach and other Europeans for fighting against white domination was a remarkable phenomenon. If Gandhi returned to India and joined the Servants of India and evoked a similar enthusiasm in the youth of India, would it not change the face of the country? Gandhi decidedly was one of those ideal missionaries Gokhale had been looking for when he founded the Servants of India Society.

Gandhi could, however, return to India only after the South African crisis was resolved. What was required was the redress of the main Indian grievances by the South African Government. And this redress seemed to be in the offing after Gokhale's interview with the Union ministers in Pretoria in November 1912. On the return voyage to Zanzibar, Gokhale talked to Gandhi at length about the affairs of the homeland and analysed for him the characters of important leaders of Indian opinion. This analysis, Gandhi wrote thirteen years later, 'was so accurate that I have hardly perceived any difference between Gokhale's estimate and my own personal estimate'. Gokhale had expected 1913 to be a year of reconciliation in South Africa; it proved to be the year of crisis.

Educational Devotion

Gokhale started life as a teacher and taught at the New English School and the Fergusson College for nearly eight years. There was scarcely an aspect of the Indian educational system to which he had not given thought. He had pleaded for the extension of female, technical, and higher education. Above all, he had advocated the diffusion of elementary education among the Indian masses. As early as 1896, when invited to deliver the annual address to the Bombay Graduates Association, Gokhale chose 'Education in India' as his subject. 'To us', he had declared, 'it [the spread of primary education] means the future salvation of our country." Universal education alone, Gokhale argued, could help the farmer to resist exploitation by the money-lender, to improve sanitation, to shake off superstition, to increase his earning capacity, to take an intelligent interest in public affairs, and to remove the reproach that Indian public life was the monopoly of a tiny minority. In the Imperial Legislative Council he pleaded vigorously for the education of the masses. It seemed to him 'a monstrous and cruel wrong' that millions and millions should be left without the rudiments of knowledge and that 'the joy of that knowledge' should be absolutely unexperienced by them. In 1910, at the very first meeting of the 'reformed' Imperial Council, Gokhale took advantage of the right given to non-official members to move resolutions, and proposed that 'a beginning should be made in the direction of making elementary education free and compulsory throughout the country, and that a mixed Commission of officials and nonofficials be appointed to frame definite proposals'. Though he withdrew this resolution on being assured by the government that his proposals would be carefully considered, Gokhale had succeeded in making elementary education a live issue. It was taken up by the Indian press; it figured in a resolution passed by the Allahabad Congress at the end of the year; it was debated by the All-India Muslim League at its annual session in Nagpur at about the same time. in November 1910, the Government of India appointed Harcourt Butler, a brilliant young officer of the Indian Civil Service, as the first Member of the Viceroy's Executive Council in charge of a newly created Department of Education. Butler called a meeting of the heads of the provincial education departments in April 1911 to discuss inter alia the problem of elementary education. On 16 March 1911, Gokhale introduced his Elementary Education Bill, which incorporated most of the suggestions he had made in the Imperial Council a year earlier. Based largely on the Irish Education Act of 1892 and the English Education Acts of 1870 and 1876, it sought gradually to introduce the principle of compulsion into elementary education.

The bill had, as he put it, 'a purely permissive character" to be applied only to selected areas where elementary education had already developed up to a point, and which were to be specially notified by municipalities and district boards. These local bodies, which were to bear part of the expenditure, were to be empowered to levy a special education tax. Compulsion was to be applied only to boys between the ages of six and ten, but it could be extended to girls of the same age-group with the approval of the provincial governments. School fees were not to be charged from parents whose income was less than ten rupees a month, and, to avoid hardship, whole classes or communities could be exempted from the operation of the bill. Gokhale deliberately brought forward a cautious measure to forestall objections on administrative and financial grounds. His speech in the Imperial Council was closely reasoned. It was a masterly survey of elementary education in India and abroad. He pointed out that in several European countries, the United States of America, Canada and Australia, whole populations could read and write, but in India only 6 per cent of the people were literate.

A mere 1.7 per cent of the population went to elementary schools in India, as against 20 per cent in the U.S.A. and western Europe, 11 per cent in Japan and 5 per cent in Russia. The expenditure on elementary education was 16s. per head in the U.S.A., 10s. in England and Germany, 4s. 10d. in France, 721d. in Japan, 7½d. in Russia, and barely a penny in India. Elementary education had been made compulsory and free in Great Britain, Ireland, France, Germany, Switzerland, Austria, Hungary, Italy, Belgium, Denmark, Norway, Canada, U.S.A., Australia and Japan;, in Holland it was compulsory, but not free. In Russia it was for the most part free, but not compulsory. If illiteracy was to be banished from India within a measurable period, Gokhale saw no escape from some form of compulsion. He pointed out that in 1870, before England introduced compulsion, only forty-three per cent of her children were at school; ten years had sufficed to bring all of them to school. Similarly, Japan had by means of compulsion made elementary education universal within twenty years.

The diffusion of education among the Indian masses was in Gokhale's opinion a great national task in which the government and the people could cooperate. He urged the government to adopt elementary education as its own policy, and to provide funds for it as 'Governments in other civilized countries are doing'. He agreed that leaders of Indian opinion, on their part, had to bring to this task energy, enthusiasm and above all the courage to court unpopularity by advocating compulsion. Gokhale made an impassioned and even indignant attack on the critics of his bill. A Bombay businessman, Sir Sassoon David, had told the Imperial Council that the time for compulsion had not yet come. 'Will he tell us', asked Gokhale, 'how and why it has arrived in Baroda and not in British territory? Will he tell us why, when the Philippino Municipalities have introduced compulsion, our own Municipalities should not? Harcourt Butler, the Education Member, rejected the analogy of Baroda on the ground that it was 'autocratically' governed. 'Western countries will not do', Gokhale retorted, 'because they are governed democratically! Baroda will not do, because it is governed autocratically! I suppose the Hon'ble Member will not be satisfied unless I produce the analogy of a country governed bureaucratically, and as there is no other country governed as India is, he is safe in insisting on such an analogy, and I must say I give it up.' After the bill had been introduced and circulated, twelve months were to elapse before it could come up before the Imperial Legislative Council again. Gokhale had a year in which to mobilize popular support for his proposals and to break down official prejudice and opposition. The bill was well received by the Indian press, and even by a few Anglo Indian newspapers such as the Indian Daily News, the Madras Mail and the Madras Times. The Senate of the Madras University, which was the only university senate consulted, ex pressed itself in favour of the bill. Public meetings were held in several places to support it. Gokhale undertook a tour to educate public opinion. He visited Calcutta, Nagpur and Madras. The visit to Madras proved the most memorable in this campaign. He had written to V. S. Srinivasa Sastri, his disciple and host in Madras, to avoid processions and public receptions. 'It is impossible', Sastri wrote back, 'to keep the young men from the platform or railway station compound, but we can take care of you and drive you home as fast as decency will allow.", On 22 July, Gokhale addressed a public meeting in the Victoria Town Hall, which was packed to capacity, its 600 seats having been reserved several days in advance. A day earlier, a petition bearing more than a hundred signatures addressed 'to the Hon'ble G. K. Gokhale, C.I.E., Madras', read : 'The Victoria Town Hall can accommodate only 600 persons. But this is a very small fraction of your admirers and sympathizers in this city, we beg that you be pleased to arrange [an] open air meeting....' An 'open air meeting' was unthinkable in those days. While Gokhale spoke on the problems of education, with the veteran S. Subramania Iyer, a former judge of the Madras High Court, in the chair, thousands waited outside the Town Hall. Next morning another meeting was held in the Victoria Hall by the students of Madras, who presented an address to Gokhale. He spoke to them on 'The Needs and Responsibilities of Public Life'. The critics of the Elementary Education Bill were not confined to the ranks of British officials.

Surendranath Banerjee opposed it, fearing that it would divert funds for elementary education from higher education-in which incidentally he was personally interested. The Bombay Corporation, under the inspiration of Pherozeshah Mehta, passed a resolution which endorsed the objects, but criticized the methods proposed in Gokhale's bill. Pherozeshah wanted the responsibility for elementary education to remain squarely on the shoulders of the Government of India; he feared that devolution of this responsibility, even partially to municipalities and district boards, would give the government a pretext for inaction. Muslim reaction was mixed. Some Muslim newspapers, such as the Observer of Lahore, supported the bill. So did the Aga Khan But Syed Ameer Ali and his friends in London struck a discordant note. Some Muslim politicians-such as Mian Muhammad Shafi of the Punjab-could hardly be expected to take a line which ran counter to the wishes of the government. But already in 1911efforts were being made to misrepresent Gokhale's proposals as communal.

The secretary of the All-India Muslim League, in a letter to the Home Department of the Government of India, suggested that the sole medium of instruction for Muslim children should be Urdu, that they should be taught the essentials of Islam, that their textbooks should draw upon Islamic sources and be prepared by Muslim writers and approved by textbook committees composed exclusively of Muslims. He went so far as to demand 'a staff of Muslim inspectors to look to the peculiar needs of the community'. Even the supervisory committees envisaged in Gokhale's Bill were to have equal representation of Hindus and Muslims. These extreme demands, the effect of which could only be to accentuate the isolation of the Muslim community from the mainstream of Indian life, could hardly have been taken seriously in 1911. Gokhale was, however, quick to recognize the justice of the demand for instruction in Urdu and other regional languages. He agreed to the introduction of a clause in his bill permitting the use of any Indian language if twenty-five children speaking it attended a school. Gokhale had known all along that because of the standing majority of the official bloc in the Imperial Council, the fate of his bill would ultimately depend upon the attitude of the government.

In March 1911, that attitude seemed to him 'cautious, but not unfriendly'. He paid a tribute to the Education Member, Harcourt Butler, who, he said, 'brings to his task a reputation for great practical capacity... the Indian sun has not dried the Hon'ble Member and... he has not shed those enthusiasms with which perhaps we all start in life and without which no high task for the improvement of humanity has even been undertaken." Butler's rise in the official hierarchy had indeed been meteoric; within three years he had risen from the post of Deputy Commissioner, Lucknow, to that of Education Member of the Viceroy's Executive Council. In 1910-11 he seemed to be enthusiastic about elementary education. Fleetwood Wilson, the Finance Member, was also sympathetic. In February 1911, he told the Viceroy that elementary education 'would make an appropriate-not to say dramatic—concession for announcement by His Majesty' at the Durbar proposed at the end of that year. With the impending loss of revenue from the opium trade with China, the prospects for Indian finance were far from bright, but Fleetwood Wilson favoured the additional expenditure on education, hoping for economies in civil and military expenditure. In May 1911, Harcourt Butler estimated that the cost of free elementary education throughout India would be rupees fifty lakhs a year. In a comprehensive note (which the Viceroy forwarded to the Secretary of State), Butler drew attention to the growing 'insistence and intensity' of the demand for free primary education. 'Hindus and Muhammedans alike have made it part of their platform', he wrote: It is advocated in Legislative Councils, at public meetings and in the press by landowners no less than by lawyers; and philanthropists and politicians are starting free institutions, night schools and the like. True, Gokhale's Bill contemplates the payment of fees by parents whose income exceeds Rs. 10 per mensem, but the public prefers the abolition of fees to the contingent introduction of the compulsory principle, and that was Mr Gokhale's own attitude in the Imperial Legislative Council a year ago.

Personally I regard the provision of free elementary education as a matter of real urgency and vital consequence not only because I foresee that we shall be forced to concede it within a year or two, nor because I think that more than any other measure it will remove the deep-rooted belief in India and outside it, that we are afraid of education and put difficulties in its path, but mainly because the economic and political conditions of the country require it.... I am convinced that unless we move in harmony with popular opinion in this matter we shall find control slipping through our fingers. Butler's appraisal of the elementary education campaign in February 1911 was a measure of Gokhale's success in making it a live issue. Even the Viceroy was deeply impressed and told the Secretary of State: It has become perfectly clear to me from the debate in [the Imperial Legislative] Council on Gokhale's Education Bill, and the comments of the Press that it is absolutely necessary that we should go in for an educational programme... [Butler and 11 are agreed that our first step should be a campaign against illiteracy and this would be best initiated by free compulsory education.... Butler estimates the cost of making elementary education free throughout India at 50 lakhs a year. I think that this money should be found without difficulty and should be the first step in a big educational programme. At the end of July 1911 Hardinge's optimism was at its peak: he went so far as to express the hope that free elementary education would be introduced in India before he left the country. Hardinge, Butler and Fleetwood Wilson may have been wholly sincere in their desire to support free and compulsory education for the masses, but they had to reckon with the resistance from the local (provincial) governments to whom mass education spelt mass sedition. The Governor of Bombay warned the Viceroy: The agitation for education [so far as Primary education is concerned] is of quite recent origin, comes from the people who are anxious to make our Rule impossible.... They well realize that their power to stir up discontent would be immensely increased if every cultivator could read.... We cannot teach the great mass of people long enough or thoroughly enough to make them permanently able even to read and write; but we can, and we shall, do much to promote general discontent. In that part of their calculations the Gokhales are perfectly right. The Bombay Governor's prejudices and-fears were typical of the British ruling class in India. The local governments were on the whole hostile to the bill. Governor Clarke's own government pronounced compulsory elementary education as 'an unwarranted interference with the liberties of the people'. The Bengal government saw no objection to the principle of mass elementary education, but ruled it out on the ground of shortage of money and trained teachers.

The Punjab government warned that the majority of the people in that province were opposed not only to compulsory education, but to any education whatsoever. The U.P. government even predicted a popular uprising if parents were compelled to educate their children! only the backward province of Baluchistan saw no danger in free and compulsory education. In July 1911 Wedderburn, at Gokhale's suggestion, organized a deputation headed by Lord Courtney to wait upon Crewe, the Secretary of State for India. Crewe expressed himself as 'wholly sympathetic, to the extension of elementary education and described Gokhale's bill as extremely moderate. Neither the public support of the Secretary of State nor the initial sympathy of the Finance and Education Members of the Executive Council and the Viceroy, however, availed against the massive opposition of the British 'steel frame' in India. By the beginning of October 1911 Gokhale had sensed that the Government of India would not support his bill, and its fate was sealed.' I Nevertheless, he decided to put up a fight when the bill came back to the Imperial Council on 18 March 1912. 'The main opposition to the bill', he said, 'has come from official quarters.' He answered objections to the bill, clarified knotty points, allayed fears, and exposed the fallacies of his critics. He conceded special arrangements for teaching the languages of cultural minorities. Of Sir Gangadhar Chitnavis and Nawab Abdul Majid, the two members of the Imperial Legislative Council who had frankly doubted the value of elementary education, Gokhale said that in this attitude they were not singular: 'There are men belonging to this class in other countries in Western countries-who have the same distrust of mass education." He reminded Sir Gangadhar that the Elementary Education Bill had been supported by the Nagpur Municipality and Nagpur District Board of which he was the chairman. To another member, Dadabhoy, who had first supported and then turned a critic of the Bill, Gokhale offered his congratulations 'not only on his conversion to official views but to his very manner of expressing those views'.

To a European member who said he had visited thousands of primary schools, Gokhale retorted: 'Sir, we have learnt in primary schools. We have experience from the inside of these schools." There were some British officials, Gokhale said, who were against mass education, because they were against all popular progress, and imagined 'in their short-sightedness that every step gained by the people is one lost by them'. Harcourt Butler described Gokhale's bill as 'a modest and unassuming measure... full of safeguards', but 'premature'. He paid a tribute to Gokhale for creating an enthusiasm for elementary education, lauded his aims, but did not support his bill. On 19 March 1911, the bill was defeated by 13 votes to 38. 'This bill', Gokhale said, 'thrown out today will come back again and again till on the stepping-stones of its dead selves, a measure ultimately rises which will spread the light of knowledge throughout the land.' On the evening of 18 March there was an official dinner at Calcutta, at which Gokhale sat next to Butler. 'We had a long talk', Butler wrote home. 'He [Gokhale] said that I had made things very difficult for him, but he rejoiced greatly at my enunciation of policy. He had seen the change that had come over the Education Departments in different provinces since I had assumed charge.... I never can fathom Gokhale, but tonight at any rate he was very human.' Gokhale was saddened, but not surprised by the defeat of his bill.

As early as October 1911, he had foreseen this possibility and planned his strategy to meet it. He had decided to visit England to canvass support for this bill in the Parliament and the. press to overcome the resistance of the British officials in India to mass education. 'It is quite clear to me,' Gokhale wrote to Wedderburn on 6 October 1911 9 'with earnest and persistent work both in this country and in England for three or four years, we should get this Bill or something similar to it placed on the statute book.' The battle for free and compulsory education turned out to be longer and harder than Gokhale had expected. Not till 1917 was the first successful measure (largely based on his bill) for enforcing compulsion in elementary education passed by a provincial legislature. Bombay was the pioneer. The following twenty years saw the enactment of similar laws by the legislatures of other provinces and Indian states.

7

GOKHALE : SELF-GOVT. AND SWADESHI

Gopal Krishna Gokhale was not happy at the social and economic backwardness of the masses of India. In the course of his speeches and writings he was keen to highlight the misdoings of the Raj which was responsible for the economic drain in our country. He always wished that each and every child should be given proper education and upbringing. While he was a teacher in Fergusson College, he dwelt upon the development of moral, physical and mental faculties of the child. He also inculcated the spirit of true nationalism among the youths. The teacher-taught and relationship took a new turn during his stewardship. The students under him felt a sense of responsibility towards our society as well as the country. He first forward the demand of self-government for India and opined that the democracy here would not tolerate such complete exclusion of the Indians from their own government. He also showed much interest in the socio-economic amelioration of Indians in Africa. He had meetings with General Botha, General Smuts and Fischer with whom he discussed the problems of Indians living there. Besides, he pleaded for the adequate employment of Indians in the public services.

Moreover, he always pleaded for the Hindu Muslim unity. His relationship in Gandhi began to develop when he found him a sincere and selfless worker struggling hard for several socioeconomic and political problems of Indians in South Africa, time and again, he advised and encouraged Gandhi for broad-based non-violent activities to achieve political concessions for Indians in South Africa. When Gandhi met him in India and sought his advice regarding his future plan of work, he was told to work ceaselessly among the masses of our country. This kind of advice was an asset for Gandhi who claimed Gokhale as his 'guru' and mentor in the long-drawn political struggle in the Indian sub-continent. Undoubtedly, Gandhi always remembered his mentor with much respect and reverence. He indeed carried on the work left by his 'guru' in 1915 when he breathed his lost. Thus, indeed Gokhale's connections with Gandhis had deep linkage with latter's political maturity after he landed on the soil of India during the global war.

Demand for Self-government

Gokhale read the following paper before the East India Association, London :

> My object in addressing you is to state before this Association briefly, and I hope clearly, what are today the ideas and aspirations of the vast majority of those Indians who have come under the influence of Western thought in regard to the government of their country. I think it will be generally admitted that the dissatisfaction in India with the existing system of administration has been for some time past rapidly growing, and we have now reached a stage when it is necessary for the rulers, if further alienation between the two sides is to be prevented, to make a bold and statesmanlike attempt to win back the confidence of the educated classes of the country. These classes have in the past been led to believe that the sole aim of British rule in India was the welfare of the Indian people, and that, under that rule, no distinction would be made between Indians and Europeans in the government of the country on grounds of race or creed or colour. The Charter Act of 1833 and the Proclamation of 1858 of the

late Queen have pledged the word of the Sovereign and the Parliament of the country the only two authorities that can claim to speak in the name of the English nation-to such a policy. And till a few years ago, whatever might have been thought of the pace at which we were going, there was no general disposition to doubt the intention of the rulers to redeem their plighted word. Today, however, the position is no longer the same. Things have moved even in dreamy and contemplative India, and many of the members of this Association who, in their time, have held high, and, in some cases, distinguished, official positions in that country, must have been startled recently to re id in the columns of such eminently Conservative journals as the Times and the Morning Post the accounts of the ferment in India witnessed by their special correspondents, and the significance they found it necessary to attach to that ferment. There is no doubt that the old faith of the people in the character and ideals of British rule has been more than shaken, and its place is being steadily taken by a conviction that, however great England may be, she is not great enough to forego voluntarily the gains of power from considerations of mere justice or national honour. I do not say that such a view is quite just to the average man or woman of this country.

Probably the democracy here will not tolerate such complete exclusion of the Indians from their own government, if the real character of the present system of administration is clearly brought home to its mind. But whatever its sympathies in the abstract may be, they are rendered inoperative, first, by its absorption in questions of domestic interest, and, secondly, by the dense and impenetrable ignorance about India that prevails in this land on all sides. Moreover, the people of India can judge of the intentions of Englishmen only from their experience of those who go out to India to exercise authority over them, and I think it is no injustice to this class to say that mast of its members show no particular anxiety to part with any portion of the power they at present enjoy, or to associate more than they can help the people of the country with themselves in the work of administration.

I know there are those who think that no serious importance need be attached to the temper or opinions of the educated classes of India: first, because, numerically, they are a small-as one Viceroy said, "a microscopic"—minority; and, secondly, because there are so many caste and creed divisions in India that united action on the part of the people in support of the views of the educated classes is impossible. It is true that, as far as mere numbers go, those who have received Western education in India form but a small proportion of the entire population, only a little over a million persons being returned at the last census as "literate in English" out of nearly three hundred millions. But there can be no greater mistake than to imagine that the influence of this class in the country is proportionate only to its numbers. In the first place, these men constitute what may be called the brain of the community. They do the thinking not only for themselves, but also for their ignorant brethren.

Moreover, theirs is the Indian press-both English and Vernacular-and the Vernacular press shapes the thoughts and sways the feelings, not only of the fifteen million "literates in Vernaculars" whom it reaches directly, but also, of many more millions who come indirectly under its influence. And whatever public opinion exists in the country reflects almost entirely the views of the educated classes. Officials sometimes look to old historic families, which in more turbulent times supplied leaders to the country, to exert a rival influence; but they have now lost their former hold on the public mind,, because in these days of peace and of transition, rusty, broken swords cannot compete with ideas as a source of importance and power. The influence of the educated classes with their country men is thus already very great, and is bound every day to grow greater and greater. As regards caste and creed divisions, even these are not now so acute as they once were. Half a century of Western education, and a century of common laws, common administration, common grievances, and common disabilities, have not failed to produce their natural effect even in India. The awakening of the Mohammedans of Aligarh to the necessity of political agitation is a significant sign of the times. It is most improbable that the Aligarh programme, when drawn up, will be found to be substantially different from the Congress programme, and though the new organisation may maintain its separate existence for a while, it must inevitably merge itself sooner or later into the larger and older organisation of the National Congress. I think those who are responsible for the government of India have now got to realize two facts, that any further alienation of the educated classes would be a course of supreme political unwisdom; and, secondly, that such alienation cannot be prevented unless the faith of these classes in the desire of the rulers to carry out the policy of the Charter Act of 1833, the Proclamation of 1858 is restored. Whatever a certain school of officials in India may say, the bulk of educated Indians have never in the past desired a severance of the British connection.

Not only was their reason enlisted on its side, but in the earlier years, at any rate, even their imagination had been captured by it. The fact that a small island' at one end of the world had by an astonishing succession of events been set to rule over a vast country, inhabited by an ancient and civilised race, at the other end; the character of the new rulers as men who bad achieved constitutional liberty for themselves, and who were regarded as friends of freedom all over the world; their noble declarations of policy in regard to India these were well calculated to cast a spell on the Indian mind; while the blessings of continued peace and order well established, the introduction into the country of the higher and more vigorous administrative standards of the West, the establishment of universities and schools, throwing open to the people the rich treasures of Western knowledge, and bringing them under the influence of Western ideas, the dispensing of equal justice between Indian and Indian, liberty of speech and liberty of writing, railways, post offices, telegraphs, and other modem appliances of material civilization these were solid and undeniable advantages brought to the people, which for a long time continued to be a theme of genuine and unsullied appreciation. The spell, however, is already broken, and even the hold on the reason is steadily slackening.

A tendency has set in to depreciate even those advantages which at one time were most cordially acknowledged. And the disadvantages of the situation-wounded self respect, inability to grow to the full height of one's stature, a steady deterioration in the manhood of the nation, and economic evils of vast magnitude inseparable from such foreign domination-these evils which, while the spell lasted, had not been restaged with sufficient clearness, have now already begun to appear as intolerable. I think there is no room for doubt that the whole attitude of the Indian mind towards British rule is undergoing a change. As yet the majority does not clearly understand this change. It would like to remain, if it could, in the old familiar groove, and it feels surprised, pained, disappointed, indignant that it cannot remain in that groove, and is being driven in a direction which it does not understand. It is a critical juncture in the relations between England and India. The highest statesmanship is needed to deal with the situation, and every day the problem grows more and more difficult of solution. After all, India's willing acceptance of the British connection can only be based on reason or enlightened self-interest. English officials in India often fail to realise the extent to which the policy laid down by the Sovereign and by Parliament has reconciled the thinking portion of the Indian community to British rule. They seem to think that, as that policy has been allowed hitherto to remain for the most part a dead letter, it could not really have any serious practical bearing.

There cannot be more complete misconception of the whole situation than this. Throughout these long years the educated classes have not lost sight of the policy even for a single moment, and, though their patience under its continued non-fulfilment—which at last has begun to give way-has worn to superficial observers the appearance of indifference, the belief that the pledges so solemnly given would not go unredeemed has, more thaw anything else, determined so long their attitude towards British rule. Once this attitude is allowed to undergo a change, such as it is now doing, the rules will not be left long in doubt as, to the great part which the Charter Act and the Queen's Proclamation have bad in insuring the loyalty of the people. It was the failure to perceive this which was responsible for the grave mistake which Lord Curzon committed more than two, years ago, when be sought in open Council to explain away the Queen's Proclamation, and practically told the people of India that, as long as British rule lasted, there could be no real equality between Englishmen and Indians in India. It is sometimes said that the existing arrangements make for efficiency of administration and in the interests of that efficiency it is necessary that they should not be disturbed. There is an air of plausibility about this plea, but those who urge it ignore the wisdom of an observation which the present Prime Minister once made, that "good government could never be a substitute for government by the people themselves!" On a closer, examination, moreover, the contention will be found to be perfectly untenable. The efficiency attained by a foreign bureaucracy, uncontrolled by public opinion, whose members, again, reside only temporarily in the land in which they exercise official power, is bound to be of a strictly limited character, and it can never compare with that higher and truer efficiency which is possible only under a well regulated system of selfgovernment. The present form of administration in India is a strongly centralised bureaucracy in which the men at the centre hold office for five years only. They then leave the country, carrying away with them all the knowledge and experience of administrative matters acquired at the expense of the country, and their places are taken by new men, who, in their turn, retire similarly after five years. As things are, there is no one ever in the government who is permanently interested in the country as only its own people can be interested. One result is that the true well-being of the people is systematically subordinated to militarism, service interests of English mercantile classes; and though under such a system peace and order may be maintained, and even a certain amount of efficient administration secured, the type of efficiency is bound to remain a low one always. Moreover, it is clear that even such efficiency of administration, as has been attained in the past by the existing system, is bound to suffer more and more, owing to the growing antagonism of the governed to that system. No man, for instance, ever laboured more strenuously for mere efficiency than Lord Curzon, and yet never was discontent deeper and more widespread than when he left India, and no Viceroy of recent times has had to succeed to a greater legacy of difficulties than Lord Minto. It may be that bureaucracies, like the Bourbons never learn, but it should really not be difficult for Englishmen to realise that you cannot have institutions like the universities working for more than half a century in India, and then expect to be able to govern the people, as though they were still strangers to ideas of constitutional freedom or to the dignity of national aspirations. Those who blindly uphold the existing system, and resist all attempts, however cautious and moderate, to broaden its bases, prefer practically to sacrifice the future to the present. No one denies the undoubted difficulties of the position, but they are by no means so formidable as those who do not want to move at all like to believe.

The goal which the educated classes of India have in view is a position for their country in the Empire worthy of the self-respect of civilised people. They want their country to be a prosperous, self-governing integral part of the Empire, like the Colonies, and not a mere poverty-stricken, bureaucratically-held possession of that Empire. The system under which India is governed at present is an unnatural system, and however one may put up with it as a temporary evil, as a permanent arrangement it is impossible, for under such a system "the noble, free, virile, fearless like," to use the words of a well-known American preacher, "which is the red blood of any nation gradually becomes torpid," and nothing can compensate a people for so terrible a wrong. Of course, we recoginse that the new selfgovernment has to be on Western lines, and therefore the steps by which the goal is reached must necessarily be slow, as, for the advance to be real, it must be from experiment to experiment only. But there is all the difference in the world between such cautious progress and no progress at all; and the bureaucracy which, by standing in the way of all reasonable instalments of reform, hopes to prevent reform altogether, is only undermining its own position by such a short-sighted and suicidal policy.

The officials in theory admit the necessity of associating the people with the Government of the country, but they object to admitting only a small proportion of the population to a share in the administration, and they ask us to wait till the mass of the people have been qualified by education to take an intelligent part in public affairs! At the same time, how much or how little is being done to push on mass education may be seen from the fact that, after more or less a century of British rule, and forty years after England herself woke up to the responsibilities of Governments in regard to mass education, seven children out of eight in India are growing up today in ignorance and darkness, and four villages out of five are as yet without a school-house! Moreover, it is ignored that what is asked at the present stage is a voice in the administration, not for the whole population, but only for those who have been qualified by education to exercise their responsibilities in a satisfactory manner. As regards the bulk of the people, it is recognised that education has got to come first, and what is urged is that this educational work should be pushed on in the most vigorous manner possible. It is true, as I have already admitted, that an Oriental, country cannot hope to advance on Western lines, except by cautious and tentative steps. But what Japan has been able to achieve in forty years, India should certainly have accomplished in a century. The attitude of the two Governments in the matter has, however, been one of the main elements of difference in the two cases. My concern, however, is more with the present and the future than with the past. And here I repeat that, unless the old faith of the educated classes in the character and ideals of British rule is brought back, England will find on her hands before long another Ireland, only many times bigger, in India. The younger generations are growing up full of what may be called Irish bitterness, and the situation must fill all who believe in the peaceful progress of the country under British rule with anxious apprehensions.

If India is to attain self-government within the Empire-an idea which to an increasing proportion of my countrymen appears to be a vain dream-the advance will have to be along several lines more or less simultaneously. Of these in some respects the most important is the admission of Indians to the higher branches of the public service. As long as India continues to be bureaucratically governed, admission to high office will be a test of the position assigned to the Indians in the system of administration. It is not a mere question of careers for young men though even that view is entitled to weight, and the bureaucracy certainly behaves at times as though the most important question before it was how to retain and, if possible, increase the existing number of openings for the employment of Englishmen in India but it is a measure of our advance towards that equality which has been promised us by the Sovereign and by Parliament. Moreover, as the ranks of the bureaucracy come to be recruited more and more from among the Indians, its resistance to the control of tax-payers' representatives will grow less and less. At present only the field of law there, too, only a portion of it-is freely open to us, and we find Indians there climbing right to the top of the tree. And if my countrymen are thought to be qualified to discharge the duties of Chief Justice and Advocate-General, it is preposterous that they should be kept out of the superior ranks of Excise and Opium and Salt and Customs and Post and Telegraph and Survey, and similar other services.

Under present arrangements India's true centre of gravity is in London. We protest against this most unnatural, arrangement and we urge most strongly that all competitive examinations for recruitment to Indian services should be held, not in London only, but simultaneously in India and in England. And we claim to be admitted now to the executive councils of the Viceroy and the Governors of Madras and Bombay, as also to the Secretary of State's Council in this country. Next, we want district administration-which is the unit of administration in India-to be decentralised. On the one hand, it must be freed from the present excessive control of the secretariat of the central Government and its numerous special departments; and on the other, the people of the district must be provided with opportunities to influence its course more and more largely, till at last the officials become in fact, as they are in theory, the servants of the people. The first step towards this is to associate with the heads of districts, for purposes of general administration, boards of leading men elected by the people, at first, perhaps, merely advisory, but gradually entrusted with increasing powers of control. In this way an administration conducted with the real consent of the governed may, in course of time, be substituted for the present system of administration carried on in the dark and behind the backs of the people concerned, with its attendant evils of confidential reports and police surveillance. Then local selfgovernment must be carried further. It still remains all over the country where it was placed by Lord Ripon a quarter of a century ago, and in some places it has even been pushed back.

Local bodies should now be made in the more advanced localities wholly popular assemblies and while the control of the Government over them must not be weakened, they should be freed from all petty and harassing interference on the part of officials. As regards Legislative Councils, the position is more difficult. Of course, the next instalment, whenever it comes, can I think, be clearly foreseen. The enlargement of the Councils, the widening of their functions so that Budgets should be really discussed and passed, an increase in the proportion of elected members up to the point at which the officials will still have a small standing majority-these changes may sooner or later appear safe enough even to the official mind. But the advance beyond that is really the thing that will matter, and it is not easy to see how it will come about. As long as the higher branches of the public service continue to be a practical monopoly of Englishmen, there is small chance of the Legislative Councils being entrusted with any substantial share of control over the actions of the Executive, and this consideration emphasises still further the necessity of steadily Indianising the service of the country. In the army, too, our position must be generally improved, and the commissioned ranks now thrown open to carefully selected Indians. Side by side with these reforms, mass education must be taken vigorously in hand, so that in twenty years from now, if not earlier, there should be free and compulsory education in the country for both boys and girls. I think that an earnest and sustained advance along these lines will go far to prevent any further alienation of the educated classes, and even their old goodwill may thus be regained. I cannot say that I have much hope that any such policy will be at once adopted. The struggle before us is, I fear, a long one and, in all probability, it will be a most bitter one. The flowing tide, however, is with us, and such a struggle can have but one issue. It only remains for me to say that it has been a pleasure to me to respond to the kind invitation of this Association. I do not expect that my views will receive any large assent at this meeting, and this only adds to my sense of the compliment which the Association has paid me.

Gokhale's Speech on Swadeshi Movement

In the second week of February 1907, the Mon. Mr. Gokhale, delivered a series of public addresses at Lucknow:

Mr. Chairman, Ladies and Gentlemen—I propose to speak to you today of the economic condition of India and the Swadeshi movement. One of the most gratifying signs of the present times is the rapid growth of the Swadeshi sentiment all over the country during the last two years. I have said more than once here, but I think the idea bears repetition, that Swadeshism at its highest is not merely an industrial movement, but that it affects the whole life of the nation-that Swadeshism at its highest is a deep, passionate, fervent, all-embracing love of the motherland, and that this love seeks to show itself, not in one sphere of activity only, but in all: it invades the whole man, and it will not rest until it has raised the whole man, Now the first thing I want to say about this movement is that it has come here to, stay. We often have movements which make a little noise for a time and then disappear without leaving any permanent mark behind. I think it safe to say that the Swadeshi movement is not going to be one of that kind, and my own personal conviction is that in this movement we shall ultimately find the true salvation of India. However, ladies and gentlemen, I do not wish to speak to you today about Swadeshism in general. The more immediate question before us is Swadeshism as applied to the present economic situation of India-its scope and character, the materials with which it has to work, and the difficulties it has to overcome before it can achieve in any degree the true industrial regeneration of the country. Gentlemen, as Mr. Ranade once pointed out, the industrial, domination of one people by another attracts much less attention than the political domination of a foreign people. The industrial domination is less visible and does its work in a more insidious manner. The disadvantages of a political domination lie very much on the surface. We see a foreign race monopolising all power and authority and keeping the people in a state of subjection.

These are facts which we observe and feel every day of our lives. Human feelings often matter more to humanity than human interests, and when your feelings are hurt in various directions, as in a state of subjection, they are bound to be—I do not mean to throw any unnecessary blame on any one—their thought fills you night and day and makes you think constantly of the fact that you are living under a foreign domination. On the other hand, the industrial domination of one people by another may come in an attractive garb. If, as has been the case with India, this foreign domination comes in the shape of more finished articles-especially articles that administer to the daily wants of a community-you unconsciously welcome the domination, you fall a victim to its temptations and its attractiveness. And it is only when the evil grows beyond certain limits, that your attention is drawn to it. Now, this is precisely what has happened in the case if India. As soon as Western education came to be imparted to the people of this country, their first thoughts were directed to their political status.

Of course they also thought of their social institutions. Those who are acquainted with the history of the last fifty years, know that the struggle for political and social reforms started almost simultaneously, but I do not wish to go into that on this occasion. What I want to point out is that the thought of the industrial domination of India by England did not really occur to men's minds at that time. At any rate, it did not occur in that pointed manner in which the thought of political domination did. The result was that the main current of our public activity came to be directed towards the realization of our political aspirations, and about 22 years ago when the Congress came into existence for the political advancement of the people, the question of this industrial domination, though it had struck a few thoughtful minds, did not receive that consideration at the hands of the leaders of the people that it deserved. However, the industrial problem and its importance are now receiving their due recognition, and today at any rate we appear to have gone so far in this direction that there is now the risk of the industrial problem actually throwing into the shade the political problem which, however to a great extent lies at the root of the industrial problem. Gentlemen, when we come to this question of India's industrial domination by England, we come to what may be described as the most deplorable result of British rule in this country. In other matters there are things on the credit side and things on the debit side. Take, for instance, the political and administrative results of British rule. We have here the shutting out of a whole race from positions of real trust and responsibility where powers of initiative can be developed, and this is producing disastrous results on the character of the people. We also see that the forcible disarming of a population is bound to crush the manhood of the nation. In these directions we find that a steady deterioration of the race has set in. But there are compensating advantages, and I am not sure that the balance is not on the latter side.

Thus, the introduction of Western education, with its liberalising influence, has been a great blessing to the people. We now understand better the necessity of equal treatment for all; we also see that unless the status of woman is raised, man by himself will not be able to advance very far; and altogether this Western education is doing most noble work in the country. Then the British have established, on the whole, equal justice between Indian and Indian as between European and Indian, that is a different matter-but between Indian and Indian it is equal, though it is costly, and that is more than can be said of previous rules. Railways, Telegraphs, Post offices and other modern appliances of material civilization have also been introduced into India by the present rules, and it is fair to acknowledge that these things have added greatly to the comforts and conveniences of life and are a powerful help to our progress. Lastly, there are the blessings of peace and of order well and firmly established. These are things which must be set against the steady deterioration of which I have already spoken, and I am not prepared to say that the balance is not, on the whole, on the side of the advantages. But when you come to the industrial field, you find that the results have been disastrous. You find very little here on the credit side and nearly all the entries on the debit side. Now this is a serious statement to make, but I think it can be substantiated.

I would ask you, first, to glance at what India was industrially before the English came into this country. It is true that there is very little direct or statistical evidence on this subject. But the statements made by travellers who came to this country supply a fair indication of how things were, though they do not enable us to establish a conclusion accurately or satisfactorily. We find, for instance, praise of India's riches in every place; we find also here and there a description of the poverty of the mass of the people. And, on the whole, I think it is fair to say this-that, compared with other countries, India could not have been worse, and very probably she was better off than most other countries, and I think this description may well apply to her right up to the end of Mohammedan rule. India's reputed wealth was the attracting cause of so many invasions.

Large wealth must, therefore, have been accumulated in some hands, and so far as the bulk of the population was concerned, as the land was fertile and the people were industrious and thrifty and, on the whole, free from vices, such as drink, it is fair to conclude that the people must have enjoyed a considerable degree of rude agricultural prosperity. It is not proper to compare the West of today, with all its production of machinery and steam, with the India of 200 years ago. Before steam and machinery were employed in the West, the West too was largely agricultural, and she had then no special advantages for the production of wealth over us. And I believe that, judged by the standards of those days, we could not have been poorer, and very probably we were richer than most Western countries. Then there was the excellence of our productions which attracted the attention of Western nations—the fine Muslims and many other things exported from this country showed what a high level of excellence had been reached by our people in industrial production. When the Mohammedan, rulers came, they settled in this country, and there was no question of any foreign drain. Things, therefore, must have, on the whole, continued as they had been before their time. Then we come to British rule. Gentlemen, I refer, on this occasion, to the past only in order that, in the light of it, we might understand the present and derive therefrom guidance and assistance for the future. The early days of the East India Company's rule were as bad as bad could possibly be from the standpoint of India's industrial system. Deliberate steps were taken by the Company to destroy the industries of the people and to make room for Western manufacturers. This has been acknowledged by English writers themselves. This was England's policy, not towards India alone, but towards America an Ireland also. America got rid, of it by shaking off England's dominion altogether. Ireland struggled to do the same, but did not succeed. India suffered the worst under the operation of the evil policy. The object aimed at by the East India Company was to reduce India to the level of a merely agricultural country producing raw material only, without factories to manufacture the same.

This was the first stage in our industrial decay. The second stage began when England forced on us the policy of free trade, i.e., of leaving the door wide open to the competition of the whole world. England's own policy for centuries had been that of Protection, and by that policy she had built up her vast industrial system. But about sixty years ago, after Protection had done its work, she decided to give up the old policy and adopt Free Trade, mainly to set right the abuses to which Protection had given rise. England depends on foreign countries for most of her raw materials, and she supplies manufactured articles practically to the whole world. It was, therefore, to the advantage of England that there should be no export or import duties, as one result of such duties was to add to the cost of the articles 'supplied to foreign countries. But forcing this policy of free trade upon a country circumstanced as India was wholly different thing and was bound to produce results of a most disastrous character. Our things were made with the hand; we did not possess anything like the combination, skill or enterprise of the West. Steam and machinery were unknown in the country. Our industries were, therefore, bound to perish as a result of the shock of this sudden competition to which they were exposed, and as a matter of course the introduction of Free Trade in this country was followed by the rapid destruction of such small industries as had existed in the country, and the people were steadily pressed back more and more on the one resource of agriculture. I should not have deplored even this destruction of our indigenous manufactures if the Government had assisted us in starting others to take their place.

The German economist—List-whose work on Political Economy is the best that Indian students can consult, explains how the state can help an old world agricultural country, suddenly brought within the circle of the world's competition, to build up a new system of industries. He says that the destruction of hand-industries is a necessary stage through which an industrially backward country must pass before she can take rank with those which use steam and machinery and advanced scientific processes and appliances in their industrial production. When handmade goods are exposed to the competition of machine-made goods, it is inevitable that the former should perish. But when this stage is reached there comes in the duty of the State. The State by a judicious system of protection should then ensure conditions under which new infant industries can grow up. And until the new industries can stand on their own legs, it becomes the duty of the State to have a protective wall around. This is what America already one of the richest nations in the world, and one which will yet reach the foremost place-has done, and the case is the same with France and Germany. The result of England's policy in India has, however, been to facilitate more and more the imports of foreign commodities, until there is no country on the face of the earth today which is so dependent on the foreign producer as India is. At the present moment about 70 per cent of our exports are raw material raised from the soil and exported in that condition. If we had the skill, enterprise, capital and organisation to manufacture the greater part of this material, there would be so many industries flourishing in the country. But the material goes out and comes back in the shape of manufactured commodities, having acquired a much higher price in the process of manufacture. Again, if you look at your imports, you will find that 60 per cent of them are manufactured goods. They are goods which have been made by other people, so that all you have got to do with them is to consume them. If this was all, if the steady rustication of India-her being steadily pushed back on the one resource of agriculture-was all that we had to deplore as the result of the present policy, the situation, bad enough as it would undoubtedly have been, would not have been so critical. But coupled with political domination, this has produced a state of things which can only be described as intolerable. The total imports of India are worth about 100 crores of rupees every year. Our total exports, on the other hand, amount to about 150 crores a year. In other words, every year about 100 crores worth of goods come to us, and we part with 150 crores worth of goods. After taking into consideration the precious metals that come into the country to redress a part of the balance, we still find that a loss of about 30 to 40 crores a year has to be borne by India. Now, I will put a simple question to those present here. If a hundred rupees come into your house every month and a hundred and fifty rupees go out, will you be growing richer or poorer? And if this process goes on year after year, decade after decade, what will be your position after a time? This has been the case with India now for many years. Every year between 30 and 40 crores of rupees go out of India never to come back.

No country not even the richest in the world-can stand such a bleeding as this. Bleeding is a strong word, but it was first used with regard to this very process by a great English statesman-the late Lord Salisbury-who was Prime Minister of England for a long time and was before that Secretary of State for India. Now this bleeding is really at the root of the greater part of the economic mischief that we have to face today. It means that this money, which would have been available to the people, if it had remained in this country, as capital for industrial purposes, is lost to us. The result is that there is hardly any capital of our own forthcoming for industrial purposes. Do not be misled by the fact that a few individuals appear to be rich and have a little money to invest. You must compare India in this matter with other countries, and then you will find that there is hardly any capital accumulated by us to be devoted to industrial development. One of the greatest students of Indian Economics-the late Mr. Justice Ranade—once calculated that our annual savings could not be more than 8 to 10 crores of rupees. Put it even at 20 crores; what is that with the hundreds and thousands of crores accumulated annually by the people of the West? This, then, is at the root of our troubles. I do not say that there are no considerations on the other side. It might, for instance, be said that the railways in this country, have been constructed with English capital. About 375 crores have been so far spent to build these railways, and it is only fair that for this capital India should pay a certain sum as interest. Englishmen have also invested British capital in indigo, tea, and other industries. A part of this capital has no doubt come out of in a vast country like India compared their own savings made in this country, but whether the money has been earned here or imported from England, the investors are, of course, entitled to a reasonable rate of interest on it. But after a deduction is made on account of this interest, there still remains a sum of over 30 crores as the net loss that India has to bear year by year. You may ask what politics has got to do with this.

Well, the greater part of this loss is due to the unnatural political position of India, and I think we shalt not be far wrong if we put the annual drain, due to political causes directly and indirectly, at about 20 crores of rupees. The greater part of the 'Home Charges' of the Government of India, which now stand at about 18 millions sterling or 27 crores of rupees, comes under this description. To this has to be added a portion at least of the annual savings of European merchants, lawyers, doctors, and such other persons, as the dominant position of the Englishman in the country gives these classes special advantages which their Indian competitors do not enjoy. Then there are the earnings of the English officials and the British troops in the country. And altogether I am convinced that it is not an extravagant estimate to put the annual cost to India of England's political domination at 20 crores of rupees, the remaining ten crores being lost on account of our industrial domination by England. This, then, is the extent of the 'bleeding' to which we are subjected year after year! It is an enormous economic evil, and as long as it is not substantially reduced, the prospect cannot be a cheering one. After all, what can you do with a small amount of capital? You must not be led away by the fact that, from time to time, you hear of a new industrial concern being started here or there. The struggle is a much bigger one than that. It is like the struggle between a dwarf and a giant. If you will form the least idea of the resources of the Western people, then you will understand what a tremendously difficult problem we have to face in this economic field. If this continuous bleeding is to cease, it is incumbent that our men should be employed more and more in the service of the State, so that pensions and furlough charges might be saved to the country.

The stores which the Government of India purchases in England should be purchased locally as far as possible. In other directions also our position must be improved. But, I think, we should not be practical, if we did not recognize that any important change in the political relations between England and India could come only gradually. It is not by a sudden and violent movement that relief will come. It will only come as we slowly build up our own strength and bring it to bear upon the Government. As this strength is increased, so will the drain be diminished. The industrial drain-due to the fact that we depend so largely for our manufactures upon foreign countries is really speaking but a small part of the drain-about one third or ten crores of rupees a year. This means that if we ever succeeded in reaching a position of entire self-reliance industrially, it would still leave about two-thirds of the present annual drain untouched. Moreover, such entire dependence upon yourselves for industrial purposes is a dream that is not likely to be realised in the near future.

I am sorry I must trouble you with a few figures, but a question of this kind cannot be adequately considered without bringing in statistics. What, than, is the position? India, as you know, is for the most part an agricultural country. Sixty-five per cent of the population, according to the last census reports—80 per cent according to the computation of Lord Curzon-depend upon agriculture. The soil is becoming, rapidly exhausted and the yield per acre is diminishing. If you compare the yield today with what it was in the time of Akbar, as given in the Ain-i-Akbar, you will be astonished to see what deterioration has taken place in the soil. This makes agricultural improvement a matter of great difficulty. You have got to abolish old methods as much as possible and effect improvements by introducing the methods of the West. You have got to introduce agricultural science and improved agricultural implements, and the question is complicated by the fact that our agricultural production in this country generally is on what is called a small scale.

Land is divided and sub-divided, and most of the holdings are so small as not to lend themselves to the use of advanced appliances. The ignorance and resourcelessness of the people also stand in the way and altogether agricultural improvement is bound to be a matter of slow growth. But this is one direction in which you young men can help the country. Instead of scrambling for Government service or overcrowding the already crowded Bar, let a few at least among you acquire agricultural education abroad, acquaint themselves with the use of advanced agricultural appliances, and then settle down to agricultural work in this country. You will thereby not only improve agriculture for yourselves, but you will also show the way to others, and they will follow when they see the good results obtained by you. The Government, which, has only recently awakened to its duty in this matter, has already taken agriculture in hand, but the greater part of this work must be done by ourselves. Our next industry, after agriculture, is the textile industry-the cotton industry. Now, taking only the production of mills, we find that last year about one-fourth of what the whole of India needed was produced in India, and three-fourths came from outside. The capital that is invested in this country, in the textile industry is between 16 and 17 crores of rupees. This may seem a large amount to some of you, but what is it compared with the capital invested in this industry in England? In Lancashire alone 300 crores of rupees are invested in this textile industry, and every year the amount is increasing by leaps and bounds. On a rough calculation you will find that if our present production is to be quadrupled, about forty to fifty crores of rupees of additional capital would be wanted. That cannot be a matter of a day. The handloom is doing good work and has some future before it. But do not let us be under a delusion. The main part of the work will have to be done by machinery. It is only in this way that we shall be able to stand the competition of producers of other countries. If we are able to find this capital in the course of the next 10 or 15 years, I for one shall be content. My own fear is that it will take more than that. If by the end of ten years we are able to produce all the cotton cloth we require, I think we shall have done exceedingly well.

We must all bend our energies in that direction and try to capture or rather recover this field as soon and as completely as possible. But then, gentlemen, I would say this. The task, even under the most favourable circumstances, is a formidable one, and it is in the highest degree unwise to add to its great difficulty by unnecessary, bitter or lamentable controversies. You require for a satisfactory solution of this problem co-operation from all quarters, including the Government of the country. We have to depend, for the present, at any rate, upon foreign countries for our machinery. If, in pursuing our object, care is not taken to avoid causing unnecessary irritation to others, there is nothing to prevent this Government from hitting back and imposing a heavy tax, say, of 20 or 25 per cent. On machinery, which would practically destroy all our chances of increasing our production of cotton goods. The problem is also largely a problem of the necessary quality of cotton being obtained in this, country. At one time India produced very fine cotton and the finest muslins were made of it. Unfortunately the cultivation of that cotton has, in course of time, owing to various causes, been given up and the present cotton is of short staple which gives you only a comparatively coarse thread. Now we know from past experience that this land can grow superior cotton. And the Bombay Government have been for a number of years making experiments to introduce into the country Egyptian cotton, and have at last been able to produce a cross between the Egyptian and the Indian, which has taken root.

If all the area irrigated in Sind-the conditions of which are similar to those of Egypt-succeeds in growing this cotton, then the finer fabric problem will have been solved. The co-operation Government in this matter is thus essential, and those who have occasion to talk of the Swadeshi question should not fail to realize that a great responsibility rests upon them. They only unnecessarily increase the difficulties in our path when they talk as though we could do without Government assistance in the matter; and thereby they damage, without meaning to do so, such chances as exist for real industrial progress. But in the case of this cotton industry, I think the outlook, on the whole, is a most hopeful one. I turn next to the sugar industry. At one time we exported sugar, but at the present time sugar comes into this country to the amount of 7 crores a year. Foreign Governments have been helping their people with bounties, and they have discovered methods whereby the cost of production has been greatly reduced. We, on the other hand, still adhere to our old-world methods of production. Sugarcane is plentiful in all parts of India, especially in your province. If we make up our minds to encourage Indian sugar as far as possible, and in this case I am glad to be able to say "have nothing to do with foreign sugar"—we should be able, with the co-operation of Government in a brief time to produce all the sugar we want. In this connection I was glad to notice a statement made by your Lieutenant-Governor the other day in the matter. He said he would rejoice if even a single ton of sugar did not come from other countries. By co-operation therefore, between the people and the Government the sugar problem would be solved practically at once. In Bengal, again, they import a good deal of salt from England though other provinces consume mostly Indian salt. With such a vast sea-board as India possesses, India ought certainly to be able to produce her own salt. Again, about 20 lakhs worth of umbrellas, 50 lakhs worth of matches and 60 lakhs worth of paper come into the country every year from abroad. All these articles are now being produced here, and with a determination on our part to use these articles as much as possible and encourage their production and consumption, we should soon be able to shut out the foreign supply. But, after all is said and done, I want you to recognise that the possibilities in the near future are not very large. I say this not to damp any one's enthusiasm, because I do want that your enthusiasm should sustain itself at its highest glow in this matter. But remember that the competition before us is like that between a giant and a dwarf. Even if we successfully make up our minds to have nothing to do with foreign goods, even then the industrial salvation of India will not have been accomplished. We are the poorest country in the world at the present moment; England, on the other hand, is the richest. The production per head in India is £2 or Rs. 30 according to Government calculation, and about Is 20 according to Indian calculation. England's production per head is £44, i.e., about 20 or 30 times greater than that of this country. Take again the buying power of the people as judged by the imports. In England the average imports per head are about £15 or Rs. 235: in the self-governing colonies of England they are —13; even in Ceylon they are £2 per head; but in India they are only six shillings or 4 to 5 rupees per head. There are other figures equally startling. Take, for instance, the deposits in banks. Of course banking is in a much more backward condition in this country than in England. But even making allowance for that, you will see that the disproportion is very great.

The deposits in English banks are about 1,200 crores of rupees for a population of about 4 crores. We are 30 crores and our deposits are only 50 crores for the whole of India, and these deposits include also the amount held by European merchants and traders in the country. Again, take the Savings Banks. In the Savings Banks and Trustees Banks in England there are 300 crores deposited today, as against about 12 crores in this country-less then seven annas per head against about Rs. 75 per head in England. You can easily see now how terrible is the disproportion between England's resources and our own. Add to this the fact that machinery has to come from England, and by the time it is set up here, there is already some improvement effected in England. The problem before us is therefore, a vastly difficult one and it is a solemn duty resting upon every one, who is a real well wisher of the Swadeshi cause, not to add to that difficulty, if he can help it. Our resources then are small, and our difficulties are enormous. It behooves us, therefore, not to throw away any cooperation from whatever quarter it may be forthcoming. Remember that, though there is a certain scope for small village industries, our main reliance now exposed as we are to the competition of the whole world-must be on production with the aid of steam and machinery. From this standpoint, what are our principal needs today? In the first place, there is general ignorance throughout the country about the industrial condition of the world. Very few of us understand where we are, as compared with others, and why we are where we are and why others are where they are. Secondly, our available capital is small, and it is, moreover, timid. Confidence in one another in the spirit of co-operation for industrial purposes is weak, and joint stock enterprise is, therefore, feeble. Thirdly, there is a lack of facilities for higher scientific and technical instruction in the country. Lastly, such new articles as we succeed in manufacturing find themselves exposed at once to the competition of the whole world, and as, in the beginning at any rate, they are bound to be somewhat inferior in quality and probably higher in price, it is difficult for them to make their way in the Indian market.

Now as our needs are various, so the Swadeshi cause requires to be served in a variety of ways, and we should be careful not to quarrel with others, simply because they serve the cause in a different way from our own. Thus, whoever tries to spread in the country a correct knowledge of the industrial conditions of the world and points out how we may ourselves advance, is a promoter of the' Swadeshi cause. Whoever again contributes capital to be applied to the industrial development of the country must be regarded as a benefactor of the country and a valued supporter of the Swadeshi movement. Then those who organise funds for sending Indian students to foreign countries for acquiring industrial or scientific education-and in our present state we must, for some time to come, depend upon foreign countries for such education or those who proceed to foreign countries for such education and try to start new industries on their return, or those who promote technical, industrial and scientific education in the country itself-all these are noble workers in the Swadeshi field.

These three ways of serving the Swadeshi cause are, however, open to a limited number of persons only. But there is a fourth way, which is open to all of us, and in the case of most, it is, perhaps, the only way in which they can help forward the Swadeshi movement. It is to use ourselves, as far as possible, Swadeshi articles only and to preach to others that they should do the same. By this we shall ensure the consumption of whatever articles are produced in the country, and we shall stimulate the production of new articles by creating a demand for them. The mass of the people cannot contribute much capital to the industrial development of the country. Neither can they render much assistance in the matter of promoting higher scientific, technical or industrial knowledge among us, but they can all render a most important and a most necessary service to the Swadeshi cause by undergoing a little sacrifice to extend a kind of voluntary protection to Swadeshi industries in their early days of stress and struggle.

In course of time, the quality of Swadeshi articles is bound to improve and their cost of production to become less and less. And it is no merit if you buy them when they can hold their own against foreign articles in quality or price. It is by ensuring the consumption of indigenous articles in their early stage, when their quality is inferior or their price is higher, or when they labour under both these disadvantages, that we can do for our industries what Protectionist Governments have done for theirs by means of State protection. Those, therefore, who go about and preach to the people that they should use, as far as possible Swadeshi articles only, are engaged in sacred work and I say to them-go forward boldly and preach your Gospel enthusiastically. Only do not forget that yours is only one way out of several of serving the Swadeshi cause. And do not do your work in a narrow, exclusive, intolerant spirit which says—'whoever is not with us is against us.' But do it in the broader, more comprehensive, more catholic spirit, which says-'whoever is not against us is with us.' Try to keep down and not encourage the tendency, which seems to be almost inherent in the Indian mind of today, to let small differences assume undue importance. Harmony, co-operation, union-by these alone can we achieve any real success in our present state. In this connection I think I ought to say a word about an expression which has, of late, found considerable favour with a section of my countrymen-'the boycott of foreign goods.' I am sure most of those who speak of this 'boycott' mean by it only the use, as far as possible, of Swadeshi, articles in preference to foreign articles. Now such use is really included in true Swadeshi; but unfortunately the word 'boycott' has a sinister meaning-it implies a vindictive desire to injure another, no matter what harm you may thereby cause to yourself. And I think we would do well to use only the word Swadeshi to describe our present movement, leaving alone the word 'boycott' which creates unnecessary ill-will against ourselves.

Moreover, remember that a strict 'boycott' of foreign goods is not at all practicable in our present industrial condition. For when you 'boycott' foreign goods, you must not touch even a particle of imported articles; and we only make ourselves ridiculous by talking of a resolution which we cannot enforce. One word more and I have done. In the struggle that lies before us, we must be prepared for repeated disappointments. We mast make up our minds that our progress is bound to be slow, and our successes, in the beginning at any rate, comparatively small. But if we go to work with firm faith in our hearts, no difficulties can obstruct our way for long, and the future will be more and more on our side. After all, the industrial problem, formidable as it is not more formidable than the political problem. And, to my mind, the two are largely bound together. Ladies and gentlemen, the task which the people of India are now called upon to accomplish is the most difficult that ever confronted any people on the face of the earth. Why it has pleased Providence to set it before us, why we are asked to wade through the deepest part of the stream-to be in the hottest part of the battle-Providence alone knows. But it is my hope and my faith that we will successfully achieve this task. The situation requires us to devote ourselves to the service of our Motherland in an earnest and self sacrificing spirit: But what can be higher or nobler or holier or more inspiring than such service? In working for India, we shall only be working for the land of our birth for the land of our fathers, for the land of our children. We shall be working for a country which God has blessed in many ways but which man has not served so well. And if we do this work as God wants us to do it, our mother land will yet march on wards and again occupy an honoured place among the nations of the world.

Issue of Hindu Mohammedan

The following is an English rendering of the speech delivered in Marathi by the Hon'ble Mr. Gokhale at a public meeting held under the auspices of the Deccan Sabha, Poona, on the 4th July 1909:

> Till recently the differences between Hindus and Mahomedans which from time to time assumed an acute form and attracted public attention were generally in regard to matters involving religious sentiment, such as cow-killing and street music. No doubt complaints were occasionally heard in the addresses presented by Mohammedan Associations to men in authority, or in the columns of the Press about the Mahomedans not securing a sufficient share of the public services, or a sufficient representation on Municipal and Local Boards. But a separate organized movement of Muslim leaders, with a comprehensive programme of their own, to win special concessions for Mahomedans as a community in the administration of the country was a matter of the last two or three years only, and while there was undoubtedly a cause for sincere congratulation that their Mohammedan brethren had at last shaken off their apathy of years in political matters, their separate organisation and the demand for special concessions did not tend to diminish their growing difficulties of their public life. After glancing briefly at the past history of the two communities and the contributions made by them to the progress of the world, Mr. Gokhale proceeded to consider their respective positions at the present day in India. The Mohammedan minority, who were a little over one-fifth of the whole population was very unequally divided among the different Provinces. In the Punjab and East Bengal they actually formed a majority of the population, being a little over one-half in the Punjab and about three-fifths in East Bengal. In Bombay, on the other hand, they were only; one-fifth, in West Bengal between one-fifth and one-sixth, in the United Provinces

one-seventh, in Madras about one-sixteenth, and in the Central Provinces less than one-twentieth. The bulk of the Mahomedans did not differ from the Hindus in race, but they had to remember that religion was a most powerful factor in life and it modified and sometimes profoundly modified race characteristics. In numbers, in wealth, in education and public spirit, the advantage at present lay with the Hindus. They had also so far contributed far more than the other community to the present national awakening in India.

But they were greatly hampered by castes, and by temperament they were mild and passive. On the other land, the Mahomedans were burdened with fewer division, their social structure rested on a more democratic basis, they had more cohesion among them, and they were more easily roused to action. The worst of the situation was that over the greater part of India the two communities had in berated a tradition of antagonism, which, though it might ordinarily lie dormant, broke forth into activity at the smallest provocation. It was that tradition that had to be overcome. And though there were certain special difficulties in their way and the task at times appeared well-nigh impossible, it was no more impossible than what Europe had to face for more than two centuries in the fierce antagonism between Protestants and Catholics. Spread of education, a wide and efficient performance of civic duties, growth of national aspirations and a quickening of national self-respect in both communities were among the forces which would ultimately overcome the tradition. The progress in that direction was bound to be slow and there were sure to be repeated set-backs. But they must believes in final success with all their will and persevere ceaselessly against all odds. It was a commonplace of Indian politics that there could be no future for India as a nation, unless a spirit of co-operation of a sufficiently durable character was developed and established between the two great communities in all public matters. They could not get over that, no matter how angry they might be at times with one another. And those among them who wished to devote themselves to the promotion of such co-operation had no choice but to refrain as far as possible from joining in controversies likely to embitter the relations between the two sides, and exercising for bearance and self-restraint themselves to counsel it in others. The speaker was of opinion that a special responsibility lay in the matter with the Hindus, who had an advantage over the other community in regard to the spread of education and who were therefore in a better position to appreciate the needs of a growing nationality. They could also do a great deal towards the establishment of better relations if some of them devoted themselves to education and other useful work among Mahomedans for the special benefit of that community. Such work could not in course of time fail to be appreciated, and it would powerfully help in gradually substituting confidence and goodwill and cooperation in place of the present distrust and suspicion and aloofness.

Mr. Gokhale having thus dealt with the general position proceeded to express his view of the controversy that had agitated the country during the last six months. Much of the excitement, he said, had been due to a misapprehension of the character and scope of the new reforms.

Mr. Gokhale stated his own position in the matter quite frankly. He had all along been in favour of special separate electorates for important minorities but he wanted such electorates to provide not the whole of the representation to which the communities were entitled but only so much of it as was necessary to redress the deficiencies and inequalities of general elections: and he wanted the same treatment to be extended to other important minorities than Mahomedans where necessary. Mr. Gokhale held strongly that in the best interest of their public life and for the future of their land they must first have elections on a territorial basis in which all communities without distinction of race or creed should participate and then special separate supplementary elections should be held to secure the fair and adequate representation of such important Minorities as had received less than their full share in the general elections. He had urged that view publicly from his place in the Viceroy's Legislative Council last March, and he had been called hard names by both sides for it. He however adhered to his view that in the present circumstances of the country, that was the only course which reasonably safeguarded the interests of all communities and prevented injustice to any one of them in practice. As far as they could see, the Government of India's original proposals had been very much on those lines. And if the Secretary of State had not unfortunately disturbed them in the first instance, very probably they would not have heard much of the demands that had since been made. No doubt, under those proposals special treatment was proposed to be accorded only to Mahomedans, but there was nothing to prevent the same treatment being extended to others later on if necessary.

The Secretary of State, however, having proposed, from the highest motives as they could all see, a scheme of his own and having afterwards found it necessary to abandon it and fall back again on the Government of India's proposaland did so in language which opened the door to large demands by the Muslim League. Straight-way the League threw the Government of India's proposals overboard and began to urge the grant of larger concessions. Mr. Gokhale made no complaint of this. Indeed so far as the League urged this substitution of election in place of nomination for all special seats, his sympathies were with the League. But when some of the leading spokesmen of the Muslim community demanded a larger representation than they were justly entitled to on, grounds such as special importance and higher loyalty traditional or otherwise, an occasion undoubtedly arose when it became the duty of the other communities in the country to protest strongly against such claims. His own feeling in the matter was the same its that of their great leader Sir Pherozeshah Mehta than whom the country had no wiser or more patriotic guide. Mr.

Gokhale associated himself fully with the telegram recently despatched, and as he knew, most reluctantly despatched by Sir Pherozeshah Mehta to the Government of India. He bad assented to that telegram, personally, having specially attended the meeting of the Presidency Association for the purpose. When any one said that his community was important and should receive fair and adequate representation, the claim was entitled to the sympathetic consideration of all. But when any one urged that his community was specially important and should therefore receive representation in excess of its fair share, the undoubted and irresistible implication was that the other communities were comparatively inferior and should receive less than their fair share. That was a position to which naturally the other communities could not assent. British rule was based on equal treatment for all communities, and the speaker trusted that the Government would never be so weak as to lean for support on any one community in particular. It was urged that the Mahomedans had ruled in India for five centuries.

It must not however be forgotten that the Hindus had ruled for countless countries before them and even afterwards, before the British came on the scene, the Mohammedan power had been broken and displaced over nearly the whole country by a revival of Hindu rule. Then it was said that there were large 'Mohammedan populations in other countries-some of, them self-governing countries and that invested the Mahomedans of India with special importance. Mr. Gokhale could not see how that mattered in determining the extent of the representation which the Government of India should grant to its own subjects, unless it was on the assumption that in the administration of this country, those whose whole heart was not with India were to have preference over those whose was. Moreover the same ground could with equal reason be urged by Indian Christians and by Buddhists. Lastly, as regards the higher traditional loyalty of Mahomedans to British rule, the claim was not historically tenable. And even during the last two or three years Mohammedan names had not been altogether absent from the lists of those speakers and writers against whom the Government had thought it necessary to proceed, though it must be admitted that the number of such names bad been extremely small. Before concluding Mr. Gokhale referred to the speech recently made by His Highness the Aga Khan. He said that he read portions of that speech with considerable astonishment, and he could not help regretting that so well informed and broadminded a gentleman as His Highness should have been labouring under so much misapprehension. His Highness had said that unless larger concessions were made to the Mahomedans, the Hindus would be exultant and triumphant.

All that Mr. Gokhale could say about this was that His Highness was evidently not in touch with Hindu feeling in the matter. Not only was there no disposition among the Hindus to exalt or to fall triumphant but there was actually a sullen feeling of resentment throughout the country, a feeling daily growing deeper and stronger than the Government had not held the balance even and that it had already learned too much on the Mohammedan side. His Highness had further said that unless additional concessions were made to Mahomedans, it would mean a monopoly of political power to the Hindus. Mr. Gokhale said that he rubbed his eyes as he read that statement. Surely the Aga Khan could not be under the impression that what the Government proposed to do was to hand over the administration of the country to elected Councils with Hindu majority in them. Not even with the Councils reconstituted as proposed the last word would still be with the officials. The enlargement of the Councils and the increase in the proportion of elected members were no doubt important matters, but they were not so important as to afford to any community the share shadow of an opportunity to obtain a monopoly of political power in the country.

As the speaker had often pointed out, the most important and valuable part of the reform of Legislative Councils was the power proposed to be conferred on members to raise discussion on administrative matters. This power, if wisely exercised, would gradually give the country an administration conducted in the light of day and under the scrutiny of public discussion in place of the present administration carried on in the dark and behind the backs of the people. For this purpose what really mattered was the capacity, the public spirit, and the sense of responsibility of the members. How many members were returned by any particular community was not of much consequence, and a member or two more or less on this side or that would not make the smallest difference in practice. Mr. Gokhale earnestly trusted that Government would soon close the question in a elite manner and he was confident that before long the present soreness of feeling would disappear and normal relations again return between the two communities. When once the new Councils commenced to work it would be realised that there was no demand or scope there for work on sectarian lines and the man who worked for all would find his service appreciated by all communities. Controversies like the present were occasionally inevitable, but if they took care not to employ words or express sentiments which would leave soreness behind, they might succeed in everything the injury which otherwise was likely to result to the best interests of their growing nationality. They were all of them trustees of those interests, and the world and their own posterity would judge them by the manner in which they discharged that trust.

Service to Motherland

Hon'ble Mr. Gokhale delivered following speech at the Students' Brotherhood, Bombay, on the 9th October, 1909:

> Gentlemen—One of the most anxious, as it is one of the most important, problems confronting us today is how to supply the guidance, at once wise and patriotic, to our young men, so that their lives may be directed into channels of high purpose and earnest endeavour in the service of the Motherland. To sustain, on the one hand, it those pure impulses and generous enthusiasms which are the special privilege of youth, and, on the other, to instill into young minds a due sense of proportion and of responsibility and a correct realization of the true needs of the country-this can never be an easy task, and in the present situation of India, it is beset with extraordinary difficulties. Influences are at work around us which bid everyone, "nor sit, nor stand, but go"!

> The very air we breathe is laden with a longing for change. Old beliefs are crumbling. New adjustments of ideas have become necessary, and amidst this general commotion which has been very properly called "unrest," it was not to be expected that our students alone should continue to stand where they did.

It is not the fact of their movement, so much as the direction in which a large proportion of them have been moving that calls for our most earnest attention and our closest inquiry. It is a well-worn truism that the students of today will be the citizens of tomorrow. Ideas and aspiration, which give a decisive bent to their minds are, therefore, matters of the deepest moment to the country, and it behooves us all seriously to examine how far they are calculated to prepare them for the responsibilities which must in due course descend to them. One complaint which is often heard may be dismissed at once. It is said in disparagement of the Indian student that he begins to feel an interest in politics long before his time, and that it is necessary to put an end to this state of things. Now, the fact itself of such precocious interest may be admitted at once, but those who speak of it as an evil that must or can be put down fail obviously to realize),that it is an inevitable result of the exceptional political situation of the country, and that it is bound to last as long as that situation continues in all essentials unaltered.

Among self-governing people, politics brings into play not only the sentiment of patriotism, but also the sense of responsibility. And young men, who feel the sentiment, but lack the sense of responsibility, naturally leave practical affairs to their elders who possess both. To the Indian student, on the other hand, Indian politics is only a struggle, in which his countrymen are engaged on behalf of the Motherland, with a body of foreign officials representing the rule of another nation. There is no room here even for the elders for any feeling of responsibility in regard to the administration of the country and for our young men who find no restraining considerations in their path, politics necessarily resolves itself into a matter of patriotic sentiment-an interest in politics is, to the Indian student, the same thing as an interest in his country. And to such interest all that is earnest, all that is self-respecting, all that is chivalrous, all that is patriotic in his nature, is continually impelling him. England herself has introduced into the country ideas which preach to us the dignity and high worth of patriotism, of freedom, of self-government and which tell us of contempt which, in the eyes of all self-governing people, covers those who accept their subjection in a slavish spirit. Our politics today is for the most part a spread of these ideas among the people, and an attempt to apply them to our present condition. And it is inevitable that the most impressionable minds in the country should be the most affected by them.

Gokhale spoke as follows at a meeting held in the Town Hall of Bombay on the 9th September 1909:

> Mr. Chairman, Ladies and Gentlemen—You will see that the first part of this resolution is practically identical not only in substance but in its very wording with a resolution which was adopted in this very Hall at the beginning of last)ear by a Public Meeting presided over by H.H. the Aga Khan. Eighteen months have elapsed since then and the fact that we have to repeat the self-same resolution again today shows that no relief has come in the interval and that the period has been one long night of tribulation and suffering to our brethren in the Transvaal. Indeed, gentlemen, the position today is far worse than it was when the last meeting was held. The actual struggle then had been only a month old, and it so happened that the very next day after the Bombay Meeting a compromise was effected between Mr. Gandhi and General Smutts, seemingly full of promise of a peaceful settlement honourable to both sides.
>
> Again out of a total Indian population of about 8,000 men in the Transvaal, 7,500 were engaged in she struggle. Today the total Indian population in that Colony has dropped tc less then 6,000; and though most of these are in deep sympathy with the struggle and are

helping it financially and in other ways, the brunt of the persecution is being brone by a brave band of about five hundred Indians, led by the indomitable Gandhi, a man of tremendous spiritual power, one who is made of the stuff of which great heroes and martyrs are made. Gentlemen, we have all been following this struggle with close interest and with deep indignation and pain, relieved only by our admiration of the heroic stand which our countrymen have made, but I think will be useful to recall briefly on this occasion the principal facts. Under the old Boer Government of the Transvaal, a law was in existence which required all Asiatics who entered the Transvaal after 1885 for purposes of trade to register themselves and to pay a registration fee of £3. There was no limit to number that might so enter and the Indian population in the Transvaal before the war was estimated-and the estimate has been accepted by the Government-at 15,000 males, leaving women and children out of account.

Another provision of this law required Indian traders to trade in locations only but it was never rigorously enforced and, in fact, an attempt to enforce it strictly was alleged by both Mr. Chamberlain and Lord Lansdowne as one of the causes that led to the war. In those days the Indians resident in the Transvaal were not only regarded as entitled but were actually encouraged to turn to the Imperial Government for protection. Before the outbreak of hostilities most of the resident Indians left the Transvaal, carrying with them passes from the Boer Government permitting them to return after the close of the war. The war ended in 1902, resulting in the annexation of the Transvaal to the British Empire. It was however soon discovered that the substitution of the British Government for the Boer, so far from bringing any relief to the Indians, actually made their position far worse. In 1903, the agents of the British Government that had gone to war with the Boers for seeking to enforce the law about locations, themselves sought to enforce that law in a far more stringent manner than the Boers had ever contemplated.

The attempt failed on an appeal to the Supreme Court, but it gave the Indians a taste of what was in store for them under the regime, and it naturally filled all right-minded men with indignation and disgust. Then the cry was started Indians were flooding the Colony and it was necessary to stop the inflex. How dishonest and unscrupulous the cry was may be seen from the fact that the Indian population in the Transvaal since the war has at no time reached the number that was there before the war. I have already said that the male population alone before the war was 15,000. In 1904, a regular census was taken when it was found that the entire Indian population, including women and children, was only 10,000. Again in 1906, a Memorandum issued by the Registrar of Asiatics showed that up to then about 13,000 permits had altogether been issued and the actual number of Indians in the Colony-men, women, and children all told-was not more than 10,000, In July 1907, when the first stage of the Passive Resistance struggle began it was estimated by the Indian leaders that there were about 9,000 Indians in the Colony. In December of that year, when the struggle reached an advanced stage it was estimated that the number was about 8,000. And today it is less than 6,000. The cry of unrestricted influx was, however, persistently and vigorously maintained by Boer and Britain alike and the Indians soon saw that the real object of the white Colonists was somehow to get rid of the Indian element altogether. Lord Milner, who could not help seeing how badly the Indians were treated, advised them in 1903 to undergo voluntary registration, and take out fresh permits, though they already had registered themselves under the Boer Government and held its passes.

The Indians did this and Lord/Milner thanked them for the manner in which they had met him in the matter. When Lord Selborne succeeded Lord Milner as High Commissioner, he inquired into the charge of unrestricted and fraudulent influx and publicly declared that the charge was unfounded. Still the cry continued that the Colony was being flooded by Indians and ultimately the Government introduced into the Legislative Council in 1906 an Ordinance called the Asiatic Law Amendment Ordinance, which provided for a fresh compulsory registration of all Asiatics entitled to be in the Colony, under very humiliating circumstances. The Asiatics protested strongly, vehemently, against the Ordinance, but to no purpose, and the Ordinance was, with small modifications, passed by the Legislative Council. This was in reality the beginning of the Passive Resistance movement. Then followed a sharp but comparatively short conflict between the Transvaal Government and the passive resisters. Many of them including Mr. Gandhi were arrested and sent to jail, but at the end of January, 1908, a compromise was arrived at, as I have already told you, between Mr. Gandhi and General Smutts. The terms of this compromise according to Mr. Gandhi's version, which those who know Mr. Gandhi will not for a moment doubt, were these—The Indians were to register themselves voluntarily within three months, the registration being free from humiliating details and the Asiatic Law Amendment Act was to be repealed and Asiatic Immigration was to be regulated under the operation of another law passed the previous year, namely, the Immigration Restriction Act, which was general in its provisions. In accordance with this compromise the whole Indian community in the Transvaal voluntarily registered itself by the beginning of May, 1908; but the Transvaal Government on its side, instead of repealing the obnoxious Asiatic Law Amendment Act, merely passed a law to validate the voluntary registrations.

The result of this action on the part of the Transvaal Government was to defeat two most important objects which the Indians had in view in agreeing to the compromise. Those objects were: first there should be no law on the Statute book of the Colony subjecting Indians as such to humiliating treatment, and secondly, it should be open to the people of this country to enter the Colony on the same legal terms as the people of European countries, i.e., by passing a literary test in one of the European languages, thereby ensuring immigration to a few cultured Indians every year. By retaining the Asiatic Law Amendment Act, however, on the Statutebook, General Smutts frustrated both these objects, as the Act subjected Indians to humiliating treatment, and by confining entry into the Colony to those Asiatics only who were pre-war residents, it effectually prevented the admission of new Indians.

The Indian community of the Transvaal naturally therefore looked upon the refusal of General Smutts to repeal the Asiatic Law Amendment Act as a gross breach of faith and finding themselves taken in, inasmuch as they had voluntarily registered themselves, they at once held a Public Meeting at which they renewed the vow to continue Passive resistance, and to re-open the struggle, and about 2,500 Indians burnt their registration certificates. This was in September of last year and since then the struggle has gone on in a very acute from. Those who will speak to the second resolution will tell you what dreadful hardships and sufferings have been endured by the passive resisters for the cause. Briefly, 2,500 sentences, mostly of hard labour, have been inflicted on them. About a thousand persons have been absolutely ruined and a thousand more have left Colony. The struggle, however, has continued unabated to the present day. Gentlemen, I have so far given you briefly the principal facts of the struggle. The first thing we have got to realize in this matter is that Mr. Gandhi and our other countrymen in the Transvaal are fighting not for themselves but for the honour and the future interests of our motherland. So far as they themselves were concerned they had satisfied the requirements of the situation by registering themselves voluntarily. But the whole battle has raged round the repeal of the Asiatic Law Amendment Act, and they have insisted on this repeal so that an invidious piece of legislation, insulting in its character to the people of this country, should be removed from the Statutebook of a British Colony.

As a practical man, Mr. Gandhi is prepared to agree that there should be no unrestricted immigration of Indians into the Colony, that Government there should in its discretion be permitted to restrict such immigration in practice. But he wants them to effect this under the operation of tile Immigration Restriction Act which is perfectly general in its application to all nationalities and which does not cast any reflection on any of His Majesty's subjects such as the Indian community. Then Mr. Gandhi's struggle is in furtherance of the future interests of our motherland. For better, for worse this country is now included in the British Empire, and our progress must be towards complete equality with our English and other fellow-subjects in that Empire. Here again as practical men, we are prepared to recognize that the attainment of such equality and the obliteration of race-distinctions which it involves can be but a slow affair.

But we have a right to insist that the movement must be in the direction of a steady removal of these distinctions which are numerous enough in all conscience and not towards adding further to them. In fighting for the principle that no humiliating disabilities shall be imposed by the Statutebook of a British Colony on Indians as Indians, Mr. Gandhi is fighting for the assertion of our claim to that equality which our hopes for the future are bound up. Gentlemen, I have heard it said by some friends, mainly Englishmen, that though they originally sympathised with the Indians in this struggle, Mr. Gandhi's resort to Passive Resistance involving as it does definance of the laws of the Colony has alienated their sympathies. Now I do not in the first place think that this is quite a fact. For we see the Committee in England, presided over by Lord Ampthill, backing up the passive resisters as strongly and cordially as ever. Again, even if a few Englishmen have grown cold in their sympathies, I am sure none of us here feels an), thing but the highest admiration for the manner in which this struggle has been carried on by our side. I think, and I say this deliberately that in the circumstances of the Transvaal, Passive Resistance such as that organized by Mr. Gandhi, is not only legitimate, but is a duty resting on all self-respecting persons. What is this Passive Resistance? Passive Resistance to an unjust law or an oppressive measure and a refusal to acquiesce in that law or measure and a readiness to suffer the penalty instead which may be prescribed as an alternative. If we strongly and clearly and conscientiously feel the grave injustice of a law, and there is no other way to obtain redress, I think refusal to acquiesce in it taking the consequences of such refusal is the only course left to those place conscience and self-respect above their material or immediate interests. Look at the splendid manner in which the whole movement has been managed. Hindus, Mahomedans, Parsis, all hold together as one man, forgetting their usual differences and sufferings with wonderful selfrestraint—surely a man who can achieve this must represent a great moral force, and must not be lightly judged. Again look at the fact that though the struggle has gone on in an acute form all these months, not even the worst opponent of Mr. Gandhi has suggested the least suspicion about his loyalty or his general attitude towards the British Government.

No, gentlemen, I am sure, we all think that Mr. Gandhi is perfectly justified in resorting to Passive Resistance when all other means of redress failed. I am sure if any of us had been in the Transvaal during these days we should have been proud to range ourselves under Mr. Gandhi's banner and work with him and suffer with him in the cause. Ladies and gentlemen, this resolution says that we again appeal to the Imperial Government and the Imperial Parliament to use their influence on our behalf at this crucial movement in the history of South Africa and thereby close this bitter question in a satisfactory manner. The present is an important moment because the four Colonies of South Africa have just been united into a federation. Surely, we trust, it is not too much to hope that at such a moment the Colonial authorities themselves must be anxious to wipe all unpleasant controversies if possible, off the slate. It is often said, and it is no doubt largely true, that the Imperial Government, whatever its sympathies, cannot coerce Self-Governing Colonies into particular courses of action. But the Imperial Government owes a duty to other subjects, besides the white residents of Self-Governing Colonies and moreover even if there may be no coercion there are numerous ways of making private representations which may prove more or less effective. For instance, South Africa is sure to want something from the Imperial Government sooner or later. That would be an opportunity for the Imperial Government to bring pressure to bear upon the Union to secure justice to us.

I fear the Imperial Government does not quite realise the bitter intensity with which the people of India feel and resent the treatment meted out to their countrymen in the Transvaal. If they did this, I do think that some way would be found out of the present difficulty, satisfactory to both sides. After all it is only a modest demand which the Indians are making, and it is difficult to believe that the Imperial Government can do nothing in the matter. But gentlemen, this resolution does not merely confine itself to an appeal to the Imperial Government. It also appeals to the Government of India whose sympathies with us in this matter are well known. The four Colonies of South Africa are now united and they are jointly responsible for any further legislation in matters affecting Indians. Now from the Indian standpoint Natal is the vulnerable point of the Union, and we call upon the Government of India to strike at this point; for if ever retaliation is justified, it is justified in this case. Natal needs Indian labour—it imported about 8,000 indentured Indian labourers in 1905; 11,600 in 1906: over 6,000 in 1907, and over 3,000 last year. The recruitment takes place in this country under the authority of the Government of India, and by simply withdrawing the authority, the Government of India can stop this migration of Indian labour to Natal.

The Government can, very well say to South Africa, as Lord Curzon said to the Transvaal five years ago, you must treat free Indians throughout South Africa in a reasonable and satisfactory manner. Otherwise we will not help you any more with Indian labour. We respectfully call upon the Government of India to take up this attitude, not only for the sake of the Indians in the Transvaal but also for the Indian in Natal itself. For it was well known that Natal treats Indians in that Colony disgracefully. The condition of our indentured labourers there is not far removed from that of slavery. Indian traders are harassed in numberless ways. There is no provision whatever for the education of the children of free Indians beyond the primary stage, and none even for the primary education for the children of indentured labourers. And there are several other grievances of a similar nature.

Last year Natal tried to pass two laws, one withdrawing the Municipal franchise from the Indians which they at present enjoy and the other intended to eliminate the whole free Indian element from the Colony in the course of ten years. Fortunately both these laws were disallowed by the Imperial Government. Natal really deserves no consideration at our hands, and I earnestly trust that the Government of India will show no such consideration. One word more and I have done The root of our present troubles in the

Colonies really lies in the fact that our status is not what it should be in our own country. Men who have no satisfactory status in their own land, cannot expect to have a satisfactory status elsewhere. Our struggle for equal treatment with Englishmen in the Empire must therefore be mainly carried on in India itself. Then again we must remember that it is bound to be a long and weary struggle. It will require again and again sacrifices and sufferings such as those of our Transvaal brethren, and it will bring up repeated failures before we achieve final success. But suffering, or no suffering, failure or success, we owe it to our motherland to carry on this struggle with stout hearts and full faith in the justice of our cause. And I for one have no doubt in my mind about the ultimate issue.

Higher and Extensive Employment

The Hon'ble Mr. Subba Rao, on 17th March 1911, moved a Resolution in the Imperial Legislative Council recommending the appointment of a Commission of officials and non-officials to consider the claims of Indians to higher and more extensive employment in the Public Service connect with the civil administration of the country. Gokhale, in supporting the Resolution, spoke as follows: Sir, before I say a few words on the resolution which my Hon'ble friend has brought forward, I would like to offer him my congratulations on the industry and care with which he has prepared his case and the ability with which he has presented it to the Council.

Sir, this question is, undoubtedly one of great importance, and, like all questions of great importance, it is beset with great difficulties. I am anxious to approach it with as much fairness as I am capable of, because there are undoubtedly two sides, and while I am keen that the aspirations of my countrymen should receive fair and reasonable recognition from the Government, I should be very unwilling not to recognise at the same time the difficulties that lie in the path of the Government in dealing with this subject. Sir, one of the fundamental conditions of the peculiar position of the British Government in this country is that it should be a continuously progressive Government. I think all thinking men, to whatever community they belong, will accept that. Now,

I suggest four tests to judge whether the Government is progressive, and further whether it is continuously progressive. The first test that I would apply is what measures it adopts for the moral and material improvement of the mass of the people, and under these measures I do not include those appliances of modern governments, which the British Government has evolved in this country, because they were appliances, necessary for its very existence, though they have benefitted the people, such as the construction of Railways, the introduction of Post and Telegraphs, and things of that kind. By measures for the moral and material improvement of the people, I mean what the Government does for education, what the Government does for sanitation, what the Government does for agricultural development, what the Government does for industrial development, and so forth. That is my first test. The second test that I would apply is what steps the Government takes to give us a larger and larger share in the administration of our local affairs-in municipalities and local boards. My third test is what voice the Government gives us in its Councils-in these deliberative assemblies, where policies are considered; and lastly, we must consider how far Indians are admitted into the ranks of the public service. Now, Sir, as regards the first test, I believe that is what one feels to be in the air—I believe that we are on the eve of important measures being taken by the Government, and in those measures both the officials and non-officials can and should heartily co-operate with one another. As regards the second, I trust that, as a result of Decentralization Commission's labours, a further advance will soon be made. A fair beginning has already been made, and when we have a further advance in the same direction, we might be expected to remain satisfied with that for some time. As regards deliberative assemblies-the Provincial and Imperial Councils-the reforms that have recently been introduced constitute an important advance, and for some time, therefore, that question may rest there. When, however, we come to the last question, we strongly feel that the time has come when something must be done to improve matters, and I hope something will soon be done. Sir, I have already observed that the Government has to be a continuously progressive Government, and that it cannot afford to rest on whatever it has done in the past in any one of these directions. Now taking this question of the employment of Indians in the higher ranks of the public service, which I admit is a very difficult question, I would like to refer briefly to what my Hon'ble friend Mr. Subba Rao has already pointed out, namely, that there are four or five distinct landmarks in regard to this matter in the history of British rule. In 1833, when Parliament laid down that there should be no distinction of race in making appointments to the public service in this country, the British nation gave a noble pledge to the people of this country of its own accord. There was no agitative here at that time-in fact, there was hardly any Western education. It was a great pledge to give, and it was given by the British nation spontaneously. The next landmark is 1854, when the competitive examination was thrown open to Indians along with Europeans. The old Haileybury system was abolished and competition was introduced, and it was thrown open to all. The Queen's Proclamation of 1858 constitutes the next landmark. Even then there was no agitation for a wide employment of Indians in the public service for the simple reason that the Universities had not then been established, and there was no large educated class. In 1861, when the Secretary of State appointed his Committee, to which my Hon'ble friend has referred, it was again more the conscience of the English people than any demand made from this side that led to the appointment of that Committee. When the Act of 1870 was passed-that is the next landmark-there was some public opinion here, and a few Indians-notably Mr. Dadabhoy Naoroji—had been agitating in England for the admission of Indians to high office; but even then, the main part of the work was done by Englishmen, by English friends of our aspirations, who felt that the arrangements existing at that time were not quite just to the people of India. When, however, the Public Service Commission was appointed in 1886-that is the next landmark-the position was much altered. By that time a large educated class had come into existence, and that class keenly felt its own exclusion from the higher ranks of the Public Service. The Commission was appointed with the declared object of devising means for the larger admission of Indians in these ranks, and as the results of the Commission's labours have, on the whole, been disappointing, there is no doubt that constitutes a legitimate ground of complaint for the people of this country. Sir, it is interesting to note at what intervals these successive steps in advance were taken.

From 1833 to 1854 or 1858, whichever you take, there was an interval of 20 or 25 years. From 1858 to 1870, when the next step was taken, there was an interval of 12 years. In 1886, when the question was again examined, it was after an interval of about 16 years. Since then, however, there has been no inquiry-that means during a period of 25 years-and that is one reason why I urge that the resolution of my Hon'ble friend should be adopted. It is true that during the last three or four years some very striking appointments to high office have been made. My friend, Mr. Ali Imam, sits on that bench there; two Indians sit in the Secretary of State for India's Council; an Indian recently held the position of Advocate-General at Calcutta, and Indians have even been appointed to act as Chief Justices of different High Courts. These striking appointments have no doubt impressed! the imagination of the people, and there can be no question that they are deeply appreciated by my countrymen. But our grievance is in regard to the bulk of appointments in the higher rank; and that grievance is not really touched by these appointments. And so far as that grievance is concerned, the labours of the Public Service Commission resulted in little substantial improvement for us in practice. And indeed in some departments, the position has been rendered actually worse. My Hon'ble friend, Mr. Subba Rao, has pointed out how in regard to the central Civil Service, the recommendations of the Public Service Commission and the orders passed by the Secretary of State on those recommendations have actually put us back, compared with the Statutory Service Rules of 1879. The rules of 1879 gave us one sixth of the total recruitment of Civilians for the country. Now, taking the cadre at about a thousand posts it may be a few more or a few less-we should have had about 160 Indians, under those rules, in the central Civil Service. The Commission, however, recommended only 108 posts for us in place of 160, and the Secretary of State cut the number down to 93; and that is the number we have at present. I believe even the whole of these 93 are not yet held by Indians. I think we are about 10 short of what the Secretary of State promised at that time leaving out of account the additions made subsequently for Burma and Assam. Now, Sir, the Secretary of State's orders were passed in about 1890 or 1891, and twenty years have elapsed since then. If for nothing else, at least for the fact that ' it is now 25 years since the appointment of the Public Service Commission ' and 20 years since the Secretary of State passed his orders on the recommendations of that Commission, I urge that there should be a fresh enquiry into the whole matter. But, Sir, I say something more. I say that as a result of the labours of the Public Service Commission, the position of Indians in many branches of the Public Service has actually been rendered worse, and that should now beset right. In the first place, Sir, the Public Service Commission recommended that there should be a division of the Public Service into Imperial and Provincial. Now that was a most unfortunate recommendation. I am quite sure that the President of the Commission-the Lieutenant-Governor of the Punjab of that time—a man of broad sympathies, undoubtedly did not want to put the Indians back; but the result actually has been to put us back, and this for two reasons. First, there is a stamp of inferiority on the Provincial men, and they are bound to feel that. Secondly, if you have these artificial divisions of Imperial and Provincial, the abler men in the Provincial Service—I mean those who are abler even than some of the men in the Imperial Service cannot help feeling that the arrangement is most unjust to them. I am, therefore, strongly of opinion that this division between Imperial and Provincial must go. I hope it will go soon, and unless it does we shall have to bring up this matter again and again before this Council.

Then, in two departments particularly, this division between Imperial and Provincial has done greater harm to us than in other departments—I mean the Education and the Public Works Department. In some of the other departments, the creation of a Provincial Service has to a certain extent improved the prospects of Indians, so far as mere numbers are concerned, because there were hardly any Indians employed in those departments before and the constitution of Provincial Service has given them some chance there. But in the Education and Public Works Departments, we have suffered a great set-back. In the Education Department, for instance, Indians were on terms of equality with their English colleagues before the creation of a Provincial Service. The scale of salary was, no doubt, two-thirds, but in other respects they were on equal terms. But they have now been put into a distinctly subordinate position and we see on every side the most flagrant cases, which hurt everybody. Thus, we find men of most distinguished attainments in the Provincial Service simply because they are Indians, and men who passed their examinations only yesterday, and who have so far earned no distinction by their work, in the Imperial Service, simply because they are Europeans. I will give only one instance.

There is a gentleman here in Calcutta, named Dr. P.C. Ray, a most distinguished man of science, a man who has been honoured by French and German savants, a man adored by his pupils, a man who has been doing original work for the last 20 years and more. But he is still in the Provincial Service, whereas young men, fresh from College, without any original work to their credit, men who are admittedly his Inferiors, are brought out to this country and put over his head, simply because he happens to be in the Provincial Service and they are brought out as members of the Imperial Service. Now, Sir, this sort of thing hurts not merely the men who are actually affected by it, it hurts the students studying under them. In other departments any injustice done to an Indian official concerns that official only. In the Education Department it affects the students as well; the bitterness passes from the professors to the students, and the whole student community comes to be affected by it. Take again the Public Works Department. At one time Indian and European Engineers were all on terms of absolute equality not only as regards status but even as regards pay. In 1892, differential rates of pay were introduced for the first time-two-thirds pay for Indian Engineers. Now under the new organisation scheme, the status of the Provincial Engineers is reduced still further, for they are now to be put on a separate list. Thus, in this Department, we were at first on terms of absolute equality with Englishmen. Then our pay was reduced to two-thirds, though in regard to other matters equality was maintained. Finally, it is now decided to do away with this equality by putting us on a separate list altogether. And not only is this applied to new men but a most unjust and unjustifiable attempt has been made to apply it to old men, recruited since 1892. There are about 100 men who are the victims of this gross injustice. There is the definite word of the Government pledged to them in 1892 that they would be on the same list as the Imperial Engineers, and yet it is :proposed now to put them on a separate list—a distinct breach of faith. These men have not yet accepted the arrangement three years have passed, and they have so far got no redress. The Secretary of State is still waiting for the despatch of the Government of India which should have gone long ago. I asked a question the other day on the subject, and the Hon'ble Mr. Carlyle gave an answer, in which I see an element of hope. I, therefore, will not press this question further today, but, if necessary, I will bring a resolution on this subject at Simla. I urge then, first of all, that this distinction between imperial and Provincial must go. The second respect in which we have lost ground since the last Public Service Commission is in regard to competition. Gradually competition has been abolished more or less throughout the country and we are now made to depend almost exclusively upon Government nomination, pure and simple. Now, I am quite alive to the defects of competition as a method of filling Government offices. Of course it is not ideally the best method, but I contend that it is the best method available.

In a country like this, governed by Englishmen, who are unfamiliar with our ways, and cannot instinctively understand the difference between one individual and another, they are at times apt to be misled by appearances, by recommendations and by a lot of other considerations owing to the very peculiarity of their position. And I submit that competition, with all its defects, is any day better than nomination, pure and simple. An Englishmen, judging of English candidates, may dispense with competition, because there is a great deal of initial knowledge that may be taken for granted on account of their belonging to the same society. Here the individuals belong to different societies and that initial knowledge is lacking and nomination, 'I contend, is bound to lead to abuses—haphazard selection and favouritism. My second point, therefore, is that competition must again be restored for making selections for Government service. I will now say a word about one or two other Departments. I have said that the Public Works and Education Departments, our position has grown worse. In the Medical Department, while it has not grown worse, it is still most unsatisfactory. The professorships are all the monopoly of the Indian Medical Service officers and the hospitals are closed to all non service men. Recently they have thrown open the Professorship of Anatomy in the Calcutta College to non-service men, but the moment it is thus thrown open to non-service men, it is rendered altogether unattractive.

There used to be a pension attached to this post till now, and private practice was hitherto allowed; but it is now declared that there is to be no pension, there is to be no private practice, and the new man will get no house allowance, when every one else is getting it. Thus, the moment the post is thrown open to non-service men it is made altogether unattractive for our best men, and I would like to have an explanation as to why this has been done.

Take again the question of the Chemical Analysers in Bombay and Karachi. Some years ago, the Secretary of State decided that these appointments should not be the monopoly of the Indian Medical Service. And there is a distinguished man in Bombay available for these appointments today, doing for years the work of Assistant Chemical Examiner. Indian Medical Service men, appointed as Chemical Analysers, receive their training under him, and then they are put over his head.

I understand the Government of Bombay is anxious to help this gentleman; but the matter rests with the Government of India, and somehow his ability and record of services receive no recognition from them. Lastly, I come to the Department of Railways. I am not going into the question in detail today because my friend the Hon'ble Mr. Mudholkar has already dealt with it exhaustively. Here we are almost entirely excluded from all higher appointments, and I hold that this is absolutely indefensible. It cannot seriously be contended that Indians are not fit for any place in the Railway Administration above Rs. 200 a month, when you can put them on the Government bench there, make them Chief Justices of High Courts or entrust them with the management of districts and divisions. To those who speak of such unfitness, I would like to mention an interesting episode. It refers not to the Railway Department, but to another Department—the Survey Department-but the principle is more or less the same. Not many years ago, there was a controversy about the position of Indians in the Survey Department, and it was contended very vigorously by the champions of European monopoly that Indians were not fit for the work, and that therefore they should be kept out. Unfortunately a report, submitted by Colonel Du Pre, who was then head of the Survey Department and who a strong advocate of Indian exclusion, came to be published, and this is what he was found to say in that report:

> I may here remark incidentally that my numerous late inspections show me that the tendency of the European surveyors is to stand and look on, while the natives are made to do the drawing and hand printing, as if they thought themselves quite above that sort of thing. This is a mistake and cannot be permitted for the future. Besides, it is suicidal for the Europeans to admit that Natives can do anyone thing better than themselves. They should claim to be superior in everything, and only allow Natives to take a secondary or subordinate part. In my old parties, I never permitted a Native to touch a theodolite or an original computation, on the principle that the triangulation or scientific work was the prerogative of the highly paid European, and this reservation of scientific work was the only way by which I could keep a distinction, so as to justify the different figures respectively drawn by the two classes-the European in office time and the Native who ran him so close in all the office duties as well as in field duties. Yet

> I see that Natives commonly do the computation work, and the Europeans some other inferior duties.

Sir, I beg, with all respect to make a present of this extract to the Hon'ble Sir T. Wynne! One word more, and I have done. Sir, I have admitted that the question is difficult one, but what I urge is that there should be continuous progress. Nobody urges that the English element should be withdrawn suddenly or even largely, but unless Indians are introduced into the higher ranks in larger and larger numbers, the discontent which the Government are anxious to remove is not likely to disappear. With these words, I strongly support the motion which my Hon'ble friend has brought forward.

Amendment to Indian Factories Bill

Gokhale on 21st March 1911, moved in the imperial Legislative Council an amendment to the Indian Factories Bill as amended by the Select Committee, making it obligatory on every factory employing more than twenty children to maintain an elementary school and provide them with free and compulsory instruction. In support 'of his amendment, he spoke as follows:

> Sir, I beg to move that to clause 23 of the Bill as amended by the Select Committee, the following sub-clauses be added: (1) Every factory, in which more than twenty children between the ages of nine and twelve are employed, shall maintain an elementary school in proper condition for their benefit and attendance at such school for not less than three hours every working day shall be compulsory in the case of each child so employed. (2) No fees shall be charged for the instruction given in such school.

Sir, I urge this amendment on the broad grounds of justice and humanity. The plea of justice is based on three considerations. In the first place, the very fact of the employment of these children in these factories disables them from availing themselves of the ordinary facilities that exist for receiving instruction at school. They have to be in the factories for certain stand hours and therefore they cannot suit themselves to the hours during which they can receive instruction in ordinary schools. Secondly, under what is known as the split shift system, their presence in the factories is not confined to the actual hours during which they have to work; but they are expected to be about the factories, on the premises or somewhere near by, because their work is divided into two parts and they have to do part of the work in the morning and the other part in the afternoon. Therefore, the total time for which they must be present in or near the factories is really much longer than the actual period for which they have to work. And thirdly, the parents of most of these children are employed in the factories, and being so employed they are prevented from exercising that supervision over their children which ordinarily they might be expected to exercise.

Therefore, Sir, on these three grounds of justice, I urge that the factory-owners should be made responsible for the education of these children. This is only fair, because the factory owners make money out of the children, make money also out of the children's parents and further work in their employ makes it impossible for the children's parents to exercise that supervision over the education and other interests of the children which they might otherwise have exercised. Then, Sir, I urge my proposal on the ground of humanity. The sole justification for a measure like this is its humanity, and humane considerations must apply most to that section of the labouring population which is least able to take care of itself. Now, children are obviously the least able to take care of themselves, and therefore, if humane considerations are to apply anywhere and the State is to extend its protection on humane grounds to any section of the labour population, that ought to be in the case of children. If the children are to be left to themselves, if after six or seven hours' work has been exacted from them they are to be turned into the street there to get into the ways of mischief-without anybody to look after them, their parents being engaged in the factories-then I say the humanity on which the State bases itself in introducing this legislation is not extended to the children. I think, therefore, Sir, that some provision ought to be made for the education of the children employed in factories, after they have performed their work. The half-timers are between the ages of 9 and 14; 1 am quite willing that the provision to be made should be for children between the ages of 9 and 12 only. Of course, it is true, as the last Factory Commission has pointed out, that there is no compulsory education for anybody in this country.

It is also true that the Commission has expressed itself against compulsory provision for the education of factory children; but even so, the Commission has recommended very strongly that something should be done to ensure the education of these children and that local bodies and the Government and the factory-owners should all concert measures together for the purpose. The earlier Factory Commission, however-that of 1890—is emphatic in its recommendation that provision ought to be made for the education of the factory children, and I prefer its recommendation to that of the latter Factory Commission. This is what the earlier Factory Commission, which first provided that children should be employed as half-timers only, recommended: If our suggestion that children should be employed as halftimers is adopted, it will be found most important to provide some means of instruction during two or three of the spare hours that the children are off work. It is not for us to discuss here the advantages of elementary education, and general control and supervision of the rising generation of operatives. These are too obvious to require any advocacy from us. What we would say is that Local Governments and municipalities should meet mill-owners half-way and, as is done in regard to children under other circumstances, contribute half the cost of teaching factory children Supposing, for instance, that a mill, employing 100 children, spends 16 rupees a month for two teachers; the Municipality or Government should double this subscription and provide two or more teachers. Looking at it from a pecuniary point of view, the expenditure is so trifling that we cannot doubt that schools would be started without delay in connection with all mills employing a large number of children. It was not to be expected that schools started under the present circumstances could be a success.

For it is impossible that a tired and jaded child (there was no class of half-timers before 1890) can work his brain to any useful purpose after his body has been thoroughly worn out with physical exertion. Then, Sir, our friend, the Hon'ble Mr. Fremantle, in a very interesting report which he submitted some time ago to the Government of the United Provinces on the condition of labour in Upper India, takes up this question and makes a very strong recommendation. I think he puts the case so well that I cannot do better than read to the Council what he says:

> The first step, says Mr. Fremantle, is to compel observance of the law as to the employment of children. When the children are really employed for only half the day, their parents will, as a rule, be only too pleased that they should be under instruction for part of the rest of the time. The schools might be maintained by the mill managers on their Premises and partly supported by grants-in-aid. With proper inspection, there should be no risk of the instruction given being insufficient. Later, if the school became popular, it might be possible to provide by law that no boy or girl under 14 should be employed in a mill unless he or she were under instruction. If this were the law, it would not be the first attempt at compulsory education in India. The Gaekwar has introduced it in parts of the Baroda State, (so it is not only I who refer to the analogy of what the Gaekwar has done; sometimes officials also do the same thing;) 'and the East Indian Railway Company in their fine estate of Giridih enforce attendance at school with excellent results. In Ceylon (here, again, we have an official mentioning the example of Ceylon) wherever there are Government schools, education is compulsory, and the Commission on Elementary Education which sat recently recommended that planters should be held responsible for the instruction of the children of their Tamil coolies. Managers of mills and factories in Upper India have never yet had their attention specially directed to this matter, and it is quite time that a beginning were made.

What Mr. Fremantle says about managers in Upper India applies equally to managers all over the country. Sir, it is true that on the Bombay side some of the mills have made attempts to provide educational facilities for the children employed in those mills; but the last Commission has come to the conclusion that these facilities were not efficiently provided, and very often they were only a thin disguise for keeping the children on the premises in order that they might be worked more than half time.

One essential condition, therefore in connection with any educational facilities offered is that there must be efficient supervision and that supervision must be provided by the Education Department or whatever body it is that inspects and supervises local schools. But I think, Sir, the first thing to do in this matter is to throw a definite responsibility on factory-owners. It is not an unfair thing to expect, as I have pointed out, that the factory owners, who make money out of the children, should hold themselves responsible for the education of those children. Of course, it is only fair that the Government and the local bodies should come to the assistance of the factory owners; the cost may be divided among the three bodies-the factory-owners, the local body concerned and the Government in such proportions as may appear to be most equitable; but somebody must first be made responsible for the education of these children, and I think it should be the factory-owners. Even though there is no general compulsory law in India, it is necessary that there should be special provision for factory children for the simple reason that these children are disabled from availing themselves of the ordinary facilities that exist. I therefore trust that the amendment which I have moved will be accepted by this Council.

Mr. Gokhale replying on the debate which ensued spoke as follows:

> Sir, I quite understand the position of the Government and I really did not expect that the Government would do more than urge on the Local Governments the necessity of looking into this matter and doing what they could to secure reasonable facilities for the education

of children employed in factories. Sir, the whole question has to be considered from a higher standpoint than that which has been taken by some of the speakers who have criticised my proposals. My Hon'ble friend Mr. Dadabhoy expresses the fear-and I am surprised to see that the Hon'ble Mr. Clark concurs in that-that if educational facilities are provided for children employed in the factories, the evil of children being overworked will be facilitated. As a matter of fact, I think, if that is done, the evil will be reduced, because children will be definitely engaged in school, instead of merely loitering about, doing nothing. Of course, I insist on the essential condition that there should be efficient supervision; and if efficient supervision is provided, there would be no risk whatever. It is when there is no school, and the children are asked to remain on the premises or close by the factories, that unscrupulous managers would find it easy to get them to work for longer hours than the law allows, under one pretence or another.

As regards the Bill, to which Mr. Dadabhoy has made reference, let me point out that the Bill has not yet become law and it will have to encounter such opposition as my Hon'ble friend offered to some of the provisions the other day, before it becomes law; and until it becomes law, it is no use speaking of it as if it was law.

Moreover, even if my Bill passes, its application will depend upon the discretion of local bodies, whereas if this amendment is accepted automatically wherever there is a factory population of children, schools will come into existence. Again, my Bill provides only for children between the ages of 6 and 10, whereas this amendment urges that facilities should be provided for the education of children up to 12. At present children from 9 upwards can be employed in factories; if my Bill becomes law, the age limit of employment will be raised by one year, as was proposed this morning by my Hon'ble friend Mr. Quin. The Hon'ble Mr. Madge spoke of the corpse of my Bill being resurrected in this amendment. The expression used by him suggests a hope on his part that my

Bill is dead. Well, we shall see about that. Sir, my object in bringing forward this amendment was to emphasize the necessity of the Government attending to this matter, and to present to the Council the view which I have submitted. That object has been attained by this discussion, and as the Government are unable to accept my amendment, I do not wish to press it.

Mr. Gokhale delivered at the Pretoria Town Hall on the 15th November 1912 the following speech :

> Mr. Chairman, Ladies and Gentlemen—I feel, I need hardly assure you, greatly honoured by the presence of you all here this evening, and I beg leave to tender at the outset my grateful and sincere thanks to you for your kindness. This is my last public utterance in South Africa, and while my thoughts are necessarily tinged with a certain degree of regret at the prospect of so soon leaving the country where I have received so much kindness and spent such a pleasant time, I cannot disguise from you the fact that I contemplate the approaching termination of my tour with a great sense of relief. Ladies and gentlemen, I doubt if 'Many people in South Africa realised how difficult was the position in which I found myself when I arrived at Capetown last month. I had come to this country with the avowed object of studying at first-hand an admittedly difficult and delicate problem—a problem which has two sides to it, and which has aroused no small feeling on both sides. And yet, 11 was compelled by the exigencies of the situation to speak publicly on matters connected more or less with the problem from the day of my arrival. But the apprehension was never absent from my mind that if, by chance, owing to any over-enthusiastic act on the part of my countrymen, who greeted me everywhere in kindly demonstration, or owing to some thoughtless act or word of ay own, an unfortunate impression was created or any feelings were inflamed which it was my earnest desire to allay and not to aggravate, I should really be injuring the cause

which I had come here to serve. All through my tour I have been weighed down with this thought; and, now that my visit is drawing to its close, I feel a great sense of relief and I thank God that no untoward incident has happened to mar the smooth progress of events. And, judging from newspaper comments, as also from private conversations I am emboldened to hope that, even it no actual good has resulted from my visit, it has, at any rate, done on harm. Ladies and gentlemen, on this, the last occasion, when I speak to the people of this country, I would like once again to tender my warm and heartfelt thanks to all who have been so kind to me. To my own countrymen, resident in South Africa, who have lavished such a wealth of affection on me wherever I have been, I have no words in which to express my gratitude, and I would only say that it is my fervent prayer that, in any difficulties they may have to face in the future, I may be privileged to be of some little assistance to them. To the members of the European community who have gone out of their way to show such great kindness to me, I tender my warmest thanks, and I tender them from the bottom of my heart. I will not abuse their generosity by interpreting it as indicating necessarily any approval of, or even sympathy with, my mission, and that only adds to the sense of obligation under which I lie to them.

Finally, I would like to repeat my respectful acknowledgments to the Union Government for the great courtesy and consideration with which they have treated me and for the generous hospitality which they have extended to me. Their attitude towards me has largely facilitated my work, and it has enabled me to meet many men of distinction in this land whom otherwise it might not have been easy for me to meet.

This morning, three Ministers General Botha, General Smutts, and Mr. Fischer-did me the honour to grant an interview, in the course of which I had an opportunity to discuss the whole

Indian problem in the sub-continent with them. We had a full, frank, and free interchange of views. I hope the Ministers saw clearly that there was no disposition on the Indian side to underrate the difficulties of their position. On the other hand, I would like to take this opportunity to express publicly my deep appreciation of the manner in which they approached the question and the sincere desire they evidenced to arrive at a just and reasonable settlement. And now, ladies and gentlemen, I think I may say a word or two on the question itself before I close. There is no doubt that there is a great deal of feeling on the question on both sides, and this makes a dispassionate examination of the matter even more difficult than it would otherwise be.

I have said, and I say it again, that, in the conclusions at which I have arrived, I have tried to keep in view the fact that the interests of both sides, must, in some way or other, be reconciled. The fundamental question is how there shall be secured just and equitable treatment for those Indians who are here now, and their number is about 150,000. Whilst here, I have heard it urged that a settlement may be found by sending these people back to India. It may be a solution of one aspect of the problem, but, assuming that it is a desirable solution, which, I think, it is not, it is, for financial and other reasons, absolutely impracticable. These 150,000 people are here, they cannot be repatriated, they must therefore remain here and they must become, more and more, an integral and a permanent part of the general population of this sub-continent. The most important question, then, is to what just and equitable treatment these people are entitled, and how such treatment may best be secured. Now one thing is quite clear, that, if a solution of this problem is to have any permanence and finality, it has to be such as will be acceptable to the European community, who are, after all, the dominant people of this country. And so long as there exists in the European mind the fear of a continued influx of Indians, there cannot be that frame of mind on its part, which would allow of any settlement being a success. The European community must therefore receive, and the Indian community must be prepared to give, the necessary assurances to remove the fear on this point.

Again there must be no room for a reasonable apprehension in the mind of the Europeans that the presence of the Indians in this land would lower the character of the political institutions under which they desire to live. I fully recognise that South Africa must be governed along the lines of Western political institutions and by men who understand the spirit of these institutions, and the European community are entitled to an assurance that this shall remain so. These assurances, however, being given-outside these questions of immigration and franchise-the aim of the Government should be to make the Indians feel that they are living under equal laws, and that these laws are administered towards them with no undue harshness, but the same as towards the other people of the country. At present, the Indians throughout South Africa feel, and justly feel, that even outside the two questions I have mentioned, they are subjected to harsh legislation specially directed against them, and, further, the administration of that legislation is, if any thing, even harsher in spirit. To take only the more important grievances, the Immigration Law is being now worked in such a rigorous manner as to cause the Indian community most serious hardships. In Cape Colony, for instance, there is the system of permits under which an Indian who may have settled in the Colony is permitted to be absent from the country for a stated period, generally one year. Only the other day an Indian trader who had gone to India on a year's permit, leaving his wife and children and his business behind, returned to the Colony, but he was prevented from landing because he had exceeded the period of absence by one day. This was owning to no fault of his, for if the steamer by which he came had run according to scheduled time, he would have arrived three days before the expiry of the permit, but it was held up on the way by a storm for four days, and this led to his arriving a day late. And yet because of this accident he has been forced to go back to India, and his business has been ruined, and his wife and children have now to follow him. The same thing is happening in Natal in connection with domicile certificates. The holders are cross-examined about their whole, life and movements in this country during long periods-sometimes as long as fifteen years-and even small discrepancies between the answers given and the facts already recorded are held to justify discrediting the certificates, and the holders are sent back to India. Now all this is grievously unjust, and I am sure only public attention has to be pointedly drawn to it to secure its stoppage, for I cannot believe that there is any desire on the part of the European community of this country to harass the Indians in this unnecessary manner. There are several other complaints to be heard everywhere about the working of the Immigration Law, but I will not go into them now.

I sincerely trust that with the removal of the fear of a continued influx of Indians into this country, the Immigration Law will be administered in a far more considerate and sympathetic spirit, and all the present soreness of feeling of the Indian community in regard to it, and all sense of insecurity produced by it, will be removed. Next there is the question of trading licenses. This appears to be in some respects the most difficult problem of all. The Europeans feel that they are gradually being crowded out by the Indians, that the Indians undersell them, and that important branches of trade are likely to fall entirely into, Indian hands. That is the European viewpoint. On the other hand, the Indians feel that their freedom is being unjustly interfered with, that all outlets are being steadily closed to them, and that gross injustice is being done to them. Now while I do not seek to minimise in any degree the argument on the European side, I must frankly say that I have always felt that the traders who are injured, if at all, by the competition of the Indians, are a very small part of the community, and that, if the argument be that the Indians sell cheaper, it must surely be to the general advantage of the community, whose interest it is to buy cheaper. But that apart, what reason can be given for the refusal to transfer a trading license from one man to another or to allow him to take his own son into partnership, as was the case only a day or two ago in Ladysmith? This is certainly neither fair nor equitable treatment, and anyone can see that its sole Object is to extinguish Indian trade, as opportunities arise.

This is absolutely unjustifiably. Moreover, what is to be the fate of those who are born here, under this policy? The matter of the control of trading licenses, in at least two Provinces of the Union, is in the hands of the local authorities and there is no right of appeal except as to renewal of licences in Natal, or on grounds of procedure, to a judicial tribunal, so that flagrant injustices are constantly perpetrated and go unremedied. That right of appeal against the interested decisions of their trade competitors must be given to Indians if anything like justice is to be done to them. I quite recognise that direct interference by the Government is impracticable, with the law as it stands, but the restraining influence of the Government may be exerted in many directions and I earnestly trust that it will be used to bring about a feeling of security in the mind of the Indian trader and remove a grievous sense of injustice and wrong. The question of the education of Indian children born in South Africa is also one about which the community has a great grievance at the present time. Very little provision for that education is made, and yet these children, when they grow up, must be absorbed into the general population to whose material and moral well-being they will be expected to contribute. Provision should therefore be made, not only for elementary, but also for the higher and for the technical education of these children. Instruction should also be given in the Indian vernaculars in school hours.

I should like the European public to lay emphasis upon this requirement, for, so long as such instruction is not given, it is a legitimate excuse for the Indian community to ask for the admission of clerks and others so instructed, for the proper keeping of their books, which are at present kept in their vernaculars, as it is impossible at present for their own children to become proficient in the Indian vernaculars in this country. These are the most important general grievances of which the Indian community has good reason to complain at present. Beyond these there are a number of specific disabilities imposed upon the Indian residents of the different Provinces, such as Law of 1885 in the Transvaal or the Gold Law and the Townships Act of 1908, which prevents Indians from residing or trading except in locations in all so-called gold areas. But I do not propose tonight to deal with them. To one such only I wish to make particular reference, and that is the 0 tax, imposed in Natal upon all ex-indentured Indians and their descendants, men and women, boys above sixteen years, and even girls above thirteen years being included, who do not return to India after the expiry of their indentures and who do not desire to re-indenture. I make bold to say that it is difficult to imagine a more harsh and unjust impost, bringing, as it does, untold misery upon those who required to pay it.

Whatever its justification may have been at a time when there was a genuine fear of the country being overrun with indentured Indians, who were being brought here in the interests of a section of the European population itself, there is no doubt that, since the stoppage of indentured recruitment in India, there no longer remains even that shadow of justification for the imposition of this tax. I discussed this subject with a large number of persons in Natal, and I did not find a single individual to justify or support it. And it was a pleasure to me to find that even those who had, two years ago, strongly upheld the impost, are now agreed that it should be abolished altogether. I may state that strong representations in this matter were made by me to the Government today, and I have every reason to believe that the matter will receive the early and sympathetic attention of the Ministers. Ladies and gentlemen, it is impossible on an occasion like this to do more than indicate in general outline the more serious and pressing of the Indian grievances in this country. And you will not understand me, in what I have mentioned, to have exhausted the whole list. Neither have I touched on that part of our disabilities which though acutely felt in the daily life of the community, cannot be put right by any direct action of the Government—I mean the social disabilities. I must say that I am astonished at the strength and intensity of the colour Prejudice that exists in this land. I had heard a good deal about it before my arrival, and I was prepared for a certain measure of it. But not till I actually was in this country did I realise the full force with which it operates nor the extent to which it prevails. However, the only hope of a remedy in such matters is in the steady improvement of the general situation and the gradual education of the heart. Meanwhile it is wise to take note of the existence of this prejudice in any solution of present difficulties that may be thought of or attempted. And now, ladies and gentlemen, I would like to say a word publicly to the Government of this country. The difficulties of its position are great and undoubted.

The delicate relations between the two European races, the special problems connected with the future of the vast native population, the powerful colour prejudice, the widespread apprehension among a section of the white population that their material interests are seriously threatened by Indian competition-all these make the position of the Government one of exceptional difficulty. And though its duty to secure the fullest justice to the resident Indian community is clear, I freely recognise that the strongest Government that may be conceived of will not be strong enough to redress all Indian grievances at once, and would be hurled from power, if it attempted to do so. I feel it is incumbent on the Indian community to realise this fully and not pitch its expectation too high-to exercise patience and self-restraint as far as possible, in order to facilitate the task of the Government, for any impatient or vehement insistence on immediate relief being granted, where the Government itself is not in a position to grant it without a considerable change in public opinion, can only retard, and not hasten, remedial action. But, while admitting all this, I feel strongly that the face of the Government must be set all through in the right direction, and the progress, slow as it may be, must be steady and continuous towards full justice to the Indian population. It is one of the primary duties of every Government to ensure justice to all who are living under its protection and the Government of South Africa owes this duty to the Indian population as much as to any other section of the community.

And the fact that the Indians have no votes only emphasises this duty still further. The Indians resident in South Africa are part and parcel of the general population, and their welfare must be an object of serious solicitude to the Government, unless the idea is to hold them down permanently as a depressed community, which I cannot believe. Those who form the Government may be dependent on the votes of the European population for their position. But once they assume the functions of Government, they make themselves responsible for even-handed justice to all, and to those who are least able to protect themselves from oppression and injustice they are bound to give their protection most. My final word tonight will be one of appeal to what I would call the better mind of the two communities, European and Indian. To the European community I would respectfully say-you have all the power and yours, therefore, is the responsibility for the manner in which the affairs of this land are, administered. You cannot believe in your heart of hearts that whatever temporary advantages may be gained by those who have power from a policy based on obvious injustice, selfishness, or unreasoning prejudice, such advantages can long endure. You owe it to your good name, you owe it to your civilisation, you owe it to the Empire of which you are part, and whose flag stands for justice and freedom and opportunities for progress for all who live under its protection, that your administration should be such that you can justify it in the eyes of the civilised world. That you have votes, and the Indians have not, only throws a double responsibility on you-the responsibility for actively promoting their prosperity and well-being as well as yours. The affairs of this country must no doubt be administered in accordance with European standards and by men who understand the spirit and working of European institutions, but the Government must exist for promoting the prosperity not of the European community only, but of all its subjects; else it is a travesty of Government to them.

To my own countrymen resident in this land, my parting appeal is-always remember that Your future is largely in your own hands. You have by no means an easy Position here, and it is not impossible that it may grow even worse. But, whatever happens, do not lose faith or give way to despair. I pray to God that such a struggle as you found it necessary to wage in the Transvaal during the last three years may not have to be waged again. But if it has to be resumed, or if you have to enter struggles of a like nature for justice denied or injustice forced on you, remember that the issue will largely turn on the character you show, on your capacity for combined action, on your readiness to suffer and sacrifice in a just cause. India will no doubt be behind you. Such assistance as she can give shall freely come to you. Her passionate sympathy, her heart, her hopes will be with you. Nay, all that is best in this Empire, all that is best in the civilised world, will wish you success. But the main endeavour to have your wrongs righted shall have to be yours. Remember that you are entitled to have the Indian problem in this country solved on right lines. And in such right solution are involved not merely your present worldly interests, but your dignity and self-respect, the honour and good name of your Motherland, and the entire moral and material well-being of your children's children. Ladies and gentlemen, I will now bring my remarks to a close. I thank you for the kind and indulgent manner in which you have listened to me. And to all of you I say good-bye and farewell.

8

Gokhale and Religious Issues

The hopes and aspiration of Gokhale was to be belied by events; in July 1906, he could have hardly foreseen the chain of events which was to culminate in the formation of the All-India Muslim League before the end of the year. His own freedom from religious passion and prejudice made it easier for him to get on with Muslim politicians, but it also somewhat disabled him from anticipating their moves. Schooled in the politics of Ranade, he was wholly free from regional and religious parochialism: 'I am neither a Hindu, nor a Muslim' was how Ranade described himself in his presidential address to the All India Social Conference at Lucknow in 1899. Gokhale never diverged from the catholic line of his master. 'The India of the future', he affirmed, it could not now be only a Hindu India or a Muhammedan India; it must be compounded of all the elements which existed in IndiaHindu, Muhammedan, Parsee, Christian, aye, and the Englishman who adopted India as his country. Some of Gokhale's best friends were to be found among the Parsis and Gujaratis of Bombay. In Poona, his home town, where religious passions occasionally rose high, Gokhale's influence was invariably cast on the side of restraint. This had brought him, and other adherents of Ranade much odium. In the early 1890s when Poona and parts of Maharashtra were in the grip of Hindu-Muslim tension and disturbances, Gokhale had tried to pour oil on troubled waters. As a member of the Bombay Legislative Council and later of the Imperial Council, he had made it a point to champion national rather than sectarian interests. 'Your ideals are and must be', the Aga Khan wrote to Gokhale, 'the ideals of every Indian who is honest and thoughtful.... 13 The promotion of 'cordial goodwill and cooperation among the different communities' was embodied in the constitution of the Servants of India Society which Gokhale had personally drafted. Every 'Servant of India' was required to 'regard all Indians as brothers' and to 'work for the advancement of all, without distinction of caste or creed'. There are few references to the Hindu-Muslim problem in Gokhale's early writings and speeches, because the problem was not in the forefront of Indian politics at the turn of the century.

After the initial confrontation between Sir Syed Ahmed and the founding fathers of the Congress, the educated section of the two communities learnt to move in their own separate grooves. Their paths did not really cross until after the partition of Bengal. The partition may not have been deliberately conceived by Curzon as a measure for playing off the two communities against each other, but after the launching of the massive agitation for the reversal of the partition, high British officials, especially in the newly created province of East Bengal and Assam, headed by Sir Bampfylde Fuller, increasingly sought Muslim support to offset a political pressure which was predominantly Hindu. Sir Bampfylde's quip about the Muslim community being his 'favourite wife' could be laughed away. But in his Studies of Indian Life and Sentiments published in 1910, he frankly explained why he looked upon Muslims as the natural allies of the British Raj. 'By their religion and political ideas, they [Indian Muslims] are less disposed than the Hindus to dissent from the assumptions which lie at the root of Imperial authority.' Within the Congress. An open clash between the Moderates and the Extremists was stayed off at Calcutta in December 1906, but in the succeeding year the two factions were again Poised for a head-on collision. Gokhale's tour of northern India at the beginning of 1907 was part of the Moderate offensive to rally the educated classes to the Congress.

This tour was remarkable for the response he was able to evoke from the Muslim community, particularly among its youth. Muslims turned up in large numbers to attend his meetings at Lucknow, Aligarh, Meerut, Lahore and other places.

At Lucknow he was entertained to breakfast by twenty Muslim leaders including Nawab Mohsin-ul-Mulk, the prime mover of the Simla deputation. The Raja of Mahmudabad the most important Muslim landowner in the province, gave a dinner in Gokhale's honour, and Syed Nabiullah, a leading barrister and a member of the Simla deputation, took the chair at the public meeting addressed by Gokhale at Lucknow. At Aligarh, a thunderous welcome awaited him; the students unhorsed his carriage and pulled it through the streets to the College Hall amidst shouts of 'Gokhale Zindabad' (Long Live Gokhale). Gokhale seems to have been deeply moved by the warmth of the reception. Dr Syed Mahmud, then a student at Aligarh, later recalled that Gokhale turned to Mohamed Ali, the future Khilafat leader, who had taken him to Aligarh, and said: 'I shall now die a happy man. When I see young Musalmans with so much enthusiasm for me and for India, little doubt remains in my heart that India will get freedom soon.' Perhaps the highest compliment from the Muslim community came to Gokhale at Lahore, when he was invited by the Muslim League to deliver a lecture on Hindu-Muslim relations. There was no problem, Gokhale declared, which was more important for the future of India, and none that required greater tact, forbearance and judgement for its solution than that of Hindu-Muslim relations. 'I now propose to examine this question', he went on, 'in a spirit entirely free from prejudice and passion and I trust that you will follow me in the same spirit.' He admitted that the relations between the two communities were 'most unsatisfactory'. In a brief historical survey he recalled the coming of Islam to India, the confrontation between Hinduism and Islam, the proselytizing zeal of early Muslim invaders, the emergence of an Indo-Muslim polity, the rise and decline of the Mughal Empire, the challenge from the Rajputs, the Marathas and the Sikhs and, finally, the British conquest. 'The British came', said Gokhale, 'at a time when the Muslims were sullen and the Hindus uncertain, and the antagonism between the two communities was in evidence here, there and everywhere, and in its worst form.' That tradition of antagonism had survived; it often lay dormant in wide areas of the country, but could at the smallest provocation become active again. Gokhale described the basic equation between the two communities. The Muslims were in a minority in all provinces except in the Punjab, and in the newly created province of East Bengal and Assam. They had lagged behind in education: only three per cent of the Muslim population could read and write in the vernacular as against five per cent of the Hindus. In higher education, the Hindus were even better off: one in 300 Hindus knew English as against one in 600 Muslims.

All the advantages, however, were not with the Hindus. The Muslims were less burdened with the divisions and subdivisions of caste and sect. Sixty million Muslims could indeed be more effective in practice than two hundred million Hindus. Gokhale had, however, no doubt that the two communities could pull together. They had not only common interests, but suffered from common disabilities. The Arms Act in British India applied equally to Muslims and Hindus. The Muslims in South Africa were not spared- the indignities heaped upon the Hindus. He urged the Hindus to realize their special responsibilities for improving the relations between the two communities. They had the advantage of numbers, education, and wealth; it was their duty to understand the genuine fears of the Muslim minority, and to treat it with tact and forbearance. The whole atmosphere could be transformed if only a few Hindus voluntarily devoted themselves to the service of the Muslim community. The Muslims on their part had to realize that the struggle of the Indian people for their rights was 'not a religious but a national struggle'; the political set-up of the future would be on national, not on religious lines.

Muslims could sympathize with the Pan-Islamic movement, but they must remember that the national ideal was spreading all over the world, that the 'Young Turks' were all for Turkey, the Egyptians for Egypt and the Persians for Persia. It did not speak well for the Muslims that they should have left the fight for India's rights to the Hindus. 'The Mahomedans of India', said Gokhale, 'must also accept India as their country and it is then that they will be able to realize their highest ideal.' 'Certain forces' were trying to keep the two communities apart. 'Some of you', he warned his predominantly Muslim audience, 'may like to side with the officials, many of whom will like to have you on their side, but you should remember that men [the British] who love patriotism and liberty cannot but despise you. There may be small favours, but when a certain limit is reached, you too will not be allowed to go further.' Gokhale had spoken candidly, but he had spoken from the heart. The spontaneity and warmth of the Muslim response delighted him as much as it surprised and disturbed the authorities. Only four months earlier, Harcourt Butler, the Commissioner of Lucknow, had testified to the bitter anti-Hindu feeling among the Muslim politicians of northern India. In February-March 1907 they seemed to be vying with each other in admiring and entertaining Gokhale. Butler and his friends were assailed by fresh doubts and fears. Would Muslim youth slide down the slippery road of political extremism? Was the Muslim middle-class about to make common cause with the Hindus? Was it possible that the antagonism between the two communities would be overlaid by a common hatred of the British Government? Soon after Gokhale's visit to Meerut, the Hindus opened a refreshment room for Muslims during 'Moharram', and the Muslims reciprocated by serving refreshments to the Hindus during the 'Holi' festival. 'This augurs well for future', wrote a correspondent to Gokhale, 'and is entirely due to your recent visit.' Gokhale's tour did not prove to be a magic wand. Indeed, even while he was making his triumphal progress in the United Provinces and the Punjab, events in East Bengal had moved to a tragic climax. As we have already seen, the partition of Bengal had ranged the Hindus and Muslims in that province on opposite sides.

Though as late as November 1906, Surendranath Banerjee was assuring Gokhale that he could get up a memorial against the partition exclusively signed by Muslims, the fact was that the

Muslims of East Bengal, especially those belonging to the landowning and professional classes, quickly acquired a vested interest in the administration of the new province. British officials in Dacca, and in the districts of East Bengal, harassed by the anti-partition agitation, were not averse to playing upon the natural antagonism of the Muslim peasantry to Hindu landlords and upon the jealousy of Muslim lawyers and landlords towards their Hindu rivals. Ambitious politicians like the Nawab of Dacca saw new vistas of power and patronage open before them. The virtual dismissal of Sir Bampfylde Fuller came as a blow both to Muslim politicians and British officials, and brought them even closer. Early in 1907 Gokhale received disquieting reports from East Bengal. He had sent V. S. Srinivasa Sastri (who had recently joined the Servants of India Society) to tour East Bengal and study the conditions there. Sastri reported that, except for the Muslim weavers (Jolas) and a few educated young men, the bulk of the Muslim community was opposed to the swadeshi movement. 'I find it hard to believe, but it seems to be the truth', Sastri told Gokhale, 'that such thorough opposition to the country's cause is the work of a band of Maulvies paid by the Nawab of Dacca and helped by the police.'

There was no doubt of the British officials' partiality towards the Muslim community in East Bengal. Indeed, accusations of official connivance at Muslim rowdyism against the Hindus were made not only in the Hindu press, but before Dunlop-Smith, the private secretary to the Viceroy, by an influential deputation consisting of the Maharaja of Darbhanga, Surendranath Banerjee, A. Chaudhury, Narendra Nath Sen, Nawab Syed Amir Husain and Sayid Shams-ul-Huda, who requested the government to wean away local officials from their blatant partisanship and policy of playing off Muslims against Hindus. Conditions in East Bengal did not, however, improve. In May 1907 Gokhale spent a fortnight in Calcutta to personally assess the situation. On his return to Poona, he summed up his impressions in a letter to Wedderburn. Gokhale to Wedderburn, 20 May 1907: 1 think the responsibility for the unhappy disturbances in East Bengal lies with all the three parties the Hindus, the Mohammedans and the officials-though necessarily in varying degrees. The anti-Partition agitation which is confined mostly to the Hindus is naturally resented by the officials who are still smarting under a sense of humiliation in connection with Sir B. Fuller's resignation.

The wild talk in which some of the more irresponsible speakers on the Hindu side have been indulging on the subject of Independence, or Swarajya without British control as they call it, is also naturally setting the officials against the Hindu community.... There is also no doubt that the officials have allowed the impression to spread (and have even openly encouraged it) that the Hindus were in their bad books and that the Mohammedan community was the special object of their favour and patronage. There is also no doubt that when the present disturbances first began, there was a marked tendency to wink at Muslim rowdyism and leave the Hindus more or less to their fate.... A number of Muslim rowdies have been preaching for some time a holy war against the Hindus, not on account of the boycott, but on religious grounds. The red pamphlet which I have seen myself and which is of a most inflammatory character has been circulated, broadcast throughout the province and in this pamphlet, the Mohammedans are called upon to rise and destroy the Hindus, so that the glory of Islam be once more re-established. I mention these things not to urge anything against the Musalmans, because these charges and counter-charges between the two communities are harmful to the real interests of both, and the quarrel is deeply painful and humiliating to those whose hopes for the future of the community lie in the two communities working together.... I do not wish even now to blame them [the Muslims of East Bengal] for they are ignorant and fanatical and know no better, but I want you to see clearly the unfairness of the Government... the whole affair has been most unfortunate and it has put the clock of progress back by several years.

9

GOKHALE : THE GREAT SUPPORTER OF INDIA

Lord Minto did not have Curzon's dominating personality, intellectual stamina and demoniac energy, but he was also free from his predecessor's flamboyance, conceit and irascibility.

Soon after his arrival in India, the new Viceroy stumbled upon the key to popularity which had eluded Curzon for six years. 'It takes a very short time in this country', Minto wrote, 'to realize how much may be done by a sympathetic appreciation of existing conditions." He noted how 'the excitable and impressionable leaders of India are curiously amenable to personal influence'. A year later, Motilal Ghose of the Amrita Bazar Patrika, a caustic critic of Curzon and official policies, was assuring Dunlop-Smith, the Viceroy's private secretary, that 'it would take two Curzons in succession to disturb the calm Lord Minto had brought'. Minto seems to have tried his charm on Gokḥale. Their meeting on 30 January 1906 went off very well. 'I had a long and most cordial interview yesterday with the Viceroy', Gokhale confided to Krishnaswami Aiyer. 'He had sent for me himself and asked my opinion about several important matters, including the Partition and expressed himself in very flattering terms about my Congress [presidential] address. A few days later, Gokhale used his influence in the viceregal camp to intercede on behalf of his friend Samuel Ratcliffe, the editor of the Statesman, who had got into trouble with the Home Department of the Government of India for publishing one of Curzon's minutes on the partition of Bengal. Enraged by this breach of the of ficial Secrets Act, the Home Department had barred the Statesman from government advertisements and other privileges.

Gokhale spoke to Dunlop-Smith, who helped in arranging an interview between Samuel Ratcliffe and Arundel, the Home Member. A compromise was reached, the Statesman published an apology and the government withdrew the ban. Gokhale's first impressions of Minto as a cool and sympathetic ruler were confirmed during the winter session of the Imperial Legislative Council. Aware that 'no Viceroy of recent times has had to succeed to a greater legacy of difficulties than Lord Minto', Gokhale was anxious not to embarrass him.

In his budget speech on 28 March, he concentrated on economic rather than political issues. He outlined a comprehensive scheme of state action for improving the condition of the masses: the reduction in the salt duty and land revenue at least in the famine-stricken areas, the amortization of rural debts, the provision of funds for local bodies, particularly for rural water supply and drainage, the extension of primary education and the establishment of a technological institute. The additional funds for this programme were to be found partly by financing railway construction through loans rather than through taxation, and partly by scrapping the costly military reorganization scheme prepared by the Commander-in-Chief, Lord Kitchener, before the Japanese victory over Russia altered the balance of power in Asia.

'The power of Russia has been broken', Gokhale argued. 'Her prestige in Asia is gone. She has on her hands troubles more than enough of her own to think of troubling others for years to come: and thus a cloud that was thought to hang for twenty years and more over our north-western frontier has passed away." Gokhale cited the example of Japan to expose the 'un-national character of the Indian army'. With an expenditure of 37 million yen, or a little under six crores of rupees, Japan had a standing army of 167,000 men with reserves which could be raised to 600,000 men. 'We spend', Gokhale reminded the Imperial Council, 'six times as much money a year and yet in return for it we have only an inexpensive force of about 230,000 men with about 25,000 Native reservists and about 30,000 European volunteers!' Indians were barred from the officers' cadre. The exclusion of the people of India, from all honourable Participation in the defence of their own country· was, said Gokhale, 'a cruel wrong to a whole peopleone-fifth of the entire population of the world'. In a telling comparison with Japan, Gokhale pointed out that though the Japanese people had come under the influence of western ideas only forty years before, they had, under the fostering care of their own government, taken their place by the side of the proudest nations of the West. Indians had been under English rule much longer, and yet continued 'to be mere hewers of wood and drawers of water in our own country and, of course, we have no position anywhere else'. 'What the country needs at this moment above everything else', Gokhale told the Imperial Legislative Council, is a government, national in spirit, even though it may be foreign in personnel—a government that will enable us to feel that our interests are the first consideration with it, and our wishes and opinions are to it a matter of some account." Gokhale concluded: 'My Lord, I have ventured to make these observations because the present situation fills me with great anxiety. I can only raise my humble voice by way of warning, by way of appeal. The rest lies on the knees of the gods.' Gokhale's speech had ended on an ardent note. It included a trenchant criticism of the government, but it did not refer to the controversial issues of the partition of Bengal and the boycott. This studied restraint could not have passed unnoticed by Minto, who presided over the deliberations of the Imperial Council.

The Viceroy and his Finance Member, E. N. Baker, seemed to have made an earnest effort to win over Gokhale, who returned to Poona from the winter session of the Imperial Council with high hopes. Gokhale to G. A. Natesan, 2 April 1905: You will be glad to know that my budget speech this year was extremely well received in the Council. The Viceroy specially sent for me at the conclusion of the proceedings and congratulated me in very flattering terms. He further assured me that it would be his ambition to advance to some extent at any rate, to work on the lines indicated by me during his regime. Mr Baker [Finance Member], with whom I had a long interview at his special request the next day, assured me that he would provide funds in next year's budget for making a beginning in the direction of free Primary Education. He said very kind things, which I need not repeat here, but you will judge how friendly he is when I tell you that he made an earnest appeal to me not to retire from the [Imperial Legislative] Council next year, as he knows it is my intention to do. He said, 'Give me two to three years and I will make a beginning in regard to most of the things you are advocating, only you must be in the Council to back me up by your criticism and your demands.' He explained to me confidentially his difficulties, but with the retirement of two of his senior colleagues, his voice will prevail more and more on the Executive Council and you may rest assured that that voice will be raised wholly in our interest.... Altogether, I feel the situation is most hopeful and I have never returned from Calcutta with such a sense of satisfaction within me as this year. Now that the Government of India have themselves taken up the question of a further reform of Legislative Council, my hands will be immensely strenghthened in pressing the question forward during my forthcoming visit to England. Gokhale was in a buoyant mood when he sailed for England from Bombay in the S.S. Egypt on 14 April. This was his fifth sea voyage, but the first which he. really enjoyed. In 1897, the thought of the ordeal awaiting him before the Welby Commission had weighed on him; the return voyage had been clouded by the 'apology incident'. In 1905, the breeze with Pherozeshah Mehta, the aftermath of the partition of Bengal and the critical responsibility of having to preside over the Benares Congress had kept his nerves on edge. In the spring of 1906 he was happily free from such anxieties, and cheerfully looked forward to being in England. He wrote from Aden on 18 April: I am enjoying the voyage immensely. The sea so far has been calm and there is a beautiful breeze all day long on the deck.... I spend my time mostly in walking and reading, with a little conversation with fellowpassengers by way of variation.... The Aga Khan is also with us and I am delighted to find that he is coming over to our way of thinking in politics more and more.", The Aga Khan expressed his happiness at the formation of the Servants of India Society, offered to contribute Rs. 5000 to its funds, and invited Gokhale to stay with him in Switzerland for a month to improve his health. As we shall see later, the Aga Khan's cordiality was not as disinterested as it seemed at the time; these conversations on the S.S. Egypt were exploited to embarrass Gokhale's mission in England. On the evening of 30 April Gokhale reached London. The train was two hours late, but about fifty Indians, headed by Dadabhai Naoroji, were waiting at Victoria station to receive him. On 1 May he met the British Committee of the Indian National Congress. The next day he called on J. E. Ellis, the Under-Secretary of State for India.

On 3 May he addressed about fifty M.P.s at a meeting of the Indian Parliamentary Committee. Two days later he was Wedderburn's guest at Gloucester where he spoke on temperance. He returned to London to address the Indian Parliamentary Committee and a meeting convened to protest against the 'Barisal Incident' in East Bengal. He visited Cambridge and Oxford, attended a peace conference at Birmingham, and addressed the East India Association. The paper that Gokhale read before the East India Association on 11 July 1906 was one of the clearest and most forthright expositions of the Indian case for self-government which he had ever attempted. It was sporting of the East India Association-comprising predominantly former governors, judges, generals, bankers and planters to invite him to speak. The consciousness of an unsympathetic or even hostile audience seems to have put Gokhale on his mettle. He asserted that the faith of the people of India in the character and ideals of British rule had been shaken, and its place was being taken by 'a conviction that, however great England may be, she is not great enough to forgo voluntarily the gains of power from considerations of mere justice or national honour'. He admitted that the English educated class in India numbered merely a million in a population of three hundred millions. There was, however, no greater mistake than to imagine that 'the influence of this class was proportionate only to its numbers'. The members of this class 'constituted the brain of the community'; they did the thinking not only for themselves, but also for their ignorant brethren. They controlled the Indian language press, which shaped the thoughts and swayed the feelings, not only of the fifteen million literates in vernaculars whom it reached directly, but also of many more who were indirectly under its influence. It was possible, argued Gokhale, that 'bureaucracies like the Bourbons' never learnt, but it should not be difficult for Englishmen to realize that you cannot have institutions like the universities working for more than half a century in India, and then expect to be able to govern the people, as though they were still strangers to ideas of constitutional freedom or to the dignity of national aspirations. Those who blindly uphold the existing system, and resist all attempts, however cautious and moderate, to broaden its base, prefer practically to sacrifice the future to the present.

The goal which the educated classes of India have in view is a position for their country in the Empire worthy of the self-respect of civilized people. They want their country to be a prosperous, self-governing, integral part of the Empire, and not a mere poverty-stricken, bureaucratically-held possession of that Empire. The system under which India is governed at present is an unnatural system, and however one may put up with it as a temporary evil, as a permanent arrangement it is impossible.... Gokhale conceded that since self-government for India had to be on western lines, the steps by which the goal was to be reached would be slow. But there was all the difference between cautious progress and no progress at all.

The bureaucracy which stood in the way of all reasonable instalments of reform was 'undermining its own position by such a short-sighted and suicidal policy'. It had been argued by British officials that India would have to wait till the mass of the people had been qualified by education to take an intelligent part in public affairs. But was it not the fault of the government that after a century of British rule, seven children out of eight in India continued to grow up in ignorance and darkness? In any case, what he was asking for immediately was a voice in the administration only for those who were qualified by education to exercise their civic responsibilities. One can only guess how the audience, consisting mostly of old India hands, must have squirmed when Gokhale told them that 'the efficiency attained by a foreign bureaucracy, uncontrolled by public opinion' was bound to be of a 'strictly limited character''[15] that as things were, there was 'no one ever in the Indian Government who is permanently interested in the country as only its own people can be interested... the true well-being of the people is systematically subordinated to militarism, service interests of English mercantile classes....' Gokhale denounced the virtual British monopoly of the higher posts in the administration in India. He warned that unless the educated classes were conciliated, 'England will find on her hands before long another Ireland, only many times bigger, in India'. 'I cannot say', Gokhale concluded, 'that I have much hope that any such policy will be at once adopted. The struggle before us is, I fear, a long one, and, in all probability, it will be a most bitter one. The flowing tide, however, is with us, and such a struggle can have but one issue. In the summer of 1906, as in his earlier visits, Gokhale's mentor in England was Sir William Wedderburn. Sir William's watchword was 'moderation'. 'The object should be', he told Gokhale, 'to show the moderation and practicality of our proposals.'

Despite occasional tours and public meetings, the emphasis during this visit was on quiet diplomacy rather than on overt propaganda. Sir William introduced Gokhale to a number of M.P.s, including Ramsay MacDonald, Sir Charles Dilke, Keir Hardie, C. P. Trevelyan and G. P. Gooch. Some of them drew upon him for facts and figures for asking questions or moving amendments to official resolutions. Many years later, G. P. Gooch, in his memoirs, described Gokhale as the most eminent Indian statesman of his time, with 'mellow wisdom and quiet strength'." Ellis, the Under-

Secretary of State for India, was extremely welldisposed to Gokhale and invited about forty members of Parliament to meet him at breakfast. The Inter-Parliamentary Conference invited Gokhale to attend the conference. From the 'Anti-Imperialist League' of America came a request that Gokhale should visit the United States and deliver a series of lectures on India. All this was very flattering, but somewhat irrelevant. The main purpose for which Gokhale had come to England was to persuade the new Liberal Government to recognize the gravity of the crisis in India and to reverse the process of alienation of the people which Curzon had set in motion. There was no time to lose. 'Now is the time for work,' R. C. Dutt wrote to Gokhale from Baroda on 24 May 1906, now or never. If this Liberal Govt. fails to give a more representative character to the Indian administration, we shall never get anything by peaceful methods, and England will be teaching to pursue Irish methods in a country which has more than 50 times the population of Ireland.' The central figure in the Liberal Government, who needed to be educated from the Indian point of view, was John Morley, the Secretary of State. Gokhale had met him during his earlier visits to England in 1897 and 1905.

These visits made it somewhat easier for Gokhale to approach Morley, who received from the young Indian politician a full exposition of Indian grievances and aspirations. 'I made a passionate appeal to Mr Morley yesterday', Gokhale wrote home on 10 May 1906, 'to realize the great responsibility of his teachings in his present office. And he was much moved and he spoke freely of his difficulties and intentions.' Eight days later, Gokhale felt that Morley was 'at last waking up to the situation and we may expect further developments yet'. 'I may tell you privately', Gokhale confided to Krishnaswami Aiyer, 'that I have been able to establish excellent personal relations with Mr Morley.' Wedderburn and his colleagues in the British Committee were glad that Gokhale was hitting it off so well with Morley. In India hopes rose high. 'You have secured the ear of Mr Morley', Gokhale's friend R. N. Mudholkar wrote to him. 'You have opened his eyes. Through him you have moved that immovable barrier, the India office.'

Another friend, Hari Narayan Apte, was delighted when he was approached on behalf of an English Radical, J. Seymour Keay, to secure Gokhale's help in finding him a safe seat in the House of Commons: When my friend... asked me to write to you in this connection [Apte told Gokhale] I was not a little overjoyed-for this shows that making India a plank in their platform has been considered advantageous by some [British] politicians at least. This gives me hope that the time is not far distant when there will be an India Party-as strong as the Labour Party in the British Parliament. I only hope you will be there to lead it. This optimism was racing ahead of events. Soon Gokhale was complaining of 'adverse influences' being at work. The anticlimax came with Morley's long-awaited speech on the Indian budget on 20 July. Three months of silent and strenuous diplomacy had nearly broken Gokhale's health, but they had not brought him visibly nearer the constitutional reforms he had been advocating. Some of the obstacles to the reforms were inherent in the structure of the British Raj; others arose at the time from conflicting pressures on John Morley.

10

Gokhale : Issues of Constitutional Reforms

Towards the end of August 1907, the Government of India's dispatch of 21 March 1907 to the Secretary of State on constitutional reforms was published, and the decision to appoint two Indians to the Secretary of State's Council announced. Early in September 1907, a Royal Commission was appointed to report on decentralization of the Indian administration. These announcements failed to evoke much enthusiasm in India.

The 'Simla proposals' as the Government of India's dispatch to the 4 Secretary of State came to be known-were based on the recommendations of a sub-committee of the Viceroy's Executive Council. The committee had been instructed to report on the enlargement of legislative councils to 'the fullest extent possible [consistently] with the necessary authority of the Government', the creation of a separate electorate for the moneyed and landed classes in order to provide 'the requisite counterpoise' to the influence of the professional classes, and the formation of an Imperial Advisory Council (consisting of ruling chiefs and territorial magnates) whose proceedings were to be private, informal and confidential. 'It would be a curious piece of irony', wrote the Statesman, 'if at a time when the Government of which he [Mr Morley] is a member are preparing an attack upon English feudalism, as represented by the House of Lords, he should have originated the doctrine that the salvation of India is to be found in the exaltation of the landed aristocracy.' That the Government of India should have thought of banking upon the princes, landlords and other vested interests in the face of growing unrest may seem odd in the light of later history. It was, however, quite in accord with the philosophy of the British ruling class in India, which Minto had readily imbibed, and which he modified only slightly under the dual pressure of Indian discontent and Morley's exhortations. It was on Minto's advice that Morley chose for his Council, not well-known public figures like R. C. Dutt and Nawab Syed Mohammed Bahadur, but K. G. Gupta, a not particularly brilliant member of the I.C.S., and Syed Husain Bilgrami (Nawab Imad-ul-Mulk), a retired civil servant from Hyderabad.

Whatever value these gestures had for Indian public opinion was largely lost after the deportation of Lajpat Rai, and the enactmentin the teeth of non-official opposition-of the Seditious Meetings Bill. The Surat Congress would have pronounced its verdict on the 'Simla proposals', had it not ended in a pandemonium. A fortnight later, when Gokhale was in Calcutta, he called on the Viceroy and urged him to accelerate the constitutional reforms. The Extremists, he told Minto, had been discredited at Surat, and would cease to be a factor of any importance in Indian politics if the constitutional reforms were framed to satisfy the reasonable aspirations of the educated classes.

In March, while speaking on the budget in the Imperial Council, Gokhale returned to the same theme. He referred to the 'sense of irritation and disappointment' caused by certain words and actions of Morley, whom educated Indians had learnt to look upon as a philosopher-statesman. 'Whatever reforms are taken in hand,' he said, 'let them be dealt with frankly and generously. And let not the words "too late" be written on every one of them. For while the Government stands considering, hesitating, 'receding, debating within itself... opportunities rush past it which can never be recalled. And the moving finger writes, and having writ moves on.' It was a sober speech, but the Viceroy, who was in the chair, took it amiss. 'Gokhale had a cut at you', Minto wrote to Morley, 'which provoked me and I dealt with what he had said somewhat testily.... Gokhale came afterwards to see Dunlop-Smith, professing to be hurt at what I had said... perhaps I was too hard on him.' This incident showed once again Minto's ambivalence: he was attracted by Gokhale's ability, but repelled by his spirit of independence. A few days later, Minto told Morley that Gokhale's note to the Decentralization Commission 'was as good as anything I have seen'. In another letter, while discussing the choice of the first Indian member of the Viceroy's Executive Council, Minto conceded that Gokhale was 'by far the ablest of that school whom we know', but added that he 'could not trust him. I don't know what there is behind him.... He is too a Maharatta Brahmin which means a great deal.' Morley complimented Minto on giving a 'rap on the knuckles' to Gokhale. Fortunately this incident did not become the starting point for the kind of hostile campaign which had brought Gokhale to a standstill during his visit to England in 1906. Much had happened in the intervening two years to raise Gokhale's stock in the eyes of the Secretary of State. Morley had never been a great admirer of the civil service, but he never forgave it for the way it misled him-and the Viceroyover the deportation of Lajpat Rai. Morley knew enough of imperial history to realize the damage done by the 'men on the spot' in misleading opinion at home and violently irritating opinion in the colonies.

'After all', he told the Viceroy, 'it is not you nor I, who are responsible for [Indian] unrest, but the over-confident and overworked Tchinovniks who have had India in their hands for 50 years past. In 1906 Morley had been reluctant to overrule his senior advisers in the India office; two years later, he felt able to assert himself. Dunlop-Smith, the Viceroy's private secretary, after meeting Arthur Godley (who had a quarter of a century's experience in the India office), wrote in June 1908: 'Poor old Godley was most pathetic. He said-he almost whined-that his position is very different from what it was... that all power has been taken away from him and he is not allowed to use his influence with other men. Godley said that Lord Morley is the most autocratic and most vain person he had seen. He will not recognize also that there is any British public in India or that men in the [civil] service can think for themselves.' In the summer of 1908, Morley had reasons to be impatient with the bureaucrats who surrounded him in London and Minto in Simla. There had been an inordinate delay in the formulation of the reforms.

With his political instinct sharpened by his sense of history, and particularly by the history of Ireland, Morley saw that the early passage of reforms was an acid test of the efficacy of the constitutional method in India and that further delay could completely alienate the educated classes. It seemed to him that the Surat Congress signified not the final defeat of the Extremists, but merely a breathing space for the Moderates, and that the Moderates were likely to be swamped by the Extremists unless they could show some tangible fruits for their labours. The 'Simla Scheme' had been a great damper for the Moderates, but Morley let it be known to their spokesmen in England (such as Wedderburn) that the Government of India's dispatch of 21 March 1907 was not the last word on the issue of Indian reform, and was subject to revision in the light of criticism. Unaware of the genesis of the 'Simla Scheme', Indian public opinion tended to attribute it to Morley and to hold him responsible for its defects. This was not only unfair to Morley but harmful to the Indian cause. Wedderburn pleaded with his Indian friends not to alienate Morley. He had no doubt that the Secretary of State's mind was still open on constitutional reforms. Morley's position in the Liberal party and the Cabinet was unassailable: to incur his ill-will would be suicidal. Wedderburn to Gokhale, 28 February 1908: It is quite clear to my mind that the only chance of getting valuable concessions is by Mr Morley's goodwill... the best help our Parliamentary friends [in England] can give us is by using friendly and encouraging pressures in the right direction.... No advocate going to a court of appeal would open his case by denouncing and insulting the judge. Now in the present instance Mr Morley is practically sole ultimate judge. He may have (and has) his weaknesses, he may be timid and vain, but what do we stand to gain for India by ceaselessly charging him with these defects and assuming that he has abandoned the principles of a lifetime? All this is bad tactics. It was primarily in order to influence Morley and the Liberal party in favour of constitutional reforms that Wedderburn and the British Committee of the Congress asked Gokhale to visit England. He arrived on 10 May 1908. To a Reuter correspondent, who met him at the Charing Cross Station, he said that his visit was in connection with the Indian Government's reforms scheme and he hoped to see Morley and other prominent men.

A few days before his arrival, Morley had become Viscount Morley of Blackburn. Wedderburn was not worried by Morley's elevation to the House of Lords. 'I have let Mr Morley know', Wedderburn wrote to Gokhale on 24 April, 'that you are coming. On the whole I think it is advantageous that he is moving to the House of Lords. It would have been disastrous if he had left just when his plans were maturing-he had to choose between the House of Commons and the India office and his choice seems to imply that he means to do something.' Gokhale met Morley on 22 May. The meeting lasted an hour and a quarter. 'We parted', Gokhale wrote home, 'with a good understanding. He has promised to consult me freely at every stage of the progress of the reforms proposals, and he has assured me that before the year is over, the reforms would not only be formulated but carried out.' A few days later, while Gokhale was at Liverpool, he received an urgent letter from the Secretary of State for India asking him to see him at once. He hurried back to London and went to the India office where he had 'a most important and on the whole highly satisfactory interview with him [Morley]. It was worth one's while to have come to this country for this interview, if for nothing else.' On 12 June, Gokhale noted that Morley had 'begun slowly to assert himself'." He found him cordial and responsive.

The doors of the India office seemed open to him at all times. 'The whole atmosphere', he noted, 'is friendly to me personally.' Morley seems to have been drawn to the young professor-politician from Poona. In one of his asides, he once confessed that he was not attracted by Orientals—Gokhale being an exception, if any'. Morley's cordiality may have stemmed from political calculation. Gokhale's intimate knowledge of Indian politics and economics could be useful to the Secretary of State in refuting the arguments of the reactionaries in the India office and the Tory party. Morley may also have hoped to use Gokhale to soften the edge of the small critical group of radical Liberals in the Commons led by Sir Henry Cotton. On 16 June, Gokhale was invited for a confidential luncheon discussion in the India office, with T. Buchanan, the Under-Secretary of State for India and four members of the India Council, Walter Lawrence, Theodore Morison, Lawrence Jenkins and S. A. Bilgrami. The initiative for his meeting seems to have come from Theodore Morison, but it could hardly have been arranged without Morley's approval. For an Indian politician, such attention from the India office was a singular compliment. 'You may take it from me', Gokhale wrote to his disciples in Poona, 'that it [the meeting] has strengthened our position in the India Council.' Meanwhile, in consultation with Wedderburn and the British Committee, Gokhale addressed a meeting of the Indian Parliamentary Committee and interviewed some prominent British statesmen, including Lords Ripon, Courtney, Reay, Welby and Fitzmaurice. He was also the chief guest at a dinner given by H. W. Nevinson of the Manchester Guardian, which was attended by the leading Liberal journalists, including A. G. Gardiner and H. W. Massingham. Wedderburn was delighted that Gokhale had an opportunity of 'getting at the brain of the Liberal Party in London'. By the middle of July, Gokhale was predicting that the reforms would take final shape before the Indian National Congress met at Madras in December.

On 10 July 1908, Gokhale to wrote to Vamanrao Patwardhan : It is almost certain (of course this is strictly confidential) that an important Indian reform Bill will be introduced in Parliament in December next and the whole scheme of reforms will be roughly settled in October and November. On December 2, I shall leave for India so as to arrive in time for the next Congress. It is considered here of the utmost importance that I should be present at the next Congress and convey a message of hope to the constitutional party.... Gokhale's optimism was somewhat tempered by the news from India. While he was on his way to England, an outrage had occurred at Muzaffarpur in Bihar. The wife and daughter of a European barrister were killed by a bomb really intended for D. H. Kingsford, the District Magistrate, who had incurred much notoriety in Calcutta for awarding savage sentences in political cases. Of the two young men who were arrested after the Muzaffarpur outrage, one shot himself, and the other made a confession which led to the discovery of an ammunition dump and the trial of thirty young men in what came to be known as the Maniktola Conspiracy case. Gokhale read the news at Marseilles.

This was not the first time that a major political crisis had occurred in his homeland as soon as he left it. In 1897, it had been the plague operations; in 1905, the Bengal partition; in 1906, the Barisal affair. And now it was this senseless assassination which threatened to put the clock back in India, and to make Gokhale's task in England doubly difficult. If the vicious cycle of. repression and retaliation continued, where was the room for sane counsels of the Moderate party? Would not the Anglo-Indian lobby in England counter his pleas for reforms by raising the spectre of anarchy in India? Gokhale took the earliest opportunity of sharing his misgivings with his disciples: I am really sorry [he wrote] that I should be out of India at such a grave juncture. There is some fatality connected with my visits to this country [England]. Every time I come here, something happens in India and throws the country into a state of wild excitement.... I fear [he added] that there will now be a fierce outburst of repression for the next two or three years, it will be a case of repression on one side and crime on the other. Ultimately, I have no doubt, crime will be stamped out, or the violence of the extreme section of the Extremists will get exhausted, but meanwhile men like ourselves can do very little useful work and we shall be compelled merely to helplessly look on.... It is not difficult at any time to create disorder in our country-it was our portion for centuries-but it is not easy to substitute another form of order for that which has been evolved by Englishmen in the course of a century.... The immediate result of the Muzaffarpur tragedy, as Gokhale had foreseen, was an Anglo-Indian clamour for the tightening of screws on Indian politicians and newspapers. 'The danger', the Viceroy wrote to the Secretary of State, 'is a very real one. It is a personal danger such as British men and women do not talk of, but they know it." Minto feared that the European population might panic and take the law into its own hands.

The Englishman was indeed making ominous suggestions on 'self-defence' by Europeans. The government lost no time in summoning the Imperial Council at Simla and rushing through an 'Explosives Bill' based on an English Act of 1853. The debate lasted for less than two hours. On the same day was passed the Indian Newspapers (Incitement to offences) Bill, which gave the executive wide powers to curb 'seditious' writings. The rigour of this bill was fortunately moderated by the intercession (at the request of Wedderburn) of Lord Ripon, who was Morley's colleague in the British Cabinet. These modifications in the press bill, Morley assured the Viceroy, would make it easier for, the Moderates to resist the Extremist attack. 'Such an attack', he wrote, 'is sure to come and it is our business, as I think, not to do anything that will give substance to extremist taunts and their moderate opponents. In 1908, as in 1897, the ruling race in India was alarmed, and traced a direct connection between political terrorism and incendiary writings in the press. Once again, the victim of the panic of the Anglo-Indian community was Tilak. Immediately after the Muzaffarpur outrage, he had denounced it publicly. This did not, however, save him from a prosecution by the Bombay Government for two articles in the Kesari, which had commented on the Muzaffarpur tragedy. He was arrested in the last week of June. The trial began on 13 July before Justice Davar of the Bombay High Court.

Tilak defended himself with great courage, skill and dignity, but was sentenced on 22 July to six years' imprisonment. It is significant that the trial was held not in Poona, where the Kesari was published, but in Bombay, and while it was in progress, Tilak was detained in an improvised lock-up in the High Court building. Nevertheless, the city of Bombay was in a turmoil for a fortnight. The mill workers of Bombay went on strike on 25 July; out of 84 mills, as many as 76 stopped working. The strike spread to railway workshops; black flags with Tilak's photographs went up in the streets; motor-cars and carriages carrying Europeans were stoned. British troops were called out. The Governor, Sir George Sydenham Clarke, conferred with prominent businessmen of Bombay and was disconcerted by the discovery that most of them at heart sympathized with Tilak. 'The business natives', he wrote, 'seemed not to have a vestige of political instinct." Vishnu Bhatvadekar, a friend of Gokhale, wrote to him from Bombay that the government 'had sought to crush Mr T. [Tilak] by a portentous prosecution, but they have only succeeded in making him a greater hero and martyr than ever'. The news of Tilak's arrest, the packed jury, the savage sentence, and the violent sequel in Bombay caused Gokhale deep concern. His heart went out to his old political rival in his hour of trial. Even from a distance of six thousand miles Gokhale could also see that these events boded ill for the cause of constitutional reform and the future of the Moderate party. Gokhale to Vamanrao Patwardhan, 17 July 1908: The telegraphic summaries of Mr Tilak's defence have made a very good impression. on friends of India in this country. This is the real Tilak, as he was and would be but for the pernicious influence of those around him.... 23 July 1908: This morning's papers contain telegrams about the shocking sentence inflicted on Mr Tilak. There is of course no doubt that he will be brought back and set free after things quiet down, if and when they quiet down. Still the conviction and sentence will really be a great blow to our party, for part of the resentment against the Government is likely to be directed also against us. Gokhale to Natesan, 24 July 1908: Yesterday's papers contained the news of Mr Tilak's conviction and sentence. I wonder what is going to happen next. It is useless to talk of reforms at a time like the present and I fear the public in India will be in no mood to appreciate them when they are produced. Gokhale's worst fears were soon confirmed. Bhatvadekar noted that the Tilak case had strengthened rather than broken the Extremists: 'The excitement caused by the press prosecutions [of the Kesari and the Kai] has made [the work of the Moderate Party] more than ever difficult... local feeling is strong and people are yet hardly prepared to listen to the voice of reason. 127 An ugly sequel to Tilak's trial was a whispering campaign against Gokhale, who was alleged to have conspired with Morley to get his rival out of the way. The Bande Mataram of Calcutta and the Hindu Panch of Poona gave currency to such insinuations. 'The rumour', in Bhatvadekar's words, was 'too puerile to be seriously considered, but some of our Extremist friends are worse than children. The chawl politicians in Bombay are loudly abusing you, P. M. Mehta and my brother and in fact all the Moderates as being responsible for the prosecution. 128 It was not only irresponsible hot-heads who helped to spread this rumour-, Tilak's devoted colleague and legal adviser, G. S. Khaparde, and the Extremist leader of Bengal, Bipin Chandra Pal, who were both in England that summer, seem to have joined in the smear campaign against Gokhale.

The public indignation against the government was thus partly diverted to Gokhale and the Moderates. During the Ganapati festival in Poona in 1909, songs were composed to depict Gokhale as the murderer of Tilak. At a public meeting in London, his detractors planned to pelt him with rotten eggs, but the plan did not materialize. There was even talk among Extremist youth of assassinating Gokhale. This was not the first time that Gokhale's opponents had hit below the belt. He had bitter memories of the 1890s, of the days of the Age of Consent Bill, of the Poona Congress, and the plague operations. 'The malevolence of these men', he wrote, 'is no new thing. It has pursued me for years past with a virulence which I alone know.... The truth is that bulk of our educated countrymen have as yet neither a true sense of justice nor true manliness nor magnanimity.' The charge that Gokhale had persuaded Morley to order Tilak's arrest was of course baseless. Gokhale to Vamanrao Patwardhan, 25 September 1908:... As I have told you before the whole accusation is a despicable and malevolent fabrication. I never had any talk whatever with Lord M. about Mr Tilak before the prosecution. I had a talk with him afterwards and in that, I expressed my deep regret at the prosecution and pointed out its great unwisdom. I know as a fact that Lord M. was himself greatly distressed when he learnt about Mr Tilak's arrest, though, of course, this must be kept confidential.... Despite an impression to the contrary prevailing in India at the time, the initiative for the prosecution had come not from Morley, nor even from Minto, but from Sir George Clarke, the Governor of Bombay, who seems to have acted against the advice of his own senior officers.

From the private correspondence of Morley with Minto and Clarke, it is now clear that Morley not only did not initiate action against Tilak, but doubted its wisdom. After reading one of the allegedly incriminating articles in the Kesari, Morley was not convinced that a prosecution was 'inevitable'. He noted that the jury which tried Tilak was composed of seven Europeans, two Parsis and not a single Hindu. After referring to 'a packed jury', Morley wrote to the Viceroy: 'I suppose the sentence will be heavy-and at all events heavy enough to produce a good deal of exasperation in the Mahratta mind and to make the Moderate game much harder to play.' One of the worst offenders in maligning Gokhale was the Marathi Hindu Panch. It charged him with secretly visiting Government House at night in order to conspire with the Bombay Governor, with poisoning the mind of Morley against Tilak in England, and playing 'the role of Iago' in the Tilak case. Gokhale's friends, infuriated by such allegations, suggested legal action against the Hindu Panch. Gokhale cabled his concurrence from England, but the disciple of Ranade was soon having qualms of conscience. He wrote on 20 September: I do not mind confessing that I have been feeling somewhat sad since despatching that telegram on Monday last.... Somehow I feel that I have not been quite loyal to the teachings and principles of my departed master [Ranade] in asking you to proceed against the offending journals as I have done. But while the heart is sad, the brain tells me that the course I have urged is the only course left open to me. Our public is so gullible that it simply swallows such stories. There was an interesting sequel to the prosecution of the Hindu Panch.

Its proprietor, Krishnaji Kashinath Phadke, was at first defiant, but his press was confiscated by the government and he was rendered penniless. Gokhale sent for him and helped him with a a subsistence allowance for several years. Phadke was deeply moved by Gokhale's magnanimity and repented the part he had played in the smear campaign against him. Incessant work and worry took their inevitable toll. By July 1908, Gokhale's health was failing. Dr Walter Carr, who had examined him earlier in May, expressed his concern at Gokhale's diabetes, which was mild, but 'such apparently mild cases are liable at any time, sometimes without any obvious reason, to become exceedingly severe. I saw last autumn a man who had been passing sugar for about 15 years, who suddenly developed symptoms and died in three weeks.' 'I fear', Dr Carr went on, 'that he [Gokhale] may sacrifice his health to his politics.' At Wedderburn's suggestion, Gokhale agreed to spend three weeks at Vichy for treatment, another four weeks in Switzerland for 'after care', and to return to London in early October. Gokhale's holiday at Vichy began well, but was marred by an injury to his left arm which caused him acute suffering and compelled him to return to London. Since the pain continued, an X-ray was taken and a bone fracture was discovered. The discovery came too late: the arm was henceforth permanently weakened and the wrist became crooked. 'I am thankful', he wrote, 'it is the left arm and not the right.'

The deformity could have been avoided if Gokhale had had an X-ray taken immediately after the accident. His passive resignation to suffering and reluctance to seek medical help promptly was not new; it had brought him to death's door in 1897 when he had injured his chest on his way to England and borne the pain in silence until his friend Wacha sent for a doctor. Once in London, Gokhale had things other than his health to worry about. The news from India again became disturbing. There were fresh outrages. On 7 November an attempt was made on the life of Sir Andrew Fraser, the Governor of Bengal. Two days later a sub-inspector of police was murdered. On 13 November the statue of Queen Victoria was defaced, and on the same day nine persons in Bengal, including Aswini Kumar Datta, were deported under Regulation III of 1818.

The British and Anglo-Indian newspapers clamoured for drastic measures. Morley refused to panic, or to withhold the constitutional reforms. On the contrary, he realized that the reforms had to be hastened if they were to conciliate the educated classes. 'I understand from a friend', Morley told Minto in November 1908, 'who has seen Gokhale that impatience is quite lively in India-because the chance of Moderates holding their own against Extremists when the Congress meets in the last week of December depends on their being able to show that we have our scheme actually ready for Parliament.' In April 1908, the Moderates held a meeting of the 'Convention' Committee at Allahabad and framed a constitution for the Indian National Congress, which was intended to provide it with elected committees and yet, by excluding the Extremists, insure it against the repetition of the internal convulsions which had culminated in the tragedy of Surat. Gokhale played a leading role in the drafting of the new Congress constitution, but he had to leave for England immediately afterwards. The recrudescence of political' terrorism, the resultant repression by the government, and the Tilak trial brought political activity in India to a low ebb. With Tilak and Aurobindo Ghose in jail, and Khaparde and Bipin Chandra Pal in England, the Extremists were almost leaderless. In the wake of the popular indignation which swept the country following the Tilak trial, the Moderates also suffered a setback. They had the misfortune of being a party with able leaders but few workers. The new electoral machinery approved by the Allahabad Convention called for a great deal of organizational effort, but there was hardly anyone to take it up seriously. Gokhale was urged by some of his Bombay friends to return to India and to put some life into the organization with the help of his Servants of India. It was not only Gokhale's friends who were appealing to him to return. Sir George Clarke, the Governor of Bombay, seems to have been rattled by the terrorist outrages and the intense excitement in his province caused by Tilak's arrest and imprisonment.

Dear Mr Gokhale [he wrote on 7 August 1908]

Will you forgive me for writing frankly to you? I feel strongly that your right place is in India at this juncture and if your health would permit it, your return would be an advantage in every way. I have no time to write about the recent events about which you will not agree with me. I will only ask you to believe [Tilak's arrest] was absolutely necessary.... The party of violence has developed much more rapidly than you can know and this has become a serious danger to the peace of India. What we need now is a leader who will dissociate himself from futile visions which, if realized, would ruin India, who will act as a check on the party of violence, who will tell the truth plainly to the people, and who will work, critically it may be, with us in carrying. out a series of gradual reforms. For India, it is now a question of orderly evolution, or of red revolution which would set back the clock for 50 years. I venture to think... that you alone can take the position I have indicated....

For a British Governor it was unusual to address an Indian politician in these terms. Sir George Clarke had only recently ordered the arrest of Tilak; in coming years he was to prove no friend of Indian aspirations. But in 1908, while his daughter Violet was alive, he impressed many Indian observers with his sympathy and sensitivity to public feeling. It is difficult to say whether he was sincerely seeking Gokhale's help in stabilizing the political situation, or merely trying to win over the ablest spokesman of Indian aspirations with soothing words. Gokhale was, however, not the man to play another man's game, and before long Sir George Clarke was to be his severest critic in official circles in India. Gokhale himself was keen to return to India; the affairs of his Society and of his party urgently required his presence. In September, he was complaining of 'homesickness'. But he could hardly leave England until the reforms scheme had taken shape.

The 'Simla proposals' of the Government of India had to be purged of their conservative and even reactionary features. The Council of Notables, a feudal concept, had to go; the increase in the size and powers of the legislative councils had to be such as to impress the educated classes; the administration had to be decentralized and Indian opinion associated with it. Above all, a dramatic gesture such as the undoing of the partition of Bengal or the appointment of an Indian to the Viceroy's Executive Council was imperative if the faith of the Indian educated classes in British bona fides was to be restored. With his better perspective of history and greater distance from the Indian bureaucratic machine, Morley viewed the reforms as a rallying point for those Indians who wanted to tread the constitutional path. By 1908, the Liberal party, after losing several byeelections, was feeling shaky, and there were possibilities of the dissolution of Parliament and a general election.

Morley did not have much time in which to get his reforms through. He had largely overcome the resistance of the Government of India by alternately lecturing and coaxing Minto through his weekly letters. In October 1908 he appointed a committee of his (India) Council, with Sir David Barr as Chairman, and gave it a twelve-point poser to cover the major points at issue in the-scheme of constitutional reforms. The committee expressed unanimity on all the points except three. These were: the appointment of an Indian to the Viceroy's Executive Council, nonofficial majorities in the provincial legislative councils and the appointment of Indian members on the Governor's Executive Councils at Bombay and Madras. On these issues the majority of the members of the committee of the India Council shared bureaucratic fears rather than Indian aspirations. On 27 November Morley sent off his despatch to the Government of India, and on 17 December made his statement on the reforms in the House of Lords. Morley thus kept his promise to Gokhale that the reforms would be announced before the Indian National Congress met for its annual session at Madras. Their last meeting on 2 December was very cordial. I had a farewell talk with Gokhale on Wednesday [wrote Morley]. He thinks he will never come to England again; no more work to be done for India here; must work in his own country; this is the moment of crisis; if nothing comes of our attempt, then the Extremists will have their own way: confusion, danger, ruin will follow-his tone both attracted and impressed me. He promises very confidently a good reception for our Reforms by the Congress. Just when the Indian constitutional cauldron was beginning to boil, Gokhale received an invitation to visit the United States and address the Civic Forum of New York in March 1909 on 'The National Movement in India'.

The Civic Forum was an important non-political platform; among those who had addressed it were Taft and Bryan, the two U.S. presidential candidates in 1908, and the leader of the Liberal Party in the Russian Duma. 'It is a great opportunity', Gokhale wrote home in July, 'to state our case to the civilized world. 131 By December 1908, he had given up the idea of going to the United States. He had been away from India for more than six months; he had plenty to do at home, and the news of student unrest and terrorist outrages disturbed him deeply. It seemed hardly feasible to return again in the spring not only for the passage of the Reforms Bill in Parliament, but for a visit to America. Three months before the Congress was scheduled to meet at Madras, Gokhale had impressed upon Krishnaswamy Aiyer the importance of making the session a spectacular demonstration of the strength and unity of the Moderate party, its adherence to constitutional methods and willingness to work the new reforms in a spirit of cooperation with the government. He suggested that the honour of presiding over the session should go to Pherozeshah Mehta, 'the foremost constitutionalist, but it was actually conferred on Rash Behari Ghose, the president-elect of the Surat session which had dissolved in chaos. Compared with the preceding three sessions at Benares, Calcutta and Surat, the: Madras Congress (December 1908) was a tame affair. The inner tensions which had brought the confrontation between the Moderates and Extremists to a head a year earlier were absent; the Extremists were in fact conspicuous by their absence. The proceedings were placid, almost dull.

There seemed to be a conscious effort not to do anything that would antagonize the government, embarrass Morley, or cast doubts on the loyalty of the educated classes, while the reforms were on the anvil of the British Parliament. A resolution on swadeshi was passed, but 'boycott' was not even mentioned. The proceedings began (to quote from the official record of the Madras Congress) with the 'Indian National Anthem' sung to the tune of 'God Save the King', and ended with 'cheers for the KingEmperor, Lord Morley and Lord Minto'.

The first resolution of the Congress tendered 'loyal homage' to His Gracious Majesty, the KingEmperor, and respectfully welcomed 'the message sent by His Majesty to the Princes and People of India on the Fiftieth Anniversary of the Memorable Proclamation issued in 1858 by his Illustrious Mother, Victoria the Good'. Rash Behari Ghose in his presidential speech refuted Anglo-Indian insinuations about Congress loyalty to the Raj. 'We must be mad', he said, 'if we were really disloyal.... Our loyalty is above all suspicion.... The Congress expressed the 'deep and general satisfaction of the country' and gratitude to Morley and Minto for the proposed reforms, which were described as 'a large and liberal instalment... needed to give the people of this country a substantial share in the management of their affairs and to bring the administration into closer touch with their wants and feelings'. Surendranath Banerjee, who moved this resolution, described the reforms scheme as the 'crowning triumph of constitutional agitation' and described Morley as the 'Simon de Montfort of the future Parliament of India'. 'Henceforth the executive will not be able to control all provincial legislation', said Rash Behari Ghose. 'In a word, we shall now have something like a constitutional government in the place of an autocratic and irresponsible government.' Strangely enough, the one man in that assembly who knew more about these constitutional reforms than anyone else did not speak on this resolution. It was only towards the end of the session, when a formal motion of thanks to Hume and Wedderburn was moved, that Gokhale expressed his views on the reforms scheme. Though he considered it 'a fruition of 23 years of Congress effort', he agreed that all that it had done was to 'modify' the bureaucratic administration. The admission of Indians to the Councils of the Secretary of State, the Viceroy, and the provincial Governors had given India a 'reasonable access to the seats of highest power and authority'. Even though the new legislative councils had limited powers, the non-official majorities in the provincial councils provided a 'preventive control' over provincial legislation. True, the veto of the government remained.

To question that, argued Gokhale, is not to understand the working of constitutional government. Even the House of Commons works under what may be called a veto, VIZ. the practical veto of the House of Lords and the theoretical veto of the Sovereign. They are a self-governing people and yet they bear all the inconveniences of this double veto. Let us grow to the full bounds of the new opportunities and it will be time enough to talk of circumscribing the veto.... None of us wants to be satisfied with things as they are, but we must prove that we can bear these responsibilities, before we ask for more. Hitherto, they had been engaged in agitation from outside; henceforth they would be engaged in 'responsible association' in administration. 'There is plenty of scope for growth here, and as we grow and discharge the responsibility that devolves on us properly, I am sure there will be progress further and further towards our having what may be called a responsible administration.' Gokhale knew that Morley's statement on the reforms was only the opening shot in his campaign.

There were strong vested interests hostile to the reforms in Britain, which were bound to exploit issues like 'boycott' and partition of Bengal, and embarrass Morley while he piloted the reforms through the British Parliament. It was on Gokhale's advice that the Madras Congress maintained a discreet silence on these vital but controversial issues. Gokhale's speech put the reforms in perspective, forestalled criticism of their rather modest aims, soothed public feeling excited by anarchical outrages and repressive legislation, and promised the support of educated India for the reforms. Morley was delighted by the verdict of the Madras Congress, which had (he noted) 'done all that we had a right to expect and will do a good deal to justify our policy in both persevering with the reforms and in making them liberal'. Gokhale was not alone in expressing enthusiasm for the reforms. on 6 January 1909, a week after the Madras Congress, Morley wrote to

Minto that R. C. Dutt and K. G. Gupta, who had dined with him, were jubilant at the way the Moderates had rallied to the defence of the reforms, and insisted 'that it will last for ever and that you have now a national party more or less committed to constitutional ways'. Three months later, Dadabhai Naoroji assured Minto and Morley that Indians would remember with gratitude their names for having courageously and sincerely made a beginning towards raising India to the status of a self-governing member and real partner in the British Empire. The Hindustan Review, edited by Sachchidananda, Sinha, eloquently summed up the optimistic mood of the Moderates: Loyal patriotism has triumphed over unreasoning fanaticism... the better mind of the people as well as of those in authority has prevailed over the narrow-minded and short-sighted extremists among Anglo-Indians and Indians alike. In all this, gratitude compels us to assign the greatest credit to the great scholar and statesman [Morley] who presides over the destinies of India.

11

Gokhale : An Overview

Gokhale was living at critical time when Liberalism was at the crossroads. In spite of the fact that for more than a decade Indian National Congress had been representing to British bureaucracy for granting some constitutional advances to the people, the outcome had practically been negligible. Even most of the Moderates began to lose faith in British sense of justice. The government of the day had acted very much against the sentiments and wishes of the people and when they expected reforms, government gave them partition of Bengal and similar other unwanted Acts. The task before Gokhale was not only to convince the people of India about the British sense of justice but also to convince the Britishers about the need of constitutional reforms in minimum possible time. It was a double sided task which required not only intelligence, calibre but also patience and tactful handling of the situation. At the time when liberalism was passing through crisis the extremists were exerting more and more pressure on political scene. It was at such a critical time that Gokhale had to work for saving liberalism and taking the people of India with him and also convincing the Britishers about immediate constitutional reforms. Not only this but he extent was also to work in a way that the youth willingly came forward as patriots having full faith in constitutionalism and peaceful methods of struggle against British government. Gopal Krishna Gokhale was very much influenced by the philosophy and working of Ram from whom he used to get inspiration and guidance.

It was under his personal supervision that he developed his philosophy and could get his present position. From Rana he learnt liberalism and constitutionalism. Like him he also believed in British sense of justice and was convinced that British rule in India was for the betterment of Indians. In the words of C.P. Ramaswami Aiyer, "Ranade was the prime factor to the growth of instructed Indian political and economic thought. He was himself a scholar politician and he trained Gokhale to follow his footsteps. At the same time, Ranade and Gokhale alike, transformed politics of India and spiritualised it by insisting on self surrender, complete dedication to the same cause of the country and purity of motive and action." K. Ishwar Dutt says, "There were three men in particular to whom Gokhale felt spiritually drawn and yield reverence from his very soul—particularly Dadabhai Naoroji, his great master, Mahadev Govind Ranade, and the incomparable Gandhiji (though his junior). In their presence he felt elevated." C.P. Ramaswamy Aiyer has also pointed out the influence of Tilak, on Gokhale by saying that "There is no doubt Gokhale, though he reacted against chauvinistic doctrines, was at the same time, perhaps unconsciously influenced by the onslaughts made by the Tilak group on British rule and its results and manifestations." In addition to this, his philosophy was influenced by his personal circumstances. He had seen poverty and worked under adverse circumstances and as such he knew the feeling of the poor and their real and practical difficulties. He had got education with great hardship and as such he personally realised. the significance and value of education in the life of person and to that extent his subsequent love for education was the direct outcome of his personal experience in life.

Gopal Krishna Gokhale is another son of Mother India, about whom nation can feel proud. He was another Maharastrian who had the privilege of guiding nation during his times and taking forward the millions of India on the path of self government. Being a Liberal he had full faith in British sense of justice and wished that the Indians should give maximum co-operation to the British in its efforts to take India on the path of constitutional development. He believed that most of the Britishers who were incharge of administration were ignorant of India's problems and efforts were needed to make them appreciate and realise our difficulties. He had also faith in the capacity of Indians to improve their conditions and come out of grinding and growing poverty. He was both a politician, social reformer and an economist. He was also one of the most brilliant parliamentarians which India produced at that time. In the word of our ex-President Dr. Radhakrishnan, "When the comforts of the world were in Gokhale's reach and could be his, he left them and gave his great talents to his service of the country. Renunciation is the principle of good life. Men are great not by what they acquire but what they renounce; those engaged in public work should not look upon it as a career with glittering prices." He was an educationist and political guru of even Mahatma Gandhi. He founded the servants of Indian Society to train the young people of India for noble cause of devoting themselves to the service of their Motherland.

Early Life. Gopal Krishna Gokhale was born on May 1,1866 in Chitpavan community in Ratnagiri District. He was hardly 13, when his father died and by the force of circumstances his mother was obliged to leave the village and shift to Kolhapur where her elder son was employed on a meagre monthly salary of fifteen rupees. It was a very critical time for this small family which even could not afford the education of the young boy who subsequently became the world famous parliamentarian, social reformer and politician. The extent of poverty can be well imagined from the fact that Gokhale had to sit beneath the street lights to study at night. After completing his early education, he joined Deccan College, Poona and Elphinstone college Bombay from where he graduated at the age of 18. After his graduation he decided to join Deccan Education society where he, on his own, accepted a meagre salary of seventy five rupees per month for a period of 20 years.

His this decision was opposed in the initial stages by his brother to which subsequently he reconciled. During his stay in the society he worked as its secretary and became so much close to it that he became its soul and life. He had the opportunity of visiting England 7 times and each time he left an impression of his ability on the people there. In 1897 he went there to give his evidence before Welby Commission which had been set up by the government to enquire into the Indian finances. In 1905 he was one of the members of the delegation sent by the Congress to persuade the British government not to go ahead with the proposal of the partition of Bengal. In 1908 he gave evidence before Hobhouse Decentralisation Commission and in 1912 he became the member of Islington Commission which was set up to enquire into the working of civil services in India. In 1912 he had to go to England in connection with the working of P. S. Commission. During one of his visits to England, Gokhale seized the opportunity of meeting Lord Morley and convinced him about the need and necessity of giving constitutional reforms to India. Perhaps no one will deny that it was due to his efforts and influence that India got her first dose of constitutional reform in 1909.

As Legislator. Gokhale became a member of Bombay Legislative Council and represented Central Division of this Presidency town. In the Council he worked for the cause of people and raised a voice against land revenue policy of the government. Even though his ideas were basically accepted by the government but after he had staged a walk-out. It however passed the Bill. He was also responsible for District Municipal Act and similar other Acts which were enacted for the betterment of municipal administration in Bombay. In 1502 he became a member of viceroy's Legislative Council when he was hardly 36 years of age and continued to stay there for full 11 years. In the Viceroy's Council he stood for administrative and financial reforms and there also he created a place for himself. His budget speeches were listened with great attention and care even by those who did not care much for Indian sentiment. In the Council he pleaded for the abolition of salt duty and bring universities under government control. Gokhale was President of Indian National Congress in 1905 and in that capacity he guided National Congress in various ways. No doubt his task was a bit difficult but still with vigour and energy he took the organisation with him. It was his influence on the Moderates that Extremists could not win their point at Surat though the unfortunate split occurred and the Extremists had to leave the Congress. Again it was due to his untiring efforts that there was unity in the Congress organisation in 1916 and both the Extremists and the Moderates again decided to sit together and to work hand in hand. A mention in his early career may also be made about his work in South Africa to improve the conditions of Indians settled there. He met South African leaders and persuaded them to abrogate and repeal those Acts which were pinching Indians. It may not he worth-while to point out that along with Gandhiji he was quite successful in his mission. Gokhale was also responsible for founding a few organisations and working in responsible capacities in few others. To quote few he was one of the secretaries of Sarvajanik Sabha, Poona, secretary of Deccan Education Society Founder member of Deccan Sabha and above all the Servants of India Society was his most important society which did the most significant and most important work in the political life of our country even long after his death.

His Perceptions

Gokhale was all praise for British rule in India. He was very much influenced by the writings, method of working and ideas of Ranade and as such his philosophy bears ample testimony of indebtedness to him. It was under his influence that he pleaded for the continuance of British rule in India. Like his great teacher Ranade and great thinkers like Dadabhai Naoroji and Raja Ram Mohan Roy he also had faith in British Liberalism. He said in the budget speech in 1902 that, "What is needed is that we should be enabled to feel that we have a government national in spirit though foreign in personal—a government which subordinates other considerations to the welfare of Indian people, which resents indignity afforded to Indian abroad as though they were afforded to Englishmen and which endeavours by all means in its power to further the moral and the material interests of the people in India and outside India." He did not therefore, go beyond that and pleaded that we want only dominion status and wish to remain within the British empire. He very boldly pleaded that British rule in India was an act of blessing of God and should be taken in that spirit.

Supporter of Peace. Gokhale's another significant idea was that he championed the cause of peace and order. In other words he wanted only status quo to the extent possible. He was deadly against violence and was very much shaken when he came to know that Indian press was being used to excite the people of India to take to violence. In order to maintain law and order he even supported notorious Indian press Act by saying that, "My Lord, in ordinary time I should have deemed it duty to resist such proposal to the utmost of my power. The risks involved in them are grave and obvious. But in view of the situation that exists in several parts of the country today, I have reluctantly come after a careful and anxious consideration, to the conclusion that I should not be justified in opposing the principles of this Bill. It is not merely the assassinations that have taken place or the conspiracies that have come to light or the political dacoities that are being committed, that fill me with anxiety. The air in many place is still thick with the ideas that are undoubtedly antagonistic to the unquestioned continuance of British rule, with which our hope of peaceful evaluation are bound up; this is a feature of The situation quite as serious as anything else. Several other causes have contributed to produce this result of which the writing in the section of the press have been one. And to the extent to which the remedy can be applied to these writings, by such executive action as is contemplated in the Bill, I am not prepared to say that the remedy should not be applied."

His Views About Decentralisation. Gokhale felt that centralisation tantamounted to monocrotic exercise of power. He therefore, felt the need and necessity of decentralisation. He wanted that actions of bureaucracy should be checked on the spot. He wanted that provincial councils should be given power of discussing provincial budget. He was not in favour of extreme concentration of power as was the case in those days and urged that some powers should be given to lower units of administration.

His Views About Rights. He stood for individual Liberty and certain basic rights which the people should enjoy. According to him, no progress is possible in our society without enjoyment of minimum basic liberties denial of which actually and virtually means denial of development of human personality.

His Views About Social Reforms. Gokhale was pained to see the evils of Hindu society, particularly treatment being meted out to the shudras and the down trodden of the Hindu society. He was equally unhappy with such practices of the society as child marriage, ban on widow remarriage etc., and wanted that the society should end these evils: Like all other thinkers of his days he believed that unless society is reformed, political progress cannot be possible. He was sure that a pure society could quickly get political reforms.

His Views About Hindu Muslim Unity. He agreed with Ranade that the Hindus and the Muslims should he made to live a harmonious and enjoyable life. He came forward saying that in this country of ours responsibility vested on the Hindus, who were in majority, that they should create such an atmosphere wherein Muslim, who are in the minority, should realise that they can live with dignity and harmony with the majority community. This, he said, could be done by respecting the sentiments of minority and by giving them what was their due. It was by this mutual adjustment that India could progress and achieve what was her due.

His Views About British Bureaucracy. Gokhale was not satisfied with the working of British bureaucracy in India and criticised ruling bureaucracy for its gross irresponsibility to the public will in having effected the partition of Bengal. He urged upon the bureaucracy not to be satisfied by claiming to be efficient but it should so govern the people of India that Indians are enabled to govern themselves according to the highest western standard. He also criticised British bureaucracy for its being costly for India.

In his own words. "The bureaucracy was becoming frankly selfish and openly hostile to national aspiration."

His Views About Local Self Government. Gokhale strongly favoured the idea of strengthening local self-government institutions. He stood for decentralisation of authority and felt that it was through this gradual decentralisation and by way of forming Advisory District Council for advising district administration that India could progress. While giving evidence before Hobhouse Decentralisation Commission, he pleaded for the system of village Panchayat and district councils for the smooth running of Indian administration.

His Views About Swadeshi. His love for Swadeshi was immense. He believed that there should be Swadeshi in everything. With Swadeshi alone a nation could solve its many problems including those of unemployment and poverty. In Banaras, while delivering his Presidential Address, he said "the devotion to Motherland which is enshrined in higher Swadeshi is an influence so profound and so passionate that its very thought thrills and its actual objects live out of oneself India needs today above everything else that the gospel of this devotion should be preached to high and low to prince and to peasant in town and in hamlet, till the service of Motherland becomes with us as over-mastering a passion as its is in Japan."

His Faith in Indians. Gokhale had very deep faith in the capacity of his countrymen to solve their own problems. According to him, Indians positively will rise with the passage of time. He had not even the shadow of doubt that they would require no foreign assistance in raising themselves to higher level from their present low level of living and thinking, provided the people had proper understanding of their problems and resolve to solve these. In 1903, in his budget speech he said, "India of the future will, under providence, not be an India of diminishing plenty, of empty prospects or of justifiable discontent; but one of expanding industry of awakened faculties, of increasing prosperity, and of more widely distributed comfort and wealth. I have faith in conscience and purpose of my own country, and I believe in almost illimitable capacities of this." In the word of Dr. S. Radhakrishnan: "The problems facing India in Gokhale's time were formidable. Though he had served all sides of our life in a brilliant and wholehearted manner he was conscious of the long distance we have to traverse before we reach the goal. He had faith in the destiny of his country." Gokhale himself said at another place, "It will no doubt be given to our countrymen of the future generation to serve India by their success, we of present generation must be content to serve her by our failure. For hard though it may be out of those failure, the strength will come which in the end will accomplish this great task."

His Views About Progressive Government. In 1911 he put forth four tests to find out if a government was progressive or not. His first test was what measures it adopts for moral and material welfare of the subjects i.e. what the government does for education, sanitation and agricultural development etc.. Second test was what steps government takes to give large share in the administration of our local affair in municipalities, in local bodies etc.. Third test is what voice the government gives in its councils where policies are considered. Lastly how far Indians are admitted into the ranks of the public services. In this way he wanted the British government in India itself to decide whether it was progressive or not.

His Views About Nationhood. He laid stress on nation building in India and that is why he pleaded for Hindu-Muslim unity. He stood for material and moral development of all as well as for dedicated pursuit of social, educational and cultural activities for building organic strength of political system but owing allegiance to the nation. He felt that nation building could be possible by cultivation of such rules and values as were rooted in the desire of the people to have material and moral advancement.

Gokhale's Economic Ideas

Gokhale was not only a politician or political thinker but he also studied economic problems of India with keen interest. He started with the basic presumption that in India agricultural land was not producing to the desired extent, with the result that India though predominantly an agricultural country, was agriculturally backward. He also started with the idea that whatever was produced that was not equitably distributed, and as such neither the means of production nor those of distribution were properly controlled by the government. In addition to this, he also believed that England, which was an industrially advanced country, was killing Indian indigenous industries which could not compete with the machine made goods of England. He, therefore, felt that Indian economy could not be set on proper footings if agriculturists were not economically well and did not possess improved tool and equipments and given necessary safeguard to enable them to continue on his land without any disturbance. He, therefore, suggested to the government that conditions of agriculturists should be improved, and way of doing that was that the government should decrease land revenue. Then he suggested that there should be steps by which infant industries in India were given adequate protection so that these were not ruined and those employed in these did not come on the road and added to already serious unemployment problems. Another step in this regard which he suggested was that government should abolish altogether such harsh duties as the I salt duty' or excise on cotton goods and so on. He also suggested that there should be more equitable distribution of means of production and distribution so that whatever was produced did not get concentrated in few hands.

His Constitutional Plan For India. With Ferozeshah Mehta and Sir Aga Khan he prepared a constitutional plan for India which aimed at making India free after some time. He recognised limited need for going separate and direct representation to the Muslims. He wanted that after the war was over India should be given provincial autonomy. Governor should have an executive council of six members, of whom three should be Indians. A legislative council of about 100 members should be constituted of which about 80% should be elected ones. Provincial government should be given complete charge of international administration and local self bodies should be given more powers. An advisory Board should beset up in every district. District Collector should consult it on every important issue.

The executive council of the viceroy should consist of six members of whom two should always be Indians. Commissions in the army and navy should be given to Indians.

Executive should he separated from judiciary and the principle of separation of powers should be followed. Military and defence expenses should be drastically reduced. He also proposed that more attention should be paid to the spread of primary education along with technical education.

From political ideas of Gokhale becomes it clear that he was very much influenced by liberalism of those days. Like Burke he also believed that we should follow a slow policy instead of violating laws and taking recourse to violence. For him, nation was above everything else. We may conclude by saying in the words of C.P Ramaswamy Aiyer, that "For over a decade, Gokhale was the acknowledged and accredited leader of non-official Indian opinion. His avowed programme was not merely to oppose mistaken government, the Indian point of view and India-oriented policies. He followed the line of toleration and comprehension of adversary's viewpoint."

His Ideas About Education

Gokhale had great faith in the system of education for improving the future of a nation. He had so much faith in education that according to him if a nation was to rise and develop that could only be done through a developed and enlightened system of education. His love for education can be judged from the fact that he very bitterly opposed Lord Curzon's Indian Universities Bill and went to the extent of even displeasing those In authority. He favoured introduction of western system of education because according to him that was more useful than our oriental system A education, if India was to go ahead with its natural progress. He says, 'No striking problems in any particular field are looked for, unless there be room for the free movement of the energies of people in all fields. To my mind, the greatest work of western education in, the present state of India is not so much the encouragement of learning as the liberation of Indian mind from thraldom of old world ideas and the assimilation of all that is highest and the best in the life thought and character of the west. For this propose not only the highest, but all western education is useful." In his budget speech in 1903 he appealed to the government in the following words, "My Lord even allowing for the difference in the purchasing power of money in this country and elsewhere, these figures ell a most melancholy tale and show helplessly behind other every civilized nation on the face of the Earth we are all in the matter of public education. It is sad to think that after a 100 year of British rule thing with us should be no better than this and unless the work is taken up with greater confidence and enthusiasm, there is small hope of any real improving in the situation taking place." He was not only in favour of improving the system of education but also made it clear that he stood for improving living condition of teachers who were responsible for imparting education to our youth. In his budget speech in 1902, he said, "Then the question of mass education must be taken in right earnest if it is so undertaken.

The present expenditure of government on public education will require a vast increase. My Lord, it is melancholy fact that while 9 children out, of every 10 are growing up in ignorance and darkness, and village out of every five without a school, our education expenditure has been almost marking time for many years past, whereas in England where every child of school going age must attend a school, the government's expenditure on education has mounted from 4.5 million to 11.25 million sterling in the course of 15 years."

Working Method

Gokhale was constitutional liberal and moderate in his outlook and as such he believed that we should always adopt constitutional means for achieving our objectives. According to him India could gain much by remaining within the British Empire but he advised his fellow countrymen not to be in haste in getting constitutional reforms. Like Burke he believed that progress should be slow and steady but at the same time he had very clear vision as to what Indians were to achieve and what government should give to the people. He outlined the ultimate object of national struggle at Banaras Congress by saying that there should be increased representation of Indians in the Legislative Council with Indian Ministers. He favoured Indianisation of administrative system. According to him there should be separation of executive and judiciary because combination of two was bound to result in tyranny. He suggested expansion of education and industrialisation of India and suggested that reduction of expenditure on non productive items like military or civil administration. He also believed that there should be progressive decentralisation of authority with the introduction of Panchayat Raj System and formation of district councils for district administration. He also suggested that India could go on the path of progress if the people of India cooperated with the government which in turn should be sincere in improving the condition of Indian masses. This could be done by improving living condition of agriculturists who were in vast majority in India. According to him, one method for achieving our objects could be adoption of such method as Swadeshi and boycott of foreign goods. His concept of Swadeshi was very wide and extensive. It covered many things including boycott of goods which were even most essential for our day-to-day life and also his boycott included passive resistance and non-payment of taxes.

From constitutional agitation he also meant exerting pressure on those who mattered in administration and mobilising public opinion in favour of those constitutional reforms. He pleaded that one of the methods for our fight was to arrange processions, to send delegation to England and to the high tip in India to acquaint them with our pitiable conditions. He also suggested that there should be various forums like those of Servant of India Society and Deccan Society where public opinion could be consulted and mobilised. But in III this arrangement there was no place for violence. In the word of Ramaswamy Aiyer, "In other words, the school of Gokhale, of Wacha and Sastri envisaged the good of political progress through constitutionalism. It was their conviction that revolutionary action, even if successful in realising their ideas, that may produce a reaction and carry things backward. In the result, as a biographer of Gokhale has stated, the follower of Mazzini hated Cavour even more than they hated the Austrians; and it is, perhaps true that some Indian politicians hated Gokhale worse than they hated the British."

Gokhale a Servant of India Society

Since Gokhale was of the opinion that there should be forums for consulting and mobilizing public opinion therefore, in 1905 he established Servant of India Society with a view to educating and training Indian youth for national cause. He desired that there should be missionary zeal among our young people for serving their nation through this society. Discussing the objects of this society he said that it was meant for creating among our young men love for Motherland and also to prepare them for every sacrifice for the nation. It was also to impart political education and to create public opinion in the country for nationalism.

One of the objects of the Society was to promote a sense and spirit of goodwill among various communities living together and to uplift socially and economically the down-trodden of Indian society. He wanted to see that there was no depressed or down-trodden in our society. The preamble of Society said, "The Servants of India Society has been established to meet, in some measure these requirements of the situation. Its members frankly accept the British connection as ordained, in the inscrutable dispensation of Providence, for India's good, self government within the Empire for their country and a higher life generally for their countrymen is their goal. This goal they recognise, cannot be attained without earnest and patient efforts and sacrifices worthy of the cause. Much of the work must be directed towards building up in the country of a higher type of character and capacity than is generally available at present, and advance can only be slowly." Each member of the society was required to take a pledge saying that he would serve the Society and through that the country to the best of his capacity and will not try to take any personal advantage out of it himself. He was also required to work for the betterment of all and to lead a pure personal life. The pledge read as under:

"(i) That the country will always be first in his thoughts and that he will give to her service the best that is in him.

(ii) That in serving the country he will seek no personal advantage for himself.

(iii) that he will regard all Indians as brothers, and will work for the achievement of all without distinction of caste and creed.

(iv) That he will be content with such provisions for himself and his family as the society may be able to make, and that he will devote no part of his energy to earning money himself.

(v) That he will lead a pure personal life.

(vi) That he will engage in no personal quarrel with any one.

(vii) That he will always keep in view the aims of the society."

Gokhale's Ends and Means. Like Mahatma Gandhi, who very closely followed his ideals, Gokhale believed in purification of means for achieving the ends. For him only good means could bring good and lasting results. He could not accept the idea that foul means could bring fair result. In other words he wanted to see pure politics by way of introducing spiritualism or religion in politics. According to him those who believed that religion and politics should be separated with each other were basically wrong as without spiritualism politics was barren and dirty. Gokhale was, therefore, of the opinion that constitutionalism could bring more faithful result than the show of force. We may conclude his method of struggle in the words of R.R. Diwakar when he says that, "He believed in vow and taking them publicly as part and parcel of his technique of mass organisation. Once free from the idea of joining Servants of India Society Gandhiji followed the traditional methods of establishing Ashrams for attracting and organising workers for carrying out the purpose in hand. It was far less sophisticated, more simple and less costly and perhaps more indigenous as well as in keeping with the genius of the people." It was due to his these remarkable method of struggle and leading the path of progress that Mahatma Gandhiji wrote in his 'The Story of My Experiment With Truth' that, "Sir Pherozeshah had seemed to me like the Himalaya and Lokmanya like the ocean but Gokhale was like Ganges. One could have a refreshing bath in the holy river.

The Himalaya was unscalable, and one could not easily launch forth on the sea but the Ganges invited one to its bosom." Gokhale is a shining star in the history of modem India. Mahatma Gandhi called him his political guru and very much appreciated his ideas and methods of working.

His Contribution to Indian Political Thought. One of his remarkable achievements was his constitutional plan which he prepared on the suggestion of Lord Willington but which subsequently became basis of Montagu-Chelmsford reforms. If then accepted there would have been a different India and perhaps the Extremist would not have come to the fore front so quickly as they came. In the words of C.P Ramaswamy Aiyer, "It would always be easy to be wise after the events, but it is worth noting that even now, after the attainment of independence, the lessons of Gokhale's life are not obsolete nor outmoded. These are relevant now, as we are comforted by enormous economic and financial problem and crisis of planning." His another contribution is in the field of education. He boldly said that the government should allocate more funds than what it was hitherto allocating for the spread of education. Perhaps no one can deny that education plays a vital role in the development of a nation and this he felt during his own times and brought it to the notice of those in power and authority. Gokhale was also remembered as a humanist and had faith in good nature of man. For him each one was noble unless he proved otherwise. In this regard his ideas are close to Locke and Rouseau rather than Hobbes. It has been said that, "thus Gokhale means to me a symbol of that steadfast vision and equipoise, which is rare in an atmosphere of political turmoil and impatience. Gokhale was not only a Maharastrian but an Indian; he was not only a Brahmin, but a humanist, who broad-mindedly fought for the rights of all the communities and creeds. It was he who advocated the desirability of education through mother tongue and criticised the lop heavy expenses on maintaining armies." Then his contribution is about his ideas about spiritualising politics.

Though subsequently after him it was accepted even by the father of our nation, Mahatma Gandhi, who laid much stress on this aspect of our political life. Credit however, goes to him for being the first thinker who gave in very clear and vivid terms this idea to the people of India. We cannot underestimate his contribution when he said that he has faith in the capacity of Indians to solve their own problems. At that stage what was badly needed was that the people should realise what was best in them they should leave lethargy and instead of remaining only beggars and having a sound sleep they should awake from the slumber to demand what was their due. That way he did his job quite nicely and successfully. His Servants of Indian Society is a living monument of his ideas in this regard. He provided an essential forum from where the nation could get trained young Indians burning with love for the country and willing to sacrifice even their life, liberty and property for Mother-India. Then we may come to his contribution in the field of legislation.

So far there was a common belief that the Indians were, not good legislators. Britishers usually had an impression that Indians could not express their feelings and opinion on the floor of the House. Very beautifully he washed away this impression and proved that Indians were good parliamentarians. It has been said about him in this regard that "Gokhale was a great parliamentarian. He had wonderful gift of analysing the problems with the cool, calculating viewpoint of a mathematician, shifting arguments for and against and communicating them convincingly". He has significantly contributed in several other ways as well. He laid stress on decentralisation of powers. He wanted that District Boards and local self government institutions should be given more powers and funds and also not be interfered in their working. He rather rightly said that too much concentration of powers was bound to do-harm both to the rulers and the ruled. His ideas about decentralisation of power and separation of executive from judiciary are being appreciated even to day and under various schemes powers are being transferred to village panchayats. Separation of executive from judiciary and encouragement to panchyati raj institutions are even enshrined in the constitution of India. His contribution also lies in his ideas about Hindu-Muslim unity and securalism. He appropriately said at that time, and it is very loudly said even to day that India cannot progress without Hindu-Muslim unity. It is secularism which can take the roots of national progress deep. He also laid down certain basic criteria for deciding whether a government was progressive or not. The criteria laid down by him at that time holds good even to day. He very beautifully said that bureaucracy should not feel satisfied only because it was efficient but its success laid in preparing the others in the art of self government.

Gokhale and Tilak. Gokhale belonged to liberal school of thought whereas Tilak was an extremist and as such both were bound to have divergent view points. But being more or less contemporary and both belonging to Maharastrian Chitpavan Brahamin families their similarity was that both had love for the country. For them both nation was above everything else and every sacrifice for the nation was less. Both were of the opinion that India's past was glorious and her future must also be bright. Both believed that ultimate aim of our national struggle was to take India forward till our ultimate object of seeing an India in which everyone could realise what was best in him, was achieved. But beyond that they both differed from each other. Their difference was primarily in the method of achieving the ultimate object. They can very easily be compared in the words of Dr. B. Pattabhai Sitaramayya who wrote in 'The History of Indian National Congress' that, "Gokhale's plan was to improve the existing constitution. Tilak was to reconstruct it. Gokhale had necessarily to work with the bureaucracy, Tilak had necessarily to fight it. Gokhale stood for competition where possible and opposition where necessary; Tilak inclined toward a policy of obstruction, Gokhale's prime concern was with the administration and its improvement; Tilak's supreme consideration was with the Nation and its holding. Gokhale's, ideal was love and sacrifice; Tilak's was service and suffering. Gokhale's method sought to win the foreigner, Tilak to replace him. Gokhale depended on other help, Tilak on self-help. Gokhale's arena was the Council Chamber; Tilak's forum was the Village Mandap. Gokhale's medium of expression was English; Tilak's was Marathi."

An Evaluation. Glowing tributes were paid to Gokhale and are being paid even today. Perhaps there is no great Indian leader who has not paid him glowing tributes for the work which he did for India. In the words of Dr. S. Radhakrishnan, "When the comforts of world were in Gokhale's reach and could be his, he left them and gave his great talents to the service of the country." C.P Ramaswamy Aiyer has characterised Gokhale as intellectual leader of flaming patriotism and self obligation with sense of discipline which Dadabhai Naoroji and Ranade fostered and which be manifested in the Deccan Education Society." R.R. Diwakar has paid him tribute by saying, "Pie name of Gokhale emerges as a brilliant star which shone for a century and contributed substantially to the purity and an orderly advance of public life and political opinion in India." Even Mahatma Gandhi said about him, "Sir Pherozeshah had seemed to me like the Himalaya and Lokmanya like the Ocean but Gokhale was like Ganges. One could have refreshing bath in the holy river. Himalaya was unscalable and one could not easily launch forth on the sea, but the Ganges invited one to its bosom."

Jawaharlal Nehru in his biography wrote, "Gokhale, fresh from South Africa attended and it was the outstanding person of the session. High strung, full of earnestness and a nervous energy he seemed to be one of the few present persons who took politics and political affairs seriously and felt deeply about them. I was impressed by him." Hoyland says about him, "He was a constructive statement of the first rank and bringer together of East and West in the common service of needy; above all an idealist, a foreseer, a prophet of new era of inner racial goodwill and co-operation. " Even Lokmanya Tilak said about him on his death, "... that he was the diamond of India, the jewel of Maharashtra and prince of workers." Dr. Pattabhai Sitaramayya said that, "Gokhale had the knack of saying the hardest thing in the gentlest language. Gokhale used soft words with clear meaning. " We may better conclude his assessment with the words of Lord Curzon when he said, "God has endowed you with extraordinary abilities and you have placed them undeservedly at the disposal of your country."

CONGRESS PRESIDENTIAL ADDRESS

(Gokhale presided over the 21st session of the Indian National Congress held at Benares in December, 1905. The text of his presidential address is reproduced below. In his address Gokhale referred to the visit of the Prince and Princess of Wales to India. He offered a most cordial and respectful welcome to the New Viceroy Lord Minto and his consort Lady Minto. He criticized Lord Curzon's administration and compared it to the times of the Mughal Emperor Aurangzeb. Gokhale was particularly critical of the partition of Bengal and he championed the Swadeshi Movement. Gokhale praised Lord Ripon, indicted bureaucracy and placed before the Government the immediate demands of the Congress).

I thank you from the bottom of my heart for the great, the signal honour, which you have conferred upon me by electing me to preside over your deliberations this year. As has been said by more than one of my predecessors, the Presidentship of the Congress is the highest distinction, which it is in the power of our countrymen to bestow upon any one; and proud, indeed, is that moment in an Indian's life when he receives at your hands this most conspicuous mark of your confidence and your favour. As I, however, stand before you today, it is not so much the honour of the position, great as that is, as the responsibility which it imposes upon me, that occupies my thoughts. When I was first invited nearly four months ago to accept this office, we were able to see on the horizon only the small cloud-no bigger than a man's hand. Since then the sky has been overcast and for some time a storm has been raging; and it is with rocks ahead and angry waves beating around that I am called upon to take charge of the vessel of the Congress. Even the stoutest heart among us may well own to a feeling of anxiety in such a situation. Let us, however, humbly trust that in this holy city of Benares, the Divine guidance, on which we may securely throw ourselves, will not fail us, and that the united wisdom and patriotism of the delegates assembled will enable the Congress to emerge from the present crisis with unimpaired and even enhanced prestige and usefulness.

Royal Highnesses

Gentlemen, our first duty today is to offer our most loyal and dutiful welcome to Their Royal Highnesses the Prince and Princess of Wales on the occasion of this their first visit to India. The Throne in England is above all parties—beyond all controversies. It is the permanent seat of the majesty, the honour and the beneficence of the British Empire. And in offering our homage to its illustrious occupants and their heirs and representatives, we not only perform a loyal duty, but also express the gratitude of our hearts for all that is noble and high-minded in England's connection with India.

The late Queen-Empress, again, was known, within the limits of her constitutional position, to exercise during her reign her vast influence in favour of a policy of justice and sympathy towards the Indian people. We can never forget that the great Proclamation of 1858, on which we take our stand so largely in our constitutional struggle, was not only in spirit but also in substance her own declaration of the principles on which India was to be governed. The present King-Emperor has announced his resolve to walk in the footsteps of his mother, and we have no doubt that the Prince of Wales is animated by the same desire to see a policy of righteousness pursued towards India. We rejoice that His Royal Highness and his noble consort have come out amongst us to acquaint themselves personally with the ancient civilization of this country and its present condition. The Congress earnestly and respectfully wishes Their Royal Highness a most successful tour through India, and it humbly trusts that the knowledge they will acquire and the recollections they will carry back with them will constitute a fresh bond of sympathy and attachment between the Royal Family in England and the Princes and people of this country. The Congress also offers a most cordial and respectful welcome to Their Excellencies Lord and Lady Minto. The new Viceroy assumes the responsibilities of his office at a critical juncture. The temper of the people, so sorely tried during the last three years, calls for the exercise of wise and statesmanlike conciliation on the part of those who are in authority, if further estrangement between the rulers and the ruled is to be prevented. I earnestly trust that such conciliation will be forthcoming.

Meanwhile, a special responsibility rests upon us all to see to it that the immediate task that confronts His Excellency is not made more difficult than it already is. The difficulties of the situation are not of Lord Minto's creating, and he has a right to expect the co-operation of both the officials and the public in his endeavours to terminate a state of tension which has already produced deplorable results and which cannot be prolonged without serious detriment to the best interests of the country.

Administration of Lord Curzon

Gentlemen, how true it is that to everything there is an end! Thus, even the Viceroyalty of Lord Curzon has come to a close! For seven long years all eyes had constantly to turn to one masterful figure in the land-now in admiration, now in astonishment, more often in anger and in pain, till at last it has become difficult to realize that a change has really come. For a parallel to such an administration, we must, I think, go back to the times of Aurangazeb in the history of our country. There we find the same attempt at a rule excessively centralized and intensely personal, the same strenuous purpose, the same overpowering consciousness of duty, the same marvellous capacity for work, the same sense of loneliness, the same persistence in a policy of distrust and repression, resulting in bitter exasperation all round. I think even the most devoted admirer of Lord Curzon cannot claim that he has strengthened the foundations of British rule in India. In some respects his Lordship will always be recognized as one of the greatest Englishmen that ever came out to this country. His wonderful intellectual gifts, his brilliant powers of expression, his phenomenal energy, his boundless enthusiasm for work-these will ever be a theme of just and unsullied praise.

But the gods are jealous, and amidst such lavish endowments, they withheld from him a sympathetic imagination, without which no man can ever understand an alien people; and it is a sad truth that at the end of his administration Lord Curzon did not really understand the people of India. This was at the root of his many inconsistencies and made him a perpetual puzzle to most men. And thus the man, who professed in all sincerity, before he assumed the reins of office, his great anxiety to show the utmost deference to the feelings and even the prejudices of those over whom he was set to rule, ended. by denouncing in unmeasured terms not only the present generation of Indians, but also their remote ancestors and even the ideals of their race which they cherish above everything else; he who, in the early part of his administration, publicly warned the official classes that "official wisdom is not so transcendent as to be superior to the stimulus and guidance of public opinion" and who declared that in the present state of India "the opinion of the educated classes is one which it is not statesmanship to ignore or to despise," ended by trampling more systematically upon that opinion that any of his predecessors, and claiming for his own judgment and that of his official colleagues a virtual character of infallibility. The fact is that Lord Curzon came to India with certain fixed ideas. To him India was a country where the Englishman was to monopolize for all times all power and talk all the while of duty.

The Indian's only business was to be governed, and it was a sacrilege on his part to have any other aspiration. In his scheme of things there was no room for the educated classes of the country; and having failed to amuse them for any length of time by an empty show of taking them into his confidence he proceeded in the end to repress them. Even in his last farewell speech at the Byculla Club in Bombay, India exists only as a scene of the Englishman's labours, with the toiling millions of the country-eighty per cent of the population-in the background. The remaining twenty per cent, for aught they are worth, might as well by gently swept into the sea! Had Lord Curzon been less self-centred, had he had more humility in his nature, he might perhaps have discovered his mistake before it was too late. This would probably have enabled him to avoid giving so much offence and causing so much pain as he unhappily did during the last two years, but I doubt if the main current of his administration would even then have flowed in another channel. Lord Curzon's highest ideal of statesmanship is efficiency of administration. He does not believe in what Mr. Gladstone used to call the principle of liberty as a factor of human progress. He has no sympathy with popular aspirations, and when he finds them among a subject people, he thinks he is rendering their country a service by trying to put them down. Thus, in his Byculla Club speech he actually stated that he had not offered political concessions to the people of India, because he "did not regard it as wisdom or statesmanship in the interests of India itself to do so!" Taking Lord Curzon at his highest, we find him engaged in a Herculean attempt to strengthen the Englishman's monopoly of power in India and stem the tide of popular agitation and, discontent by rousing the members of the bureaucracy to a sense of duty similar to his own and raising the standard of administrative efficiency all round. The attempt has failed, as it was bound to fail. Never was discontent in India more acute and widespread than when the late Viceroy laid down the reins of office; and as regards the bureaucratic monopoly of power, I think we are sensibly nearer the time when it will be successfully assailed. One claim Lord Curzon advanced in his farewell speech at Bombay, which it is necessary to examine a little. He told his hearers, as he had done once before-on the occasion of the last Budget debate-that even if he had incurred the hostility of educated Indians, the masses would be grateful to him for what he had done for them. This attempt to distinguish between the interests of the educated classes and those of the bulk of their countrymen is a favourite device with those who seek to repress the legitimate aspirations of our people. It is significant that Lord Curzon had never resorted to it till he had finally broken with the educated classes. We know, of course, that the distinction is unreal and ridiculous, and we know also that most of those who use it as a convenient means to disparage the educated classes cannot themselves really believe in it.

Lord Curzon mentions the reduction of the salt duty, the writing off of famine arrears, the increased grants to primary education and to irrigation, the attempt at Police reform as measures on which he bases his claim. The suggestion here is that he adopted these measures for the good of the masses in spite of the opposition-at any rate, the indifference-of the educated classes, when the plain fact is that it was the Congress that had been urging these measures year after year on the attention of Government and that it was only after years of persistent agitation that it was able to move the Government in the desired direction. Four years ago, when with a surplus of seven crores or nearly five millions sterling in hand, the Government of India did not remit any taxation, and I ventured to complain of this in the Council and to urge an immediate reduction of the salt duty, I well remember how Lord Curzon sneered at those who "talked glibly" of the burdens of the masses and of the necessity of lowering the salt tax as a measure of relief! Lord Curzon was fortunate in coming to India when the currency legislation of Lord Landsowne and Sir David Barbour, had succeeded in artificially raising the rupee to its present level, thereby enabling the Government of India to save about four millions sterling a year on its Home remittances.

This, with the recovery of the opium revenue, placed huge surpluses at Lord Curzon's disposal throughout his administration and he never knew a moment of that financial stress and anxiety which his predecessors had to face for a series of years. Considering how large these surpluses have been, I do not think the relief given by Lord Curzon to the taxpayers of the country has by any means been liberal. He himself estimated last March the total amount of this relief at 7 millions sterling. He did not mention that during the same time he had taken from the taxpayers 33 millions sterling over and above the requirements of the Government. Again, how paltry is the relief given by the reduction of the salt duty and the writing off of famine arrears compared with the enormous injury done to the mass of our people by the artificial raising of the value of the rupee, which led to heavy and immediate depreciation of their small savings in silver, and which makes a grievous addition to their permanent burdens by indirectly enhancing their assessments and increasing their debts to the money-lender as prices adjust themselves to the new rupee. Much has been made of Lord Curzon's increased grants to primary education. Considering how little the State does in India for the education of the masses it would have been astonishing, if with such surpluses Lord Curzon had not made any addition to the educational expenditure of the country. But if he has given a quarter of a million more to education, he has given five millions a year more to the Army; and with reckless profusion he has increased the salaries of European officials in many departments and has created several new posts for them. "A spirit of expenditure," to use an expression of Mr. Gladstone's, has been abroad in all directions during his time, and he has never practised the old fashioned virtue of economy, with which the real interests of the people are bound up.

Of course a ruler cannot labour as devotedly as Lord Curzon has done for seven years for increased efficiency without removing or mitigating important administrative evils; but that is quite different from a claim of championing the special interests of the masses as against their natural leaders and spokesmen, the educated classes of the community.

Bengal's Division

Gentlemen, the question that is uppermost in the minds of us all at this moment is the Partition of Bengal. A cruel wrong has been inflicted on our Bengalee brethren and the whole country has been stirred to its deepest depths with sorrow and resentment, as has never been the case before. The scheme of partition, concocted in the dark and carried out in the face of the fiercest opposition that any Government measure has encountered during the last half a century, will always stand as a complete illustration of the worst features of the present system of bureaucratic rule-its utter contempt for public opinion, its arrogant pretensions to superior wisdom, its reckless disregard of the most cherished feelings of the people, the mockery an appeal to its sense of justice becomes and its cool preference of Service interests to those of the governed. Lord Curzon and his advisers-if he ever had any advisers-could never allege that they had no means of judging of the depth of public feeling in the matter. All that could possibly have been done by way of a respectful representation of the views of the people had been done.

As soon as it was known that a partition of some sort was contemplated, meeting after meeting of protest was held, till over five hundred public meetings in all parts of the Province had proclaimed in no uncertain voice that the attempt to dismember a compact and homogeneous province, to which the people were passionately attached and of which they were justly proud, was deeply resented and would be resisted to the uttermost. Memorials to the same effect poured in upon the Viceroy. The Secretary of State for India was implored to withhold his sanction to the proposed measure. The intervention of the British House of Commons was sought, first, by a monster petition, signed by sixty thousand people, and later by means of a debate on the subject raised in the House by our ever watchful friend-Mr. Herbert Roberts.' All proved unavailing. The Viceroy had made up his mind. The officials under him had expressed approval. What business had the people to have an opinion of their own and to stand in the way? To add insult to injury, Lord Curzon described the opposition to his measure as 'manufactured' the opposition in which all classes of Indians, high and low, uneducated and educated, Hindus and Mahomedans, had joined, the opposition than which nothing more intense, nothing more widespread, nothing more spontaneous, had been seen in this country in the whole course of our political agitation! Let it be remembered that when the late Viceroy cast this stigma on those who were ranged against his proposals, not a single public pronouncement in favour of those proposals had been made by any section of the community; and that among the foremost opponents of the measure were men like Sir Jotindra Mohan Tagore and Sir Gurudas Bannerji, Raja Peary Mohan Mukerji and Dr. Rash Behary Ghose, the Maharajas of Mymensingh and Kassimbazaar—men who keep themselves aloof from ordinary political agitation and never say a word calculated in any way to embarrass the authorities, and who came forward to oppose publicly the Partition project only from an overpowering sense of the necessity of their doing what they could to avert a dreaded calamity. If the opinions of even such men are to be brushed aside with contempt, if all Indians are to be treated as no better than dumb-driven cattle; if men, whom any other country would delight to honour, are to be thus made to realize the utter humiliation and helplessness of their position in their own, then all I can say is "Good-bye to all hope of cooperating in any way with the bureaucracy in the interests of the people!" I can conceive of no graver indictment of British rule than that such a state of things should be possible after a hundred years of that rule!

Feasible Substitute

Gentlemen, I have carefully gone through all the papers which have been published by the Government on this subject of

Partition. Three things have struck me forcibly—a determination to dismember Bengal at all costs, an anxiety to promote the interests of Assam at the expense of Bengal, and a desire to suit everything to the interests and convenience of the Civil Service. It is not merely that a number of new prizes have been thrown into the lap of that Service-one Lieutenant-Governorship, two Memberships of the Board of Revenue, one Commissionership of a Division, several Secretaryships and Under-Secretaryships—but alternative schemes of readjustment have been rejected on the express ground that their adoption would be unpopular with the members of the Service.

Thus, even if a reduction of the charge of the Lieutenant-Governor of Bengal had really become inevitable—a contention which the greatest living authority on the subject, Sir Henry Cotton, who was Secretary to the Bengal Government under seven Lieutenant Governors does not admit-one would have thought that the most natural course to take was to separate Behar, Orissa and Chota Nagpore from Bengal and form them into a separate province. This would have made the Western Province one of 30 millions in place of the Eastern. But this, says the Government of India, "would take from Bengal all its best districts and would make the Province universally unpopular." This was of course a fatal objection, for, compared with the displeasure of the Civil Service, the trampling under foot of public opinion and the outraging of the deepest feelings of a whole people was a small matter! But one can see that administrative considerations were really only secondary in the determination of this question. The dismemberment of Bengal had become necessary, because, in the view of the Government of India, "it cannot be for the lasting good of any country or any people that public opinion or what passes for it should be manufactured by a comparatively small number of people at a single centre and should be disseminated thence for universal adoption, all other views being discouraged or suppressed." "From every point of view," the Government further states, "it appears to us desirable to encourage the growth of centres of independent opinion, local aspirations, local ideals and to preserve the growing intelligence and enterprise of Bengal from being cramped and stunted by the process of forcing it prematurely into a mould of rigid and sterile uniformity." You will see that this is only a paraphrase, in Lord Curzon's most approved style, of the complaint of the people of Bengal that their fair Province has been dismembered to destroy their growing solidarity, check their national aspirations and weaken their power of co-operating for national ends, lessen the influence of their educated classes with their countrymen, and reduce the political importance of Calcutta.

After this, let no apologist of the late Viceroy pretend that the object of the partition was administrative convenience and not political repression! Gentlemen, it is difficult to speak in terms of due restraint of Lord Curzon's conduct throughout this affair. Having published his earlier and smaller scheme for public criticism, it was his clear duty to publish similarly the later and larger scheme which he afterwards substituted for it. But in consequence of the opposition which the first scheme encountered, he abandoned the idea of taking the public any more into his confidence and proceeded to work in the matter in the dark. For more than a year nothing further was heard of his intentions, and while he was silently elaborating the details of his measure, he allowed the impression to prevail that the Government had abandoned the partition project. And in the end, when he had succeeded in securing the Secretary of State's sanction to the scheme, it was from Simla, where he and his official colleagues were beyond the reach of public opinion, that he sprang the final orders of Government upon an unprepared people. Then suddenly came his resignation. And the people permitted themselves for a while to hope that it would bring them at least a brief respite, especially as Mr. Brodrick had promised shortly before to present further papers on the subject to Parliament, which was understood to mean that the scheme would not be brought into operation till Parliament reassembled at the beginning of next year.

Of course, after his resignation, the only proper, the only dignified, course for Lord Curzon was to take no step which it was difficult to revoke and the consequences of which would have to be faced not by him, but by his successor. He owed it to Lord Minto to give him an opportunity to examine the question for himself; he owed it to the Royal visitors not to plunge the largest Province of India into violent agitation and grief on the eve of their visit to it. But Lord Curzon was determined to partition Bengal before he left India, and so he rushed the necessary legislation through the Legislative Council at Simla, which only the official members could attend, and enforced his orders on 16th October last—a day observed as one of universal mourning by all classes of people in Bengal. And now, while he himself has gone from India, what a sea of troubles he has bequeathed to his successor! Fortunately, there are grounds to believe that Lord Minto will deal with the situation with tact, firmness, and sympathy, and it seems he has already pulled up to some extent Lord Curzon's favourite Lieutenant, the first ruler of the new Eastern Province. Mr. Fuller has evidently cast to the winds all prudence, all restraint, all sense of responsibility. Even if a fraction of what the papers have been reporting be true, his extraordinary doings must receive the attention of the new Secretary of State for India and the House of Commons. There is no surer method of goading a docile people into a state of dangerous despair than the kind of hectoring and repression he has been attempting. But, gentlemen, as has been well said, even in things evil there is a soul of goodness, and the dark times through which Bengal has passed and is passing, have not been without a message of bright hope for the future. The tremendous upheaval of popular feeling, which has taken place in Bengal in consequence of the partition, will constitute a landmark in the history of our national progress. For the first time since British rule began, all sections of the Indian community, without distinction of caste or creed, have been moved, by a common impulse and without the stimulus of external pressure, to act together in offering resistance to a common wrong. A wave of true national consciousness has swept over the Province and, at its touch, old barriers have, for the time at any rate, been thrown down, personal jealousies have vanished, other controversies have been hushed! Bengal's heroic stand against the oppression of a harsh and uncontrolled bureaucracy has astonished and gratified all India, and her sufferings have not been endured in vain, when they have helped to draw closer all parts of the country in sympathy and in aspiration.

A great rush and uprising the waters such as has been recently witnessed in Bengal cannot take place without a little inundation over the banks here and there. Those little excesses are inevitable when large' masses of men move spontaneously-especially when the movement is from darkness into light, from bondage towards freedom and they must not be allowed to disconcert us too much. The most astounding fact of the situation is that the public life of this country has received an accession of strength of great importance, and for this all India owes a deep debt of gratitude to Bengal. Of course the difficulties which confront the leaders of Bengal are enormous and perhaps they have only just begun. But I know there is no disposition to shrink from any responsibilities, and I have no doubt that whatever sacrifices are necessary will be cheerfully made. All India is at their back, and they will receive in the work that lies before them the cordial sympathy and assistance of the other Provinces. Any discredit that is allowed to fall on them affects us all. They on their side must not forget that the honour of all India is at present in their keeping.

Swadeshi—A Patriotic and Economic Movement

Gentlemen, I will now say a few words on a movement which has spread so rapidly and has been hailed with so much enthusiasm all over the country during the last few months—the Swadeshi movement. It is necessary, at the outset, to distinguish it from another movement started in Bengal, which has really given it such immense impetus-the boycott of British goods.

We all know that when our Bengalee brethren found that nothing would turn the late Viceroy from his purpose of partitioning Bengal, that all their protests in the Press and on the platform, all their memorials to him, to the Secretary of State and to Parliament were unavailing, that the Government exercised its despotic strength to trample on their most cherished feelings and to injure their dearest interests and that no protection against this of any kind was forthcoming from any quarter, they, in their extremity, resolved to have recourse to this boycott movement. This they did with a twofold object-first, as a demonstration of their deep resentment at the treatment they were receiving, and, secondly, to attract the attention of the people in England to their grievances, so that those who were in a position to call the Government of India to account might understand what was taking place in India. It was thus as a political weapon, used for a definite political purpose, that they had recourse to the boycott; and in the circumstances of their position they had every justification for the step they took. And I can tell you from personal experience that their action has proved immensely effective in drawing the attention of English people to the state of things in our country.

But a weapon like this must be reserved only for extreme occasions. There are obvious risks involved in its failure and it cannot be used with sufficient effectiveness, unless there is an extraordinary upheaval of popular feeling behind it. It is bound to rouse angry passions on the other side, and no true well-wisher of his country will be responsible for provoking such passions, except under an overpowering sense of necessity. On an extreme occasion, of course, a boycotting demonstration is perfectly legitimate but that occasion must be one to drive all the classes, as in Bengal, to act with one impulse, and make all leaders sink their personal differences in the presence of a common danger. It is well to remember that the term 'boycott', owing to its origin, has got unsavoury associations, and it conveys to the mind before everything else a vindictive desire to injure another.

Such a desire on our part, as a normal feature of our relations with England, is, of course, out of the question. Moreover, if the boycott is confined to British goods only, it leaves us free to purchase the goods of other foreign countries, and this does not help the Swadeshi movement in any way. Gentlemen, the true Swadeshi movement is both a patriotic and an economic movement. The idea of Swadeshi or 'one's own country' is one of the noblest conception's that have ever stirred the heart of humanity. As the poet asks:

Breathes there the man with soul so dead,

Who never to himself hath said,

This is my own, my native land!

The devotion to motherland, which is enshrined in the highest Swadeshi, is an influence so profound and so passionate that its very thought thrills and its actual touch lifts one out of oneself. India needs today above everything else that the gospel of this devotion should be preached to high and low, to prince and to peasant, in town and in hamlet, till the service of motherland becomes with us as overmastering a passion as it is in Japan. The

Swadeshi movement, as it is ordinarily understood, presents one part of this gospel to the mass of our people in a form which brings it within their comprehension. It turns their thoughts to their country, accustoms them to the idea of voluntarily making some sacrifice for her sake, enables them to take an intelligent interest in her economic development and teaches them the important lesson of co-operating with one another for a national end. All this is most valuable work and those who undertake it are entitled to feel that they are engaged in a highly patriotic mission.

But the movement on its material side is an economic one; and though self-denying ordinances, extensively entered into, must serve a valuable economic purpose, namely, to ensure a ready consumption of such articles as are produced in the country and to furnish a perpetual stimulus to production by keeping the demand for indigenous things largely in excess of the supply, the difficulties that surround the question economically are so great that they require the co-operation of every available agency to surmount them. The problem is, indeed, one of the first magnitude. Twelve years ago, the late Mr. Ranade remarked at an Industrial Conference held at Poona: The political domination of one country by another attracts far more attention that the more formidable, though unfelt domination, which the capital, enterprise and skill of one country exercise over the trade and manufactures of another. This latter domination has an insidious influence which paralyzes the springs of all the varied activities, which together make up the life of a nation. The question of production is a question of capital, enterprise and skill, and in all these factors our deficiency at present is very great. Whoever can help in any one of these fields is, therefore, a worker in the Swadeshi cause and should be welcomed as such. Not by methods of exclusion but by those of comprehension, not by insisting on every one working in the same part of the field but by leaving each one free to select his own corner, by attracting to the cause all who ire likely to help and not alienating any who are already with us, are the difficulties of the problem likely to be overcome. Above all, let us see to it that there are no fresh divisions in the country in the name of Swadeshism. No greater perversion of its true spirit could be imagined than that. Take the question of cotton piece-goods, of which we import at present over 22 millions sterling worth a year. This is by far the heaviest item among our imports and our present Swadeshi agitation is directed mainly towards producing as much of these goods in our own country as possible. I have consulted three of the best experts available in India on this subject-Mr. Bezanji of Nagpore, the right-hand man of the late Mr. Tata in mill matters, the Hon. Mr. Vithaldas Damodardas, who has written an admirable paper on the Cotton Industry for the Industrial Conference and has kindly placed a copy of it at my disposal, and our friend Mr. Wacha. They are all agreed about the requirements and the difficulties of the situation.

So far as the cotton fabrics are concerned, even strict Free Traders should have nothing to say against the encouragement which the Swadeshi movement seeks to give to their manufacture in India. In the first place, many of the usual objections that may be urged against a system of State protection do not apply to helpful voluntary action on the part of consumers, such as the Swadeshi movement endeavours to promote. Moreover, the essence of Free Trade is that a commodity should be produced where the comparative cost of its production is the least and that it should be consumed where its relative value is the highest; and if accidental circumstances have thwarted such an adjustment in a given case, any agency which seeks to overcome the impediment works in the "end in the interests of true Free Trade. Now everyone will admit that with cheap labour and cotton at her own door, India enjoys exceptional advantages for the manufacture of cotton goods; and if the Swadeshi movement helps her to regain her natural position in this respect—a position which she once occupied but out of which she has been driven by an extraordinary combination of circumstances—the movement works not against but in' furtherance of true Free Trade. Even at present the cotton industry in India is an important one. It is the largest industry after agriculture in the country; it is also one-agriculture excepted in which the Indians themselves have a substantial share.

It is represented by a paid-up capital of about 17 crores of rupees or a little over 11 millions sterling, the number of mills being about 200, with five million spindles and fifty thousand power-looms. In addition to this, there are, according to the census of 1901, about a quarter of a million persons engaged in hand-loom weaving in the country. Our mills consume nearly 60 per cent of the cotton produce of India and produce 58 crore lbs. of yearn. Of this quantity, Mr. Vithaldas tells us, about 231/2 crore lbs. is exported to China and other foreign countries, about 13½ crore lbs. is used in our weaving mills and about 19 crore lbs. is woven by handloom weavers, the remaining 2 crore lbs. going to the manufacture of rope and twine. In addition to this, 3 crore lbs. Of yarn is imported from the United Kingdom, and is consumed by the handlooms. The hand-loom industry of the country thus absorbs, in spite of its hard struggles, about 22 crore lbs. Of yarn, or nearly double the quantity woven by power-looms, and this is a most interesting and significant fact. The yarn used by the weaving mills produces about 55 crores of yards of cloth, of which about 14 crore yards is exported to foreign countries and about 41 crores is left for consumption in the country. If we put down the production of the hand-looms at about 90 crore yards, we have about 130 crore yards as the quantity of Swadeshi cloth consumed at present in India. The quantity of piece-goods imported from the United Kingdom and retained for use in the country is about 205 crore yards a year. Of the total cloth consumed, therefore, over one-third is at present Swadeshi. This is an encouraging feature of the situation. But the imported cloth is almost all superior in quality. "While our mills," Mr. Vithaldas says, "produce the coarser cloth, say, from yarn up to 30's count and in a few cases up to 40's, the bulk of the imported cloth is of the finer quality, using yarn over 30's count. The Indian weaving mills are obliged to restrict themselves for the most part to weaving coarser cloth owing to the inferior quality of cotton now grown in the country". It may be noted that even from existing cotton, 'hand-looms can, owing to their greater delicacy of handling the yarn, produce finer cloth than the power-looms. Fortunately, owing to the exertions of the Agricultural Department of the Bombay Government—exertions for which it is entitled to the best thanks of the whole country-Egyptian cotton has just been successfully introduced into Sind and this year a thousand bales of a quality equal to very good Egyptian have been produced. A much heavier crop is expected next year and there is no doubt that its cultivation will rapidly extend. The main difficulty in the way of our manufacturing the quality of cloth that is at present imported is one of capital. Mr.

Wacha estimates that if the whole quantity of 205 crore yards is to be produced by mills, the industry requires an additional capital of about 30 crores of rupees.

Even if we proposed to spread this over ten years, we should require an addition of 3 crores of rupees every year. Now if we turn to the Statistical Abstract of British India, we shall find that the total increase in the capital invested in cotton mills during the last ten years has been only about 3 crores for ten years, an amount that Mr. Wacha wants every year. The normal development of the mill industry is thus plainly unequal to the requirements of the situation. Moreover, it is well to remember what Mr. Bezanji says that the present mill-owners must not be expected to be very keen about the production of finer cloth, because its manufacture is much less paying than that of the coarser cloth. This is due to various causes, the principal one among them being that English capital, similarly invested, is satisfied with a smaller range of profits. Capital from other quarters must, therefore, be induced to come forward and undertake this business. If we again turn to the Statistical Abstract, we shall find that our people hold about 50 crores of rupees in Government Securities and about 11 crores in Postal Savings Banks. The private deposits stand at about 33 crores of rupees, but there are no means of ascertaining how much of the amount is held by Indians. Considering the extent of the country and the number of the population, these resources are, of course, extremely meagre.

Still they might furnish some part of the capital needed. In this connection may I say that a special responsibility now rests in the matter on the aristocracy of Bengal? And this is not merely because the Swadeshi movement is being so vigorously advocated in their Province, but also because, owing to the Permanent Settlement of Bengal, they are enabled to enjoy resources, which, in other parts of India, are swept into the coffers of the State. If sufficient capital is forthcoming, Mr. Bezanji's patriotism may, I am sure, be relied on to secure for the undertaking whatever assistance his great capacity and unrivalled knowledge can give. It must, however, be admitted that capital will come forward only cautiously for this branch of the business. But the handlooms are likely to prove of greater immediate service. Mr. Vithaldas looks forward to a great revival of the handloom industry in the country, and I cannot do better than quote what he says on this point in his paper: "The village industry," he says, "gives means of livelihood not only to an immense number of the weaver class, but affords means of supplementing their income to agriculturists-the backbone of India-who usually employ themselves on hand-looms when field work is unnecessary, and also when, owing to famine, drought or excessive rains, agricultural operations are not possible. Now the apparatus with which they work is nearly two centuries behind the times. Mr. Havell, Principal of the Calcutta School of Arts, Mr. Chatterton of the Madras School of Arts, and Mr. Churchill of Bangalore, along with many others, are doing yeoman's service by taking keen interest in the question of supplying economical and improved apparatus to the hand-loom weavers Mr. Havell has pointed out that in preparing the work our handloom weavers are incapable of winding more than two threads at a time, though the simplest mechanical device would enable them to treat 50 or 100 threads simultaneously. The latest European hand-loom which successfully competes with the power-loom in Cairo and in many places in Europe, can turn out a maximum of 68 yards of common cloth in a day. Mr. Havell is satisfied that the greater portion of the imported cotton cloth can be made in the Indian handlooms with great- profit to the whole community. The question of the immediate revival of the hand-loom weaving industry on a commercial basis demands the most earnest attention of every well-wisher of India and evidence gives promise of a successful issue to efforts put forward in this direction." The outlook here is thus hopeful and cheering; only we must not fail to realize that the co-operation of all who can help including the Government-is needed to overcome the difficulties that lie in the path.

Expectation of the People

Gentlemen, this is the twenty-first session of the Indian National Congress. Year after year, since 1885, we have been assembling in these gatherings to give voice to our aspirations and to formulate our wants. When the movement was first inaugurated, we were under the influence of that remarkable outburst of enthusiasm for British rule, which had been evoked in the country by the great Viceroyalty of the Marquis of Ripon. The best beloved of India's Viceroys was not content to offer mere lip-homage to the principle that righteousness alone exalteth a nation. He had dared to act on it in practice and he had braved persecution at the hands of his own countrymen in India for its sake. Lord Ripon's noblest service to this country was that he greatly quickened the processes by which the consciousness of a national purpose comes to establish itself in the minds of a people.

The Congress movement was the direct and immediate outcome of this realization. It was started to focus and organize the patriotic forces that were working independently of one another in different parts of the country so as to invest their work with a national character and to increase their general effectiveness. Hope at that time was warm and faith shone bright, largely as a result of Lord Ripon's Viceroyalty, and those who started the Congress believed that, by offering their criticism and urging their demands from a national platform where they could speak in the name of all India, they would be able to Secure a continuous improvement of the administration and a steady advance in the direction of the political emancipation of the people. Twenty years have since elapsed, and during the time much has happened to chill that hope and dim that faith, but there can be no doubt that work of great value in our national life has already been accomplished. The minds of the people have been familiarized with the idea of a united India working for her salvation; a national public opinion has been created; close bonds of sympathy now knit together the different Provinces; caste and creed separations hamper less and less the pursuit of common aims; the dignity of a consciousness of national existence has spread over the whole land. Our record of political concessions won is, no doubt, very meagre, but those that have been secured are of considerable value; some retrogression has been prevented; and if latterly we have been unable to stem the tide of reaction, the resistance we have offered, though it has failed of its avowed purpose, has substantially strengthened our public life. Our deliberations have extended over a very wide range of problems; public opinion in the country is, in consequence, better informed, and the Press is steadily growing in authority and usefulness. Above all, there is a general perception now of the goal towards which we have to strive and a wide recognition of the arduous character of the struggle and the immense sacrifices it requires. The goal of the Congress is that India should be governed in the interests of the Indians themselves, and that, in course of time, a form of Government should be attained in this country similar to what exists in the Self-Governing Colonies of the British Empire. For better, for worse, our destinies are now linked with those of England, and the Congress freely recognises that whatever advance we seek must be within the Empire itself.

That advance, moreover, can only be gradual, as at each stage of the progress it may be necessary for us to pass through a brief course of apprenticeship before we are enabled to go to the next one; for it is a reasonable proposition that the sense of responsibility, required for the proper exercise of the political institutions of the West, can be acquired by an Eastern people through practical training and experience only. To admit this is not to express any agreement with those who usually oppose all attempts at reform on the plea that the people are not ready for it. "It is liberty alone," says Mr. Gladstone in words of profound wisdom, "which fits men for liberty. This proposition, like every other in politics, has its bounds; but it is far safer than the counter doctrine, wait till they are fit." While, therefore, we are prepared to allow that an advance towards our goal that be only by reasonably cautious steps, what we emphatically insist on is that the resources of the country should be primarily devoted to the work of qualifying the people by means of education and in other ways for such advance. Even the most bigoted champion of the existing system of administration will not pretend that this is in any degree the case at present. Our net revenue is about 44 millions sterling. Of this very nearly one-half is now eaten up by the Army. The Home Congress, exclusive of their military portion, absorb nearly one-third. The two, between them, account for about 34 millions out of 44. Then over 3 millions are paid to European officials in civil employ. This leaves only about 7 millions at the disposal of the Government to be applied to other purposes. Can any one, who realises what this means, wonder that the Government spends only a miserable three-quarters of a million out of State funds on the education of the people-primary, secondary and higher, all put together! Japan came under the influence of Western ideas only forty years ago, and yet already she is in a line with the most advanced nations of the West in matters of mass education, the State finding funds for the education of every child of school-going age. We have now been a hundred years under England's rule, and yet today four villages out of every five are without a school-house and seven children out of eight are allowed to grow up in ignorance and in darkness! Militarism, Service interests and the interests of English capitalists-all take precedence today of the true interests of the Indian people in the administration of the country. Things cannot be otherwise, for it is the government of the people of our country by the people of another and this, as Mill points out, is bound to produce great evils. Now the Congress wants that all this should be governed, first and foremost, in the interests of the Indians themselves. This result will be achieved only in proportion as we obtain more and more voice in the government of our country. We are prepared to bear-and bear cheerfully-our fair share of the burdens of the Empire, of which we are now a part, but we want to participate in the privileges also, and we object most strongly to being sacrificed, as at present, in order that others may prosper.

Then the Congress asks for a redemption of those promises for the equal treatment of Indians and Englishmen in the government of this country, which have been so solemnly given us by the Sovereign and the Parliament of England. It is now three-quarters of a century since the Parliament passed an Act, which, the Court of Directors pointed out, meant that there was to be no governing caste in India. The governing caste, however, is still as vigorous, as exclusive as ever. Twenty-five years later the late Queen Empress addressed a most memorable Proclamation to the princes and people of India. The circumstances connected with the issue of that Proclamation and its noble contents will always bear witness to the true greatness of that great Sovereign and will never cease to shed lustre on the English name. The Proclamation repeats the pledges contained in the Charter Act of 1833, and though an astounding attempt was made less than two years ago by the late Viceroy to explain away its solemn import, the plain meaning of the royal message cannot be altered without attributing what is nothing less than an unworthy subterfuge to a Sovereign, the deep reverence for whose memory is an asset of the Empire. That the Charter Act of 1833 and the Queen's Proclamation of 1858 have created in the eyes of reactionary rulers a most inconvenient situation is clear from a blunt declaration which another Viceroy of India, the late Lord Lytton," made in a confidential document and which has since seen the light of day. Speaking of our claims and expectations based on the pledges of the Sovereign and the Parliament of England, he wrote: We all know that these claims and expectations never can or will be fulfilled. We have had to choose between prohibiting them (the natives of India) and cheating them, and we have chosen the least straightforward course.... Since I am writing confidentially, I do not hesitate to say that both the Government of England and of India appear to me up to the present moment unable to answer satisfactorily the charge of having taken every means in their power of breaking to the heart the words of promise they had uttered to the car. We accept Lord Lytton as an unimpeachable authority on the conduct of the Government in evading the fulfilment of the pledges. We deny his claim to lay down that our "claims and expectations never can or will be fulfilled." Our whole future, it is needless to say, is bound up with this question of the relative position of the two races in this country. The domination of one race over another-especially when there is no great disparity between their intellectual endowments and their general civilization-inflicts great injury on the subject race in a thousand insidious ways.

On the moral side, the present situation is steadily destroying our capacity for initiative and dwarfing us as men of action. On the material side, it has resulted in a fearful impoverishment of the people. For a hundred years and more now India has been for members of the dominant race a country where fortunes were to be made to be taken out and spent elsewhere. As in Ireland, the evil of absent landlordism has in the past aggravated the racial domination of the English over the Irish, so in India what may be called absentee capitalism has been added to the racial ascendancy of Englishmen. A great and ruinous drain of wealth from the country has gone on for many years, the net excess of exports over imports (including treasure) during the last forty years amounting to no less than a thousand millions sterling. The steady rise in the death rate of the country from 24 per thousand, the average for 1882-84, to 30 per thousand, the average for 1892-94, and 34 per thousand, the present average— a terrible and conclusive proof of this continuous impoverishment of the mass of our people. India's best interests material and moral-no less than the honour of England, demand that the policy of equality for the two races promised by the Sovereign and by Parliament should be faithfully and courageously carried out. Gentlemen, as I have already observed, the manner in which the Partition of Bengal has been carried out furnishes a striking illustration of the worst features of the present system of bureaucratic rule.

Happily these features are not always so conspicuously in evidence. No one also denies that a large proportion of the members of the bureaucracy being to their work a high level of ability, a keen sense of duty and a conscientious desire, within the limits of the restricted opportunities permitted by the predominance of other interests, to do what good they can to the people. It is the system that is really at fault—a system which relegates the interest of the people to a very subordinate place and which, by putting too much power into the hands of these men, impairs their sense of responsibility and develops in them a spirit of intolerance of criticism. I know many of these men are on their side constantly smarting under a sense of unfair condemnation by our countrymen. They fail to realize that if the criticism that is passed on their actions is sometimes ill-informed and even unjust, this is largely due to the veil of secrecy which carefully hides official proceedings from the view of the people in India.

Moreover, theirs are at present all the privileges of the position and they must bear without impatience or bitterness its few disadvantages. I have already said that our advance towards our goal can only be gradual. Meanwhile, there is a great deal of work to be done for the country in which officials and nonofficials could join hands A considerable part of the way we could both go together, but it can only be on terms consistent with the self-respect of either side. In old times, when British rule was new and its higher standards and its more vigorous purposes excited general admiration, the Englishman's claim to a privileged position, even outside the sphere of official duties, was allowed to pass unchallenged. That is now no longer possible, and those officials, who expect the Indians to approach them with bated breath and whispering humbleness-and the type is not confined to the new

Eastern Province exclusively-not only make useful relations between the two sides impossible, but do more harm to their own class than they imagine. In one respect, the gulf between the official and educated classes of the country is bound to widen more and more every day. The latter now clearly see that the bureaucracy is growing frankly selfish and openly hostile to their national aspirations. It was not so in the past. In a most remarkable letter which I had the honour to receive, while in England two months ago, from Mr. Hodgson Pratt—a great and venerated name among all lovers of peace-hè tells us with what object Western education was introduced into this country. "Fifty years ago," writes Mr. Pratt, who in those days was a member of the Bengal Civil Service, "while India was still under the Government of the East India Company, it was considered both just and wise to introduce measures for national education on a liberal scale, with adequate provision of schools, colleges, and universities. This event was hailed with lively satisfaction by the native population as heralding a new era of social progress, and as satisfying the active intelligence of the Hindus. Now it must be observed that the character of the teaching thus inaugurated by Englishmen would necessarily reflect the ideals which have for centuries prevailed among them. In other words Indian youths would be brought up to admire our doctrines of political liberty, popular rights, and national independence; nor could it ever have been supposed that these lessons would fall upon deaf ears and cold hearts.

On the contrary, the inevitable result of such teaching was clearly perceived by the Government of those days, and was regarded in a generous spirit. In support of this assertion I may attention that at the time of the inauguration of these measures I accompanied the then Lieutenant-Governor of Bengal (Sir Frederick Halliday) on one of his winter tours through the province. Naturally, he called the attention of those who attended the public meetings held by him to the new education policy, and he always took occasion to declare that the schools would promote one of the leading purposes of British rule, which was to prepare the people for self-government. It certainly was not supposed that at any subsequent time a policy would be adopted, which would disappoint the legitimate hopes thus created." Now, however, that the time has come for the bureaucracy to part with some of its power in favour of the educated classes, all kinds of excuses are brought forward to postpone what is no doubt regarded as the evil day. One favourite argument is that the educated classes are as yet only a very small fraction of the community. The hollowness of this plea was well exposed by the late Mr. George Yule in his address as President of our National Congress in 1888. Quoting Prof. Thorold Rogers, he pointed out that a hundred years ago, not one man in ten or one woman in twenty knew how to read and write in England. Going another century or two back, he added, the people of England, man and boy, high and low, with the exception of a mere handful, were steeped in the grossest ignorance, and yet there was a House of Commons. We have now in this country about 15 million people who can read and write, and about a million of these have come under the influence of some kind of English education. Moreover, what we ask for at present is a voice in the government of the country, not for the whole population, but for such portion of it as has been qualified by education to discharge properly the responsibilities of such association. Another argument brought forward in favour of maintaining the present bureaucratic monopoly of power is that though the educated classes make a grievance of it, the mass of the people are quite indifferent in the matter. Now, in the first place, this is not true. However, it may suit the interests of the officials to deny the fact, the educated classes are, in the present circumstances of India, the natural leaders of the people. Theirs is the Vernacular Press, the contents of which do not fail to reach the mass of our population; in a hundred ways they have access to the minds of the latter; and what the educated Indians think today, the rest of India thinks tomorrow.

Moreover, do the officials realise how their contention condemns their rule out of their own mouths? For it means that only so long as the people of India are kept in ignorance and their faculties are forced to lie dormant, that they do not raise any objection to the present system of administration. The moment education quickens those faculties and clears their vision, they range themselves against a continuance of the system! Gentlemen, a number of important questions will come up before you for discussion during the next two days, and following the practice of previous Congresses, you will, no doubt, record after due deliberation, your views on them in the form of resolutions. This is, of course, necessary; but may I suggest that, for purposes of effective agitation in the immediate future, we should now concentrate our main energies on certain selected portions of our programme? Speaking broadly, most of the reforms that we have been advocating may be grouped under four heads: (1) Those which aim at securing for our people a larger and larger share in the administration and control of our affairs; these include a reform of our Legislative Councils, the appointment of Indians to the Secretary of State's Council and the Executive Councils in India, and a steady substitution of the Indian for the European agency in the public service of the country; (2) those which seek to improve the methods of administration, such as the separation of Judicial from Executive functions, Police Reform, and similar proposals; (3) those which propose a readjustment of financial arrangements with the object of securing a reduction of the burdens of the tax-payers and a more efficient application of our resources; under this head come a reduction of military charges, the moderating of land assessments and so forth; and (4) those which urge the adoption of measures calculated to improve the condition of the mass of the people; these include a vigorous extension of primary education, facilities for industrial and technical instruction, grants for improved sanitation, and a real attempt to deal with the alarming indebtedness of the peasantry. Now what I would most earnestly and respectfully suggest is that we should select from each group such reforms as may be immediately urged with the greatest effect and press them forward in this country and in England with all the energy we can command. In my humble opinion, our immediate demands should be:

(a) The creation of Advisory Boards in all Districts throughout India, whom the heads of districts should be bound to consult in important matters of administration concerning the public before taking action. For the present, heir functions should be only advisory, the Collectors or District Magistrates being at liberty to set aside their advice at their discretion. Half the members of a Board should be only advisory, the Collectors or District Magistrates being at liberty to set aside their advice at their discretion. Half the members of a Board should be elected representatives of the different Talukas or sub-divisions of the district, an the other half should consist of the principal District officers and such nonofficial gentlemen as the head of the district may appoint. These Boards must not be confounded with what are known as District Local Boards. There is, at present, too much of what may be called Secretariat rule with an excessive multiplication of central departments. District administration must be largely freed from this, and reasonable opportunities afforded to the people concerned to influence its course, before final decisions are arrived at. If such Boards; are created, we may, in course of time, expect them to be entrusted with some real measure of control over the district administration. The late Mr. Ranade used to urge the importance of such Boards very strongly. If ever we are to have real local Government in matters of general administration, the creation of these Boards will pave the way for it. One great evil of the present system of administration is its secrecy. This will be materially reduced, so far as district administration in concerned, by the step proposed.

(b) A reform of our Legislative Councils, i.e. raising the proportion of elected members to one-half, requiring the budgets to be formally passed by the Councils, and empowering the members to bring forward amendments, with safeguards for bringing the debates to a close in a reasonable time. The presidents of the Councils should have the power of veto. The Viceroy's Legislative Council consists at present of 25 members, of whom only five are elected, one by the Chamber of Commerce of Calcutta—a body of Europeans-and the other four by four provinces. We must ask for the proportion of elected members to be now raised to 12. Of this number one seat might be given to commerce and one to certain industries, and the remaining ten should be assigned to different provinces, two to each of the three older provinces, and one each to the remaining.

And, to begin with, the right of members to move amendments may be confined to one amendment each. The two members for commerce and industries will generally be Europeans, and they will ordinarily vote with Government. Thus, even if all the ten provincial members voted together, they would be only 10 out of 25. Ordinarily they will not be able to carry a motion against the Government, but on exceptional occasions they may obtain the support of two or three men from the other side, and then the moral effect of the situation will be considerable. In the Provincial Legislative Councils, we must have an increase in the number of members,. each district of a proving being empowered to send a member. The objection that these bodies will, in that case, be somewhat unwieldy is not entitled to much weight.

(c) The appointment of at least three Indians to the Secretary of State's Council, to be returned, one each, by the three older provinces.

(d) The separation of judicial and Executive functions.

(e) A large extension of primary education.

(f) The recruitment of the judicial branch of the Indian Civil Service from the legal profession in India.

(g) A reduction of military expenditure.

(h) An experimental measure to deal with the indebtedness of the peasantry over a selected area.

(i) Facilities for industrial and technical education!

I think, gentlemen, if we now concentrate all our energies on some such programme, we may within a reasonable time see results which will not be altogether disappointing. One thing is clear. The present is a specially favourable juncture for such an effort. In our own country, there is sure to be a great rebound of public opinion after the repression to which it has been subjected during the last three years. And in England, for the first time since the Congress movement began, the Liberal and Radical party will come into real power. My recent visit to England, during which I enjoyed somewhat exceptional opportunities to judge of the situation, has satisfied me that a strong current has already set in there against that narrow and aggressive Imperialism, which only the other day seemed to be carrying everything before it.

The new Prime Minister is a tried and trusted friend of freedom. And as regards the new Secretary of State for India, what shall I say? Large numbers of educated men in this country feel towards Mr. Morley as towards a Master, and the heart hopes and yet it trembles, as it had never hoped or trembled before. He, the reverent student of Burke, the disciple of Mill, the friend and biographer of Gladstone-will he courageously apply their principles and his own to the government of the country, or will he too succumb to the influences of the India office around him, and thus cast a cruel blight on hopes, which his own writings have done so much to foster? We shall see; but in any case his appointment, as Secretary of State for India, indicates how strongly favourable to our cause the attitude of the new Ministry is Mr. Ellis, the new Under Secretary of State for India, is openly known to be a friend of our aspirations. A more gratifying combination of circumstances could not be conceived, and it now rests with us to turn it to the best advantage we can for our motherland.

Essence

Gentlemen, one word more and I have done. I have no wish to underrate the difficulties that lie in our path, but I am convinced more than ever that they are not insuperable. Moreover, the real moral interest of a struggle, such as we are engaged in, lies not so much in the particular readjustment of present institutions which we may succeed in securing, as in the strength that the conflict brings us to be a permanent part of ourselves. The whole life of a people, which is broader and deeper than what is touched by purely political institutions, is enriched even by failures, provided the effort has been all that it should be. For such enrichment the present struggle is invaluable. "The true end of our work," said Mr. Ranade nine years ago, "is to renovate, to purify, and also to perfect the whole man by liberating his intellect, elevating his standard of duty, and developing to the full all his powers. Till so renovated, purified, and perfected, we can never hope to be what our ancestors once were—a chosen people, to whom great tasks were allotted and by whom great deeds were performed. Where this feeling animates the worker, it is a matter of comparative indifference in what particular direction it asserts itself and in what particular method it proceeds to work. With a liberated manhood, with buoyant hope, with a faith that never shirks duty, with a sense of justice that deals fairly by all, with unclouded intellect and powers fully cultivated, and, lastly, with a love that overleaps all bounds, renovated India will take her proper rank among the nations of the world, and be the master of the situation and of her own destiny. This is the goal to be reached-this is the promised land. Happy are they, who see it in distant vision; happier those who are permitted to work and clear the way on to it; happiest they, who live to see it with their eyes and tread upon the holy soil once more. Famine and pestilence, oppression and sorrow, will then be myths of the past, and the gods will once again descend to the earth and associate with men, as they did in times which we now call mythical." Gentlemen, I can add nothing that may be worthy of being placed by the side of these beautiful words. I will only call to your minds the words of another great teacher of humanity who asks us to keep our faith in spite of trying circumstances and warns us against the presumption of despairing, because we do not see the whole future clearly before our eyes:

Our times are in His hand
Who saith a whole I planned,
Youth shows but half; trust God; see all, nor be afraid.

BIBLIOGRAPHY

B.R., Nanda, Gokhale, Gandhi and the Nehrus.

——, Gokhale: The Indian Moderates and the British Raj, Oxford University Press, 1977.

D.B., Mathur, Gokhale, a Political Biography. A Study of his Services and Political Ideas, Bombay, 1966.

D.G., Karve, and Ambedkar, D.V., Speeches and Writings of Gopal Krishna Gokhale, Vol. II-Political, Asia Publishing House, 1966.

——, Speeches and Writings of Gopal Krishna Gokhale, Vol. III-Educational, Asia Publishing House, 1967.

John Somervell, Hoyland, Gopal Krishna Gokhale, Calcutta, 1933.

M.K., Gandhi, Gokhale—My Political Guru, Ahmedabad, 1955. Gandhi, Satyagraha in South Africa.

O.P., Goyal, Political Thought of Gokhale, Allahabad, 1965.

P.R., Damle, Gopal Krishna Gokhale, Poona, 1961. Gandhi, M.K., Gokhale: My Political Guru, Ahmedabad, 1955.

R.P. Patwardhan, and Ambedkar, (eds.) The Speeches and Writings of Gopal Krishna Gokhale, Vol. I-Economic, Asia Publishing House, 1962.

R.P., Paranjpye, Gopal Krishna Gokhale, Poona, 1915.

Sarojini, Naidu, Reminiscences of Mr. Gokhale, Poona, 1915.

Sastri, V.S., Srinivasa, Life of Gopal Krishna Gokhale, Bangalore, 1937.

Sir Dinsha Edulji, Wacha, Remembrances of the Late Hon. Mr. G.K. Gokhale, Bombay, 1915.

Stanely A., Wolpert, Tilak and Gokhale Revolution and Reform in the Making of Modern India, Berkeley, 1962.

T.N. Jagdisan, (ed.), My Master Gokhale: A Selection from the Speeches and Writings of Rt. Hon'ble VS. Srinivasa Sastri, Madras, 1946.

T.V., Parvate, Gopal Krishna Gokhale: A Narrative and Interpretative Review of his Life, Career and Contemporary Events, Navjivan Publishing House, Ahmedabad, 1959.

Vaman Govind, Kale, Gokhale and Economic Reforms, Poona, 1916.

INDEX